W0246643

Darjeeling Reconsidered

Map of Darjeeling and Environs

Source: Prepared by Philip McDaniel of UNC Libraries, North Carolina, USA.

Note: This map does not represent the authentic national and international boundaries of India. This map is not to scale and is provided for illustrative purposes only.

Darjeeling Reconsidered

Histories, Politics, Environments

edited by

TOWNSEND MIDDLETON

and

SARA SHNEIDERMAN

UNIVERSITY PRESS

OXFORD
UNIVERSITY PRESS

Oxford University Press is a department of the University of Oxford. It furthers the University's objective of excellence in research, scholarship, and education by publishing worldwide. Oxford is a registered trademark of Oxford University Press in the UK and in certain other countries.

Published in India by
Oxford University Press
2/11 Ground Floor, Ansari Road, Daryaganj, New Delhi 110 002, India

First Edition published in 2018

ISBN-13 (print edition): 978-0-19-948355-6
ISBN-10 (print edition): 0-19-948355-8

ISBN-13 (eBook): 978-0-19-909397-7
ISBN-10 (eBook): 0-19-909397-0

Typeset in Adobe Jenson Pro 10.5/13
by Tranistics Data Technologies, Kolkata 700 091
Printed in India by Rakmo Press, New Delhi 110 020

For the people of Darjeeling

Contents

Tables and Figures

Tables

Figures

Acknowledgements

Darjeeling Reconsidered is the product of countless conversations and contributions, many of which extend beyond the pages of this book. The individual authors who comprise this volume will, no doubt, share their own thanks with the many who influenced their respective chapters. But as editors, we speak for everyone in expressing our first and greatest thanks to the people of Darjeeling, without whom this book would not have been possible. At the end of the day, we hope the book will be understood as our small contribution to the larger project of documenting their struggles, successes, and aspirations over time.

The project originated out of a series of long-running discussions between the editors, authors, and others doing research in the Darjeeling region, dating back to the early 2000s. In time, these discussions have helped forge a network around Darjeeling Studies, constituted by a community of scholars and practitioners of which we are honoured to be a part. In October 2015, we brought many members of this community together for a one-day workshop in Madison, Wisconsin—the exchanges of which proved formative for the book at hand. The organizers of the Annual Conference on South Asia at the University of Wisconsin–Madison graciously hosted and supported this workshop as one of their selected pre-conferences for that year. We benefited immensely from the participation of discussants Bengt G. Karlsson and Arjun Guneratne, who read and commented at length on all of the working papers presented that day. Although they may not be named authors, their insights remain at the core of this book's constitution. While editing this volume, we have been grateful for support from our home institutions—for Sara Shneiderman, the University of British Columbia or UBC (Department of Anthropology, the School of Public Policy and Global Affairs/ Institute of Asian Research, and the Peter Wall Institute for Advanced Studies.); for Townsend Middleton, the University of North Carolina at Chapel Hill (Department of Anthropology).

We would also like to acknowledge the tremendous contributions of our editorial assistant, Zoë Johnson, who took on this project as a fourth-year undergraduate at UBC, and has completed it as a postgraduate headed to Oxford for an MPhil in Development Studies. Her tireless work behind-the-scenes quite literally brought this manuscript together, shaped its overall contours, and ensured a level of quality that would have otherwise been impossible. Philip McDaniel and Hannah Reckhow at UNC's Digital Research Services graciously made the map featured at the outset. The manuscript received generous reviews from two anonymous reviewers, whose engagements with the text and detailed suggestions markedly improved the volume. We owe enduring thanks to our colleagues at Oxford University Press, India—and in particular our editors at Oxford University Press, whose acumen and enthusiasm for the project have propelled us throughout.

Such projects have a way of inserting themselves in our personal as well as professional lives. Townsend Middleton conveys a special thanks to all the family and friends who have supported his life's various projects, including this book—and to his wife, Emily Esmaili, whose footprints preceded his in the Darjeeling hills. Sara Shneiderman thanks her children Sam and Nina for their patience during the long life of this project, and her husband Mark Turin—with whom she first travelled to Darjeeling in the late 1990s, subsequently conducting much joint research there—for his many direct and indirect contributions to this work.

Acronyms and Abbreviations

ABMS	Akhil Bharatiya Mangar Sangh
AIGL	All India Gorkha League
AITBA	All India Tamang Buddhist Association
ASER	Annual Status of Education Report
BGP	Bharatiya Gorkha Parisang
BJP	Bharatiya Janata Party
BLTS	Bhai Larke Thami Samaj
CBI	Central Bureau of Investigation
CPI	Communist Party of India
CPI(M)	Communist Party of India (Marxist)
CPRM	Communist Party of Revolutionary Marxists
CRPF	Central Reserve Police Force
DGHC	Darjeeling Gorkha Hill Council
DTMTC	Darjeeling Tea Management Training Centre
EIC	East India Company

FLO	Fair Trade Labeling Organization International
GDNS	Gorkha Dukha Niwarak Sammelan
GJM	Gorkha Janamukti Morcha
GLO	Gorkhaland Liberation Organization
GLP	Gorkhaland Personnel
GNLF	Gorkha National Liberation Front
GNLF(C)	Gorkha National Liberation Front (C.K. Pradhan)
GTA	Gorkhaland Territorial Administration
HPSU	Hill People's Social Union of Darjeeling
INC	India National Congress
JAP	Jana Andolan Party
MGNREGA	Mahatma Gandhi National Rural Employment Guarantee Act
MSB	Mangar Sangh Bharat
NBU	North Bengal University
NGO	Non-Governmental Organization
NITM	National Institute of Tea Management
OBC	Other Backward Class
PMGSY	Pradhan Mantri Gram Sadak Yojana
SC	Scheduled Caste
SHG	Self-Help Group
SKS	Sanu Krishak Sanstha (Small Farmers' Organization)
ST	Scheduled Tribe
TB	Tuberculosis
TMC	Trinamool Congress
TRA	Tea Research Association

Note on Language

Nepali is the lingua franca of Darjeeling, and therefore is the non-English language we most often encounter in these essays. However, readers will also find words from Hindi, Bengali, and Lepcha in various parts of the text. This diversity highlights Darjeeling's complex ethno-linguistic composition. While there are several formal systems for the transliteration of Nepali and other South Asian languages that rely on diacritical marks or the use of double letters such as 'aa' or chh', we have opted to present non-English terms in simplified forms that will be accessible to non-specialist readers (and we beg forgiveness from speakers and scholars of the languages at hand). All non-English terms are italicized, with the exception of proper names, place names, and terms that have been adopted into English such as 'coolie'. We have endeavoured to make language use consistent across the entire volume, but in some cases, authors may take slightly different approaches to the same word or concept, and we have allowed each author to maintain their own voice to the extent possible. A glossary is included at the end of the book for reference.

Introduction

Reconsidering Darjeeling

Sara Shneiderman and Townsend Middleton

Darjeeling occupies a special place in the South Asian imaginary. With its Himalayan vistas, lush tea gardens, and brisk mountain air, Darjeeling became the consummate hill station for the British—a place somehow different from the rest of India in the plains below and an escape from the proverbial heat of the Empire. The romance with the 'queen of the hills' lives on, as thousands of Indian and foreign tourists flock annually to the region to taste its world-renowned tea, soak up the colonial nostalgia, and glimpse mighty Mount Kanchenjunga. Darjeeling's fame has now gone global, as its teas fetch top dollar on the world market and its legacy continues to fuel Hollywood and Bollywood fantasies. These romantic images, however, tell only a part of Darjeeling's story.

Offering new perspectives, this book aims to challenge—and ultimately, rethink—Darjeeling's legendary status in the postcolonial imagination. Understandings of the region are rapidly transforming, as a new generation of scholars engages Darjeeling from fresh analytical perspectives. This collection of essays brings together researchers from across Europe, North America, and India to shed fresh light on Darjeeling's past and offer timely insight into the critical issues facing its people today. At present, Darjeeling finds itself mired in a range of political, economic, and environmental crises that belie the popular narratives of Darjeeling being somehow 'above it all'—a land of Himalayan mystique, colonial splendour, and exquisite teas; a place to be visited and consumed. These real and imagined qualities have done much to shape the region. Yet these narratives have also all too conveniently obscured the hard realities of life in this particular corner of India. This collection of essays proposes a more grounded understanding of the region and its people. Historiographically, these essays break with the hackneyed colonial accounts of the hill station's founding to present alternative readings of the systems of colonial governance, labour, and migration that made Darjeeling a categorically exceptional place. Turning to the present, the essays offer in-depth ethnographic accounts of dynamics that define life in twenty-first century Darjeeling: among them, the realpolitik of subnationalist and indigenous struggles in the region; the controversial inner workings of Darjeeling's tea industry and Fair Trade implementation; gendered inequality, ecological transformation, and water rights controversies; and the enduring struggle of Darjeeling's communities to find their place amidst the turbulent political and economic transformations of twenty-first century India.

The goals of this book are twofold: First, to explore how perspectives from the contemporary social sciences and humanities may open up new understandings of Darjeeling's past, present, and future. Second, to ask what Darjeeling might teach us about South Asia, the Himalayan region, and the postcolonial world more generally. Placed within these broader frameworks of area studies and postcolonial theory, Darjeeling figures as a key site for research. Geopolitically, the Darjeeling region—which for the purposes of this book we consider to include both the Kalimpong and Darjeeling districts—sits at a crucial nexus of South Asia (see the map in the frontispiece), yet it productively refuses many conventional demarcations within South Asian Studies. It is part of West Bengal, but has remained largely peripheral to the well-established intellectual community focused on Bengali history, literature, and politics. The region likewise serves as a gateway to India's North-East—namely, through the Siliguri Corridor and rapidly growing city of Siliguri—but it seldom figures in scholarly attention from both Indian and foreign scholars to the eight states that comprised the North-Eastern Council,[1] as this does not include West Bengal. Likewise, within Himalayan Studies, Darjeeling has historically been understood as a key node of Nepali-speaking networks, but, with the prominent exception of its literary history,[2] has remained largely beyond the scope of researchers focused on Nepal. The same may be said of Tibet and Tibetan Studies: several recent studies of Tibetan history,[3] death rituals,[4] and trade[5] have been based in whole or part on research conducted in Darjeeling, yet the sociopolitical realities of the place itself are often obscured from view. Located accordingly, Darjeeling's anomalous place in South Asia provides both a challenge and opportunity to reconsider the internal and external boundaries that have defined this area of study.[6]

Darjeeling's intellectual promise also extends beyond the subcontinent. Most notably, Darjeeling figures as a different kind of space for postcolonial critique. From this space so steeped in colonial lore, we gain critical insights into the historical and present workings of frontier capitalism; the less-understood dynamics of internal neocolonialism that followed decolonization in South Asia;[7] the ongoing turbulence of economic liberalization;[8] and the formative intersections of political

[1] The eight states are Arunachal Pradesh, Assam, Manipur, Meghalaya, Mizoram, Sikkim, Nagaland, and Tripura. Some recent examples of relevant scholarship about India's North–East may be found in McDuie–Ra (2016); Vandenhelsken and Karlsson (2015).

[2] Chalmers (2003a, 2003b, 2009); Hutt (1997, 1998); Onta (1996a, 1996b).

[3] McGranahan (2010).

[4] Gerke (2012); Zivkovic (2013).

[5] Harris (2013).

[6] A recent edited volume, *Transcultural Encounters in the Himalayan Borderlands: Kalimpong as 'Contact Zone'* (Viehbeck 2017) and a recent special issue of *Transcultural Studies* points in a positive direction by exploring the 'connected histories of Darjeeling, Kalimpong, and the Himalayas' (Harris et al. 2016) in a manner that bridges gaps between several of the domains we describe here. The current volume builds upon this impetus both by connecting history with the present through ethnographic and political analysis, and by further expanding the frame to engage with 'South Asia' and 'West Bengal' as sites of connection.

[7] Banerjee and Basu (2015); Sökefeld (2005).

[8] Gupta and Sivaramakrishnan (2011).

ecology and identity-based politics. Crucially, the contributions to this volume provide insights into how all of these phenomena are experienced by those on the margins of 'mainstream' India. These views from Darjeeling provide, moreover, incisive looks into the forging of postcolonial territory, the quandaries of postcolonial citizenship; and the entanglements of social movements, governance, and economic transformation that have come to define life at the margins of India and beyond. Darjeeling accordingly figures as an alternative—and critically productive—site through which to engage a range of outstanding concerns in modern South Asia and the postcolonial world writ large. Indeed, part of this book's project is to introduce Darjeeling to postcolonial thinking and, in turn, to explore what this critical tradition might teach us about Darjeeling today.

By reconsidering Darjeeling, this book seeks not to tell *the* definitive story of this region and its people, but rather to challenge prevailing narratives through an assortment of perspectives and voices. In keeping with the spirit of postcolonial critique, the essays embrace the possibilities of interdisciplinary collaboration. We feel privileged to count among the contributors to this volume anthropologists, development practitioners, geographers, historians, and political scientists, as well as scholars who define themselves in interdisciplinary terms that bridge social science with cultural, environmental, and literary studies. Readers will find the same place explored through several different methodological approaches, further refracted through a range of disciplinary frameworks for analysis. The chapters are grouped not by discipline, but rather by theme, in three sections: *Histories of Exception, Political and Social Movements*, and *Environments and Labour*. In each section readers will find multiple approaches to a shared set of issues—often developed in productive tension—which, taken together, illuminate Darjeeling in new ways. Through these diverse commitments, we venture a multifaceted engagement with the legend and hard realities of this oft-romanticized region and its people. Reconsidering Darjeeling's past and present in this way, we hope, can also help open new ways of imagining its future. To establish a foundation for the analyses that follow, we begin with a short history of the region and its people.

Colonial Darjeeling

The Darjeeling hills have been an historic crossroads of South Asia. Subject to the ebb and flow of regional powers, Darjeeling's borders and the territorial claims that define them have shifted periodically through time. The region's status as a geopolitical frontier—at once strategic and sensitive—has inflected its standing in the context of South Asia from the precolonial period to the postcolonial present. Throughout much of the eighteenth century, the territory between the Mechi and Teesta rivers (see the map in frontispiece) was claimed by the Chogyal of Sikkim. Nepal's military expansion eastward in the final decades of that century brought the tract under the control of Nepal's Gorkha Empire. The areas east of the Teesta River meanwhile remained part of Bhutan. Nepal's rule over Darjeeling came to an end in 1815, when the British mandated Nepal return the tract to Sikkim at the conclusion of the Anglo-Nepalese War (1814–16) by way of the Treaty of Segowlee or Sugauli (1815) and subsequent Treaty of Titalia (1817).[9] If this marked the start of British territorial meddling in the area, it would not be long before the Empire began to make more direct claims upon the region and its people.

The stories of Darjeeling's colonial founding are by now legion.[10] In 1829, Captain George Lloyd and J.W. Grant were passing through Darjeeling en route to settle a border dispute between Sikkim and Nepal. The location was then known by local Lepcha peoples as *Dorje-ling*, or 'Place of the Thunderbolt'. The crescent shaped ridge of Dorje-ling struck Lloyd as an ideal location for a hill station sanatorium where colonial officials could find respite from the swelter of the plains below. Lloyd conveyed his vision to the Governor General of India, Lord William Bentinck, who agreed that Dorje–ling would make an excellent sanatorium and strategic military outpost for monitoring the Himalayan frontier. Deputy Surveyor General of India Captain J.D. Herbert subsequently visited Darjeeling in February and March 1830 to survey the site and concurred.[11] Taking the plan forward, in 1835, the British East India Company (EIC) secured rights to a roughly 24 × 6 miles stretch of land from Sikkim by way of an official Deed of Grant (1835). With a lease on this land, the British set to work transforming the ostensibly 'uninhabited' hill tract into a proper hill station. The EIC appointed Dr A. Campbell as Darjeeling's first superintendent in 1839, and, deeming the tract a 'Nonregulated Area', gave him far-reaching authority to develop the hills as he saw fit. The first decades of British rule brought major infrastructural and environmental transformations,

9 Kennedy (1996); Mullard (2011); Pradhan (1991); Subba (1989a: 1–5).

10 See, for instance, O'Malley (1907).

11 Herbert (1830).

as forests were cleared, roads were built, and bungalows were erected to meet British desires. The 'practically uninhabited' ridge of Dorje–ling thus began its rapid metamorphosis into a colonial hill station.

These transformations required labour—far more than the local inhabitants (largely Lepcha and Limbu) could provide. The British consequently lured workers from Sikkim, Bhutan, and Nepal by promising wages, shelter, and freedom from the oppressive tax and forced labour regimes that marked life in these neighbouring countries.[12] Tens of thousands poured into Darjeeling, marking the start of profound demographic changes that forever altered the ethnic landscape of the hills. In their contributions to this volume, Middleton and Sharma detail these patterns of mobility from historical perspectives, along with some of their legal and representational challenges. While integral to the hill station's formation, these migrations also caused tension between the EIC and its Himalayan neighbours, who disapproved of these imperial encroachments on their human resources. British relations with Sikkim deteriorated throughout the 1840s, culminating in the purported kidnapping of Campbell and renowned botanist and explorer Joseph Hooker in 1849. Campbell and Hooker were released without incident, but the British leveraged the confrontation to permanently annex the region between the Mechi and Teesta rivers in 1850. The British expanded further into the region in the 1860s, using the Anglo-Bhutanese War (1864–5) and consequent Treaty of Sinchula (1865) to incorporate Kalimpong and the lands east of the Teesta River into British control. Thus came into existence the region now commonly referred to as the Darjeeling hills: an area that loosely corresponds to the contemporary administrative districts of Darjeeling and Kalimpong.[13]

[12] Subba (1989a); also Dutt (1981: 1052); Hutt (1997, 1998); Middleton (2015); Sharma (2016a, 2016b); Shneiderman (2015: Chapter 4); Warner (2014).

[13] Kalimpong became a separate district in February 2017, after decades as a subdivision of Darjeeling. The creation of the new Kalimpong district prompted new subdivisional lines to be drawn within Darjeeling district as well, such that it now consists of the subdivisions of Darjeeling, Kurseong, Mirik, and Siliguri. The city and subdivision of Siliguri—located, as they are, in the plains of West Bengal and vested with considerable geopolitical import—fit uneasily within the framing 'Darjeeling hills' and, indeed, remain a source of considerable territorial contention between local, regional, and national political actors.

The British 'discovery' of Darjeeling has become standard fare in the historiography of the region. But it is misguided to suggest that Darjeeling's history began with the advent of colonial rule. Prior to British arrival, the Darjeeling hills (and Kalimpong in particular) had been major points in trans-Himalayan trade networks, with goods and traders from Nepal, Sikkim, Tibet, Bhutan, and further afield criss-crossing the region and, at times, making it home.[14] Sovereignty during the pre-colonial period was contested and fluid. As historian Catherine Warner has noted, local populations paid tribute to, and strategically allied themselves with, different powers at different times.[15] British rule effectively reterritorialized the region, however. The borders separating British India and Nepal, Sikkim, and Bhutan hardened as new sovereign claims were laid upon the region and its people.[16] As the British and others made claims upon the region's fluid populations, the question of who exactly was living in Darjeeling at the time became a point of concern and longstanding uncertainty. Such ambiguities continue to this day. Early colonial accounts claim that the region was sparsely inhabited by the indigenous Lepcha, Limbu, and Bhutia. These colonial demographics are, at best, incomplete. Given the crosscurrents of trade, migration, and sovereignty that defined the region throughout the pre-colonial period, the local population was likely more heterogeneous and numerous than the British accounted for. Many local writers and historians have argued for the autochthony of all of the Nepali-speaking peoples of Darjeeling. These revisionist histories have been closely associated with different ethnic groups' claims to rights and belonging in India, as detailed in Nilamber Chhetri's contribution to this volume. Despite the challenges of identifying conclusive evidence, such claims should be understood in context as important assertions of belonging. While it is impossible to verify the precise dates and routes of migration for different groups, what remains clear is that British colonial rule triggered significant migration into the area, and, with it, long-lasting demographic transformations.

Tea proved formative. Experiments in the 1840s demonstrated that tea thrived in the hills of Darjeeling. By the 1850s, European investors were acquiring and converting massive tracts of land into the tea gardens that have become iconic of Darjeeling today. To meet the significant

[14] Harris et al. (2016).

[15] Warner (2014).

[16] Warner (2014).

labour needs of this budding industry, the British looked to neighbouring Sikkim, Bhutan, and especially Nepal for coolies to care for this global cash crop. The industry expanded rapidly throughout the 1850s and 1860s. Darjeeling subsequently transformed into a place not only of colonial convalescence, but also capitalist production.[17] By 1870, there were 56 gardens employing roughly 8,000 labourers. By 1900, there were more than 100 gardens employing an estimated 64,000 labourers—nearly all of them categorized as 'Nepali' by the colonial records.[18] However, other data suggests that colonial records did not adequately account for differences between those born in Darjeeling and those newly migrated from Nepal. This lack of clarity regarding citizenship in a context of multiple identities shaped by high mobility remains a key vector in contemporary identity politics, as will be explored in further detail below.

These economic qua ecological developments prompted attendant transformations to Darjeeling's cultural landscape. As members of various ethnic groups from across the Himalayas found work in the up-and-coming hill station, the new arrivals brought with them their own languages, customs, and religious practices. These were the building blocks of the ethnic plurality that is the region's signature. The ethnically diverse settlers found common ground in their Himalayan heritage, and the Nepali language soon became (and remains) Darjeeling's lingua franca. Over the generations, as members of different ethnic groups mixed and intermarried, many of the discrete linguistic and religious practices of their ancestors gave way to new hybrid cultural forms. Today, many community members of groups like the Tamang, Gurung, Newar, and others do not speak the languages of their ancestors and contemporaries in Nepal, but rather grow up speaking and studying Nepali, English, Hindi, and Bengali.[19] But where languages and customs were lost, new forms of solidarity and cultural identity were gained. These dynamics of cultural loss, hybridity, and ethnogenesis over the last two centuries have yielded Darjeeling's distinctive multicultural identity and made the hills a unique site of Himalayan cosmopolitanism.[20]

[17] On the history of the tea industry, see Besky (2013); Bhowmik (1996, 2016); Chatterjee (2001).

[18] Besky (2013: 53); Kennedy (1996: 188–190).

[19] Turin (2014).

[20] Sharma this volume (2016a, 2016b).

Despite the fact that the Nepali-speaking population quickly became the region's demographic majority, they faced difficult circumstances. Because neighbouring countries like Nepal and Sikkim did not approve of the immigration patterns that brought much of this workforce to Darjeeling, the British refused to officially claim the settlers as British subjects.[21] The paradox was unmistakable. With one hand, colonial officials and planters lured labourers with the promise of wages and housing, as an alternative to the forced labour regimes, caste-based agrarian exploitation, and excessive taxation schemes of their homelands in Nepal. With the other hand though, British officials denied the settlers rights and a sense of security in India. Fears of being forcefully returned to their country of origin were rampant amongst the coolies.[22] These anxieties, coupled with the jarring new capitalist circumstances that workers found themselves in, made precarity a formative condition of colonial life. 'Going to Mugalan' (as India was then called in Nepal) may have posed an enticing alternative to the oppressive hierarchies of nineteenth century Nepal,[23] but the colonial conjuncture introduced a novel set of difficulties that would haunt the Nepali speakers of Darjeeling for generations to come. These communities' anxieties over being-in and being-of India intensified as they encountered racial discrimination, xenophobic misrecognition as being 'foreigners', and various forms of structural exclusion from the India of the plains below.[24] The colonial archive, not surprisingly, tells us little of these hardships, but they remain integral to the sociopolitical life of Darjeeling today.

In the twentieth century, the people of Darjeeling increasingly sought political formulations to secure the autonomy, well-being, and belonging in India that they desired. According to local histories, calls for rights and equitable representation for the Nepali-speaking majority were sounded as early as 1907. In 1917, the Hillmen's Association—an ethnically heterogeneous organization comprising Nepali, Lepcha, and Bhutia—formalized these claims with a memorandum to the Government of Bengal calling for native self-rule in the hills. The call for ethnic autonomy was taken up by numerous organizations in subsequent decades. In 1934, S.W. Laden La founded the Hill People's Social

21 See Middleton, this volume; (2013a).

22 Middleton (2015: 34–7).

23 Hutt (1998).

24 Middleton (2013a).

Union (HPSU), which advocated for rights and social improvement across the hills.[25] The HPSU's journal *NeBuLa* (representing its Nepali, Bhutia, and Lepcha constituents) bolstered awareness of the collective identity and needs of Darjeeling's Nepali-speaking majority. The All India Gorkha League (AIGL)—originally launched in Dehradun in 1923 and subsequently revived in Darjeeling in 1943—worked within similarly pan-Nepali frames to advocate for Nepali speakers' rights in India. These and other organizations forged a thriving public sphere, which would lay the groundwork for a distinctive political and literary culture in the hills in the years to come.[26] The calls for autonomy, however, were met with few results, and socio-economic change was slow to come. As British rule drew to a close in the middle of the twentieth century, the people of Darjeeling found themselves in an increasingly difficult situation. Lacking clearly recognized citizenship rights in independent India, facing pernicious discrimination, and stuck on the lowest rungs of the local economy, frustrations mounted.

Postcolonial Darjeeling and the Gorkhaland Movement

India's independence from British rule in 1947 brought significant changes to Darjeeling, but also troubling continuities. Darjeeling's governmental and economic structure remained largely intact—as did its legend. Importantly though, as British officials vacated their posts and British tea planters sold off their tea estates, it was not the local Nepali-speaking populations that filled these vacancies, but Indian politicians and businessmen from the plains below. The postcolonial era paradoxically ushered in a new wave of colonial domination—an internal neocolonialism—that persists into the twenty-first century.[27] Economically, Darjeeling's tea industry quickly came to be dominated by Bengali and Marwaris, as well as large-scale corporate conglomerates based elsewhere in India.

[25] On Laden La, see Rhodes & Rhodes (2006).

[26] Chalmers (2003: 202–14); Hutt (1997); Onta (1996a, 1996b); Shneiderman (2015: Chapter 5).

[27] This is akin to the situation that Martin Sökefeld (2005) describes for Pakistan's northern areas.

Politically, the story was similar. The region's geopolitical importance assumed a new valence as independent India looked to establish its place vis-à-vis its South Asian neighbours and its rival to the north, China. That Darjeeling served as a gateway to Nepal, East Pakistan (which became Bangladesh in 1971), Bhutan, Sikkim, Burma (Myanmar), and of course China, ensured it would remain the subject of governmental scrutiny and significant military presence. The Partition of 1947, and the demarcation of East Pakistan only redoubled the region's geopolitical significance—namely by carving out the precarious sliver of territory known as the Siliguri Corridor, linking India's 'mainland' to its ethnically divergent North-East. Darjeeling's consequent place as both a frontier and crossroads of not only South Asia, but Asia writ large—and thus a national security hotspot for India—has directly and indirectly influenced its political circumstances. The 1950 Indo-Nepalese Friendship Treaty established an open border between the two countries, but made it difficult for Nepali speakers to claim full belonging as Indians. Since independence, Darjeeling has remained territorially part of, and fully under the administrative thumb of, the state of West Bengal. For much of this period, West Bengal maintained the longest running popularly elected communist government in the world. Yet despite the Communist Party of India's (Marxist) [CPI(M)] commitment to oppressed peoples, the regime accomplished little to bring the people of Darjeeling the autonomy and economic mobility they desired and deserved. Since the CPI(M) represented the state government of West Bengal, political mobilizations for autonomy in Darjeeling have often been aligned with anti-communist forces, an apparent paradox given the class status of the plantation workers who made up significant proportions of the Nepali population. Swatahsiddha Sarkar and Babika Khawas explore these class questions in their contribution to this volume.

The conditions of postcolonial life fuelled an array of political demands among Darjeeling's people. By the 1970s, the various Nepali-speaking communities of the hills had congealed into a powerful multi-ethnic community that increasingly went by the ethnonym 'Gorkha.' Throughout this period, people of Nepali heritage were served unnerving reminders of their precarious place in India. Bouts of ethnic cleansing targeting Nepali speakers in Mizoram in 1967, in Assam and Meghalaya in 1979, and in Manipur in 1980 violently emphasized the everyday discriminations that Nepali speakers faced throughout India. The flight of tens of thousands of Nepali-speaking citizens from Bhutan in the early 1990s in response to alleged ethnic cleansing in the Buddhist kingdom that borders Darjeeling further heightened tensions in the region.[28] These events imbued the people of Darjeeling with a sense of unease that continues to haunt and animate sociopolitical life in the hills.[29] Responding to this long-standing climate of prejudice, the All India Nepali Language Committee, in 1972, began a protracted struggle to make Nepali a national language of India. This all-India movement had strong activist roots in Darjeeling, but struggled throughout the 1970s to gain linguistic recognition for the millions of native Nepali speakers in India.[30] In 1979, India's then Prime Minister Morarji Desai exacerbated the Gorkhas' frustration by publically declaring Nepali to be 'a foreign language spoken by foreigners in India'.[31] Given the anxiety-ridden histories outlined above, Desai's remarks struck a painful nerve in Darjeeling.

Throughout the 1970s and early 1980s, local political outfits such as the AIGL and the Pranta Parishad elaborated the demands for ethnic autonomy, but to no avail. Spurred on by the aforementioned ethnic violence against Nepalis in the North-East and the various forms of structural violence that persistently relegated the people of Darjeeling to a literal and figurative corner of the nation-state, there was a growing sense that the Gorkhas of Darjeeling needed a place to call their own. In 1986, a new party, the Gorkhaland National Liberation Front (GNLF), launched a violent agitation for a separate state of Gorkhaland within India. Spearheaded by the GNLF's charismatic leader Subash Ghisingh, the logics of the Gorkhaland Movement were clear. First, the people of Darjeeling demanded their own state within India, free from the oppression of West Bengal. Second, despite being stigmatized as 'outsiders' and 'foreigners', the Gorkhas of Darjeeling were loyal Indians. A state bearing their own ethnonym would thereby establish their rightful place in the nation-state. In Ghisingh's words:

> We Indian Nepalis who have nothing to do with Nepal are constantly confused as 'Nepalis', that is, citizens of Nepal, a foreign country. But if there is Gorkhaland then our identity as Indian, belonging to an Indian state ... will be clear.[32]

[28] Hutt (2003).

[29] See Middleton's discussion of 'anxious belongings' (2013a).

[30] Booth (2011).

[31] Dhakal (2009: 157); Samanta (2000: 101).

[32] 'Nothing Short of a Separate State,' *India Today*, 66, October 31, 1986. Cited in Lama (1996: 50).

Taking up arms for Gorkhaland, the Gorkhas sought to opt out of West Bengal and into India on their own terms as citizens of an independent state in the federal union. Ethnic autonomy, further, seemed to promise redress for histories of discrimination and oppression.

The 1980s Gorkhaland Movement lasted three years (1986–8). Society-wide strikes known as *bandhs*, endless protests, and sporadic violence against the government's paramilitary forces (primarily the Central Reserve Police Force (CRPF)) crippled life in the hills. The subnationalist agitation resulted in an estimated 297 deaths and 1,164 homes destroyed.[33] Public memories of the agitation are haunted by the imagery of decapitated heads appearing in the bazaar, CRPF raids, razed homes, disappearances of loved ones, and other traumas. But in the end, the Gorkhaland Movement failed to deliver a separate state. Ghisingh, West Bengal, and the central Government of India in New Delhi (often referred to as 'the Centre'), instead negotiated for a conciliatory administrative set-up known as the Darjeeling Gorkha Hill Council (DGHC, established 1988): a new form of governmental exceptionalism in the hills. Under this arrangement, Darjeeling received limited autonomy, but the district remained under the government of West Bengal. Ostensibly, the DGHC arrangement would respond to the Gorkhas' plea for autonomy (thereby answering the region's 'ethnic question'), while preserving the established sovereign chain of command over this geopolitically strategic area (thereby heeding the 'security perspective').[34] Ghisingh and the GNLF assumed control of the DGHC for the next two decades, but the arrangement was ultimately rendered a toothless entity that quickly drew rancour from all sides. Despite its failures, the Gorkhaland Movement nevertheless put Darjeeling on the national radar as something other than a Himalayan paradise. It moreover established the contours of a distinctive political culture in the hills, charged with unrequited and periodically volatile demands for rights, recognition, and autonomy in India. These subnationalist desires would take a range of forms in the years to come.

[33] Samanta (2000: 54).

[34] Some elements of the arrangement were echoed in the establishment of the Ladakh Autonomous Hill Council in the western Indian Himalayan region a few years later in 1995, the limitations of which are well described in van Beek (2000).

Alternative Routes to Recognition

In the wake of the 1980s agitation, many citizens of Darjeeling sought alternative routes to rights and recognition in India. Inspired by the proliferation of indigenous movements around the world, individual ethnic groups that comprised the greater Gorkha conglomerate mobilized for recognition as Scheduled Tribes (ST) of India—a designation that affords affirmative action benefits, often referred to in India as 'reservations'.[35] If these 'tribal' movements tapped into a global arena of indigenous struggle, they were also part and parcel of more regional—and specifically Himalayan—networks of ethnic mobilization. The links with Nepal's *janajati* movement for indigenous rights during the 1990s were formative. In Nepal, the comparatively strong presence of international development agencies encouraged ethnic activists to connect with global indigenous discourses through initiatives like the United Nations's Year of Indigenous Peoples in 1993—ideas which further circulated to Darjeeling.[36] As groups like the Gurung, Tamang, Thangmi, and others mobilized to overcome their historic marginalization in the Hindu kingdom of Nepal, their ethnic counterparts in Darjeeling borrowed tactics, information, and inspiration from Nepal's *janajati* movement to add new contours to the politics of identity in India.

But as per the terms of the postcolonial state, in India the sought-after identity was not *janajati*, 'indigenous', or 'ethnic'. Rather, these movements would go by the designation 'tribe'. The Tamang and Limbu communities led the way towards ST status throughout the early 1990s, with other communities following suit. By the 2000s, the quest for ST status became a pan-ethnic phenomenon across the hills, as every major ethnic group that was not yet an ST applied for tribal status.[37] The

[35] See Shah and Shneiderman (2013).

[36] See Middleton and Shneiderman (2008) and Shneiderman (2009) for further exploration of the connections and comparisons between ethnic mobilization in Nepal and India during this period. Karlsson (2013) presents a case study of one Tamang ethnic activist that further demonstrates these links. Shneiderman (2013) highlights entanglements between indigenous mobilization and international development in the region. For further background on Nepal's *janajati* movement, see Gellner (2007); Hangen (2010); and Onta (2006).

[37] Four communities of Darjeeling (the Bhutia, Lepcha, Sherpa, and Yolmo) had enjoyed ST status since 1950. The Tamang and Limbu achieved ST status in 2003.

turn to tribal politics coincided with renewed programmes of ethnic revitalization, as Nilamber Chhetri details in this volume. Partnering with their *janajati* contemporaries in Nepal, communities launched initiatives to recover the 'lost' languages and cultural practices of their ancestors. Scouring the anthropological literature and sending study teams to Nepal, the findings deepened ethnic awareness amongst these groups, becoming at once the stuff of ethnic rebirth and the content of these groups' applications to the state for tribal recognition. This 'tribal turn' marked a profound shift in Darjeeling's politics—effectively shifting the banner of ethnic mobilization from Gorkha (in the 1980s) to 'tribe' in the 1990s and 2000s.[38]

The calculus of becoming tribal grew more complicated in 2005, when Ghisingh and the GNLF sought to make Darjeeling a 'tribal area', as per the Sixth Schedule of the Indian constitution. Originally designed for the tribal communities of India's North–East, this would afford qualified autonomy and special territorial and cultural rights. In late 2005, Ghisingh, West Bengal, and the Centre signed a Memorandum of Settlement declaring the intention to bring Sixth Schedule status to the hills. There thus emerged a synergy between the bids for ST status and Sixth Schedule autonomy. Indeed, between 2005 and 2007 becoming tribal was the order of the day. In hindsight, the Sixth Schedule proposal was hamstrung from the start. According to census statistics, only 32 per cent of Darjeeling was then recognized as tribal, making it difficult to meet the constitutional criteria for Sixth Schedule status.[39] The jurisdiction of the proposed 'tribal area', moreover, was unclear—as was the internal structure of governance. Sixth Schedule areas are supposed to incorporate traditional tribal political structures, but since Darjeeling did not have a single uniformly agreed upon set of such structures, how it would be governed as a 'tribal area' remained uncertain. These doubts began to chip away at public enthusiasm.

That is when an unexpected saga overtook Darjeeling. In 2007, Darjeeling's own Prashant Tamang won the popular national reality

[38] For broader context see Middleton (2015); Middleton and Shneiderman (2008); Shneiderman and Turin (2006); Shneiderman (2015).

[39] The applications for ST status remained pending at the time of writing in mid-2017, despite several flurries of activity on this front since Narendra Modi took office as Prime Minister of India in 2014 and stated that he would resolve these long-standing issues.

television show, *Indian Idol*. Prashant's run to victory elicited powerful emotions of pride from the people of Darjeeling and Nepali speakers throughout South Asia. The jubilation at Tamang being crowned Indian Idol turned to outrage, however, when a radio DJ in New Delhi made discriminatory remarks about Prashant's ethnicity. A riot followed, in the streets of Siliguri (the district's most important economic hub in the plains), which left hundreds of Tamang supporters trapped in the district courthouse, seeking safety from the projectile-wielding Bengali mob outside. Eventually, the army had to be called in to free them. Running a gamut of emotions, the Indian Idol saga served Nepali speakers an all-too-familiar reminder of their precarious place in India. As a result, it became a watershed moment. Within days, the beloved and feared henchman of the GNLF—Bimal Gurung—launched a new party, the Gorkha Janamukti Morcha (GJM), demanding nothing short of a separate state of Gorkhaland. Enervated by the recent chain of events, the public flocked to Gurung's new party. The GJM stormed to power in 2008, ousted Ghisingh and the GNLF, and chased the opposition from the hills. Under Gurung's firebrand leadership, the GJM launched the second Gorkhaland Movement in as many generations.

The GJM declared this second Gorkhaland Movement to be a non-violent Gandhian struggle, but the party's muscular ways soon became evident. Interparty violence, intimidation, and coercion were integral to their power. Initially backed by overwhelming popular support, the charismatic Bimal Gurung promised Gorkhaland or death. But as the years of agitation wore on, the GJM had little to show for their efforts. Opposition leaders like Madan Tamang of the AIGL took the GJM to task for the failed promises, especially as the agitation appeared headed for another conciliatory set-up that looked suspiciously like the DGHC, which had ended the first Gorkhaland Movement in 1988. This was because both administrative arrangements accorded personal power to the leader of the moment (first Ghisingh, then Gurung), without substantive economic or political reform that might have created broader positive impact for common citizens. With their failures becoming clear, the GJM clamped down on the opposition. In an effort to prevent democratic assembly, a GJM mob attacked Madan Tamang and his party on 21 May 2010, killing him in broad daylight in the centre of Darjeeling bazaar. This was perhaps the most infamous event linked to the 'rowdy' political culture that Mona Chettri describes in this volume. The assassination sent shockwaves through Darjeeling and turned many against the GJM.[40] The case has since implicated the GJM's top brass, including Bimal Gurung. At the time of writing in 2017, the assassination case remains open, a dark cloud hanging over the hills.

The Gorkhaland Movement meanwhile has waxed and waned. In 2012, the GJM did indeed agree to a conciliatory set-up known as the Gorkhaland Territorial Administration (GTA), which, once again, provided only limited autonomy that has since been met with disappointment. The GJM has used the local administration and its resources to consolidate its power through patronage. The party continues to rule with a heavy hand, even though the Madan Tamang murder case has clipped the party's ability to violently forestall democracy due to equivocal popular support. Capitalizing on the disappointments of the second Gorkhaland Movement and all that has followed, opposition parties like the Jana Andolan Party (JAP), the GNLF, the AIGL, and West Bengal's Trinamool Congress (TMC) have made significant political inroads in recent years. The demand for Gorkhaland, meanwhile, has made periodic returns, as illuminated at different political moments by Bethany Lacina and Miriam Wenner in this volume. In 2017, the Gorkhaland Movement flared up with unexpected force. In June, GJM protests sparked by Trinamool Congress Chief Minister Mamata Banerjee's assertion that the Bengali language would be made a mandatory subject in Darjeeling schools were met with police violence, leading to multiple deaths in the streets. The state violence galvanized a new phase of the Gorkhaland Movement that quickly spread through the region, uniting people and parties from across the political spectrum. The government rushed additional CRPF forces into the area and enforced an internet blackout, but the agitations gripped the body politic with an intensity not seen since the 1980s. An ensuing 104 days of continuous strikes crippled both the economy and everyday life, leading to curfews, food shortages, and significant suffering. The agitation was punctuated by sporadic violence amounting to roughly a dozen deaths (from both sides) and significant destruction of property. But in the end, the 2017 Gorkhaland Movement yielded little. The toll of the agitations split the ruling GJM. When the agitation concluded in September of 2017, GJM party-founder Bimal Gurung was out of power, wanted for arrest, and the subject of a massive manhunt. Meanwhile, on 20 September 2017, Mamata Banerjee installed the more moderate GJM leader, Binoy

40 Middleton (2018).

Tamang, as the Chairperson of a reconstituted Gorkhaland Territorial Administration—effectively instituting a revamped status quo, arguably more favourable to the interests of West Bengal. After a summer of strife, this would prove a tough pill to swallow. Even as this book goes to press, the people of Darjeeling are still coming to terms with the bewildering aftermaths of the 2017 Gorkhaland Movement. This recurrence and volatility of subnationalist agitation in the hills powerfully underscores the need for sustained engagement with Darjeeling's contemporary political culture, and the often-unsettling histories that undergird it. Gorkhaland remains the ultimate political goal, but amid the struggles and serial disappointments of the recent past, many are left questioning the available avenues to that end.

These recent struggles have unfolded in a context of unprecedented socio-economic transformation across India. Since the 1990s, India's economic liberalization has rewritten the script of socio-economic mobility on the subcontinent. Yet as India embraced neoliberal reform and globalization, the people of Darjeeling have largely found themselves on the outside looking in at a quickening national mainstream. At home, the tea industry and its entanglements with the local state and NGOs dominate the local economy, as Debarati Sen explains in her contribution to this volume. Employment opportunities for educated and uneducated alike are few and far between. Facing these conditions, Darjeeling's youth now see their futures being elsewhere, despite their strong feelings of belonging at home, as Sarah Besky's chapter poignantly demonstrates. But when Nepali speakers venture to places like Bengaluru, Kolkata, and New Delhi in search of education and employment, they face the familiar forms of racial discrimination and socio-economic exclusion that have dogged them for generations. India's neoliberal advance has consequently only intensified the marginalization of Darjeeling and its people.

Many of Darjeeling's woes are derived from the declining colonial era infrastructure, especially the region's inadequate motorable roads and antiquated water delivery systems, as explored by Georgina Drew and Roshan Rai in this volume. While it is these quaint colonial trappings that have always been part of Darjeeling's allure for tourists—along with its commodified landscape, as Rune Bennike's contribution to this volume highlights—for residents who rely on these resources for daily livelihood and well-being, patience is stretched thin. Traffic has increased exponentially in recent years, as private vehicles have become a desired hallmark of the post-liberalization Indian middle class. New high-rise buildings have obscured the views for which Darjeeling was once famous. At the same time, they have further burdened sparse resource bases. These new forms of urbanization, and the resource scarcities they entail, stand in telling juxtaposition to the long-standing rural concerns about exploitative practices on Darjeeling's tea plantations that have played a significant role in each wave of the Gorkhaland Movement. Figured alongside the historic struggles for autonomy and recognition described earlier, these contemporary issues call for new analytical approaches that actively explore the relationships between political economy and cultural politics. Several authors in this collection take up this imperative by focusing attention on the conjunctures and disjunctures between culture, politics, infrastructure, and resource management—in the past and, more pressingly, in the present.

Reconsidering Darjeeling

Amid these conditions, we believe the time is now for a critical reconsideration of Darjeeling's past, present, and future. There is no doubt that Darjeeling is a special place—one of remarkable beauty, distinctive cultures, exquisite teas, and all the rest. These real and imagined qualities have proven formative of the Darjeeling we know today. In rethinking this legacy, however, the challenge is not to do away with the legend of Darjeeling altogether, but rather to acknowledge how such idyllic framings have shaped life in the hills, yet also failed to capture its dynamism and difficulties. So long as the legend of Darjeeling continues to cast its long shadows across the hills, the postcolonial romance with this 'queen of the hills' will continue to obscure and occlude understandings of the region—and more importantly, the prospects of those who call it home. Figured in this way, the project of reconsidering Darjeeling stands as both an intellectual *and* political project; one that beckons a multitude of voices well beyond the covers of this book. The perspectives that follow provide some grist for the conversations to come, the emergent contours of which are brought into focus for future consideration by Tanka Subba's Afterword, which at once commends and critiques the contributions. Tracing the shadows of Darjeeling's postcolonial legend and casting light on lives lived otherwise, these essays, we hope, can help clear a space for rethinking Darjeeling on its own terms. Indeed, this book is underwritten by the possibility that reconsidering Darjeeling's past and present may, in time, prove a vital step towards reimagining its future.

The essays presented here build upon several lineages of knowledge production and scholarship, all of which we recognize as foundational to any proposal for contemporary Darjeeling Studies. First is the legacy of census data and other writings by colonial scholar–administrators such as George Grierson and Brian Houghton Hodgson. Whether we like it or not, it is these early enumerative texts that provide a starting point for building our historical knowledge of Darjeeling, a subject which has recently been treated in exciting new ways by scholars such as Catherine Warner, and is further addressed in the contributions by Middleton, Bennike, and Sharma here. Second is the work on Nepali identity produced by Nepali writers such as Parasmani Pradhan and I.B. Rai within Darjeeling's vibrant literary sphere in the first half of the twentieth century, as has been well-documented by contemporary scholars such as Pratyoush Onta, Michael Hutt, and Rhoderick Chalmers. This scholarship has established a platform for exploring the cultural and sociopolitical connections between Darjeeling, Nepal, and the Himalayan region writ large. Third is the contemporaneous Tibetan language sphere of literary production, exemplified by publications like the monthly Kalimpong-based *Tibet Mirror* published from the 1920s–1960s, and the subsequent and ongoing body of Tibetological literature published by Western scholars based on research in the Darjeeling region. The recent *Transcultural Studies* special issue on Darjeeling and Kalimpong follows most closely in this tradition. Fourth is the scholarship on the political economy of tea and agrarian relations, which began to gather momentum in the 1960s as primarily Indian scholars, trained in Marxist social scientific lineages, turned to the region as a fieldsite that was both accessible and 'remote'. Darjeeling's proximity to Naxalbari—the home of India's Naxalite (Maoist) movement—has helped bring bring the hills of this region into focus as an alternative site for examining questions of class, labour, gender, indigeneity, and social upliftment. In this volume, Besky and Sen build upon this rich legacy. Fifth are studies of the Gorkhaland Movement. Perhaps best exemplified by Subba's *Ethnicity, State, and Development: A Case Study of the Gorkhaland Movement in Darjeeling* (1992), this genre is of course in constant need of updating as the movement has reformulated itself, and there are many more recent relevant studies, including Bethany Lacina's recent monograph (2017) and the contributions of Lacina and Wenner here. Sixth is the body of work on cultural politics and belonging published by regionally based scholars such as Subba, A.C. Sinha, and Mahendra Lama in several monographs and edited volumes. This scholarship has also inspired several recent monographs by contributors to this volume, including Mona Chettri (2017), Townsend Middleton (2015), and Sara Shneiderman (2015), and is also taken forward in Nilamber Chhetri's contribution here. Seventh, we wish to acknowledge the recent efflorescence of scholarship on Sikkim by authors such as Vibha Arora, Anna Balikci-Denjongpa, Mabel Gergan, Saul Mullard and Mélanie Vandenhelsken. We see this as an important, adjacent body of literature to that on Darjeeling, which interested readers should consult in conjunction with this volume. While Sikkim has experienced a very different trajectory of integration into the Indian polity than the district of Darjeeling—embedded in West Bengal as it is—the histories of the two regions are intertwined and must be understood in tandem. Eighth and finally, we see this book as furthering an ongoing conversation between Darjeeling and the study of India's North–East. With the Siliguri Corridor providing critical passage to the North–East, Darjeeling stands in provocative relationship to the histories and contemporary issues that define the North–East as a region of study. The seminal works of Sanjib Baruah, Sanjoy Hazarika, Duncan McDuie–Ra, Bengt Karlsson, and others provide comparative means for thinking through both the operative connections and similarities between Darjeeling and the North–East, as well as their differences. Such comparative work figures as part of a broader effort to reconsider Darjeeling's place in India, South Asia, and the postcolonial world more generally.

Outline of the Book

Here, however, we focus primarily on Darjeeling on its own terms. The first section, *Histories of Exception*, provides readers with three historical perspectives on the territorial, legal, and representational particularities that have made Darjeeling what it is today. This requires locating Darjeeling within a broader pattern of colonial exceptionality, while also isolating those factors that distinguish Darjeeling from other exceptional spaces, be they the tea growing regions of Assam or the various colonial 'hill-stations' scattered across the subcontinent.[41] Townsend Middleton begins with an exploration of the relationship between colonial governance, planter capital, and labour mobility, demonstrating how Darjeeling was intentionally produced as an exceptional space for the

[41] Kennedy (1996).

purposes of capitalist exploitation. Rune Bennike takes these arguments further by showing how Darjeeling was subsequently commodified as a tourist space, through a series of representational moves that obscured the reality of exploited labour upon which it was built in order to portray the Darjeeling hills as the perfect 'summer place' for both colonial and Indian residents of the plains. Jayeeta Sharma adds an intersectionally attuned lens to the considerations of labour, mobility, and cosmopolitanism, exploring diverse subaltern perspectives on the production of Darjeeling's space.

The second section, *Politics and Social Movements*, builds upon these historical foundations to offer five engagements with the challenging contemporary dynamics of ethnicity, class, and mobilization that underlie Darjeeling's ongoing political transformations. Bethany Lacina applies insights from the comparative study of electoral politics to the Gorkhaland Movement by tracing the political biographies of three of its important leaders from different historical phases: Deoprakash Rai, Subash Ghisingh, and Bimal Gurung. Miriam Wenner considers how political activism is often 'camouflaged' as social work, and considers the implications for mobilization from a perspective attentive to both the specificities of Gorkhaland, and the broader context of political science theorization. Mona Chettri draws upon regional South Asian literatures regarding patronage and corruption to consider how the culture of 'rowdies'—young party cadres who enforce a regime of violence—remains a consistent feature of the political landscape despite its supposed ideological shifts. Moving from the realm of mainstream party politics to the parallel yet structurally different world of ethnic politics, Nilamber Chettri explores the variegated histories of ethnic associations in Darjeeling to offer a diachronic study that tracks how communities have responded to external political conditions in shaping their self-representations and strategies for ethnic mobilization. Finally, Swatahsiddha Sarkar and Babika Khawas reintroduce 'the class question' to Darjeeling Studies by revisiting the works of the late pioneering scholar Kumar Pradhan, who strove to provide a model for understanding the relationship between Nepali national identity formation and class formation.

The third and final section, *Environments and Labour*, demonstrates how the histories of exception and long-standing waves of political mobilization detailed in the first two sections affect contemporary citizens of Darjeeling through their everyday experiences of livelihood and resource management. Sarah Besky shows how 'training' is a political space shot through with the challenges of emplacement and belonging in Darjeeling, as demonstrated through her ethnography of the Darjeeling Tea Management Training Center. Georgina Drew and Roshan Rai address the question of exclusion through the lens of water management, investigating how local social organizations enable better access to these crucial resources for many Darjeeling residents today. Finally, Debarati Sen shows how women tea plantation workers must engage in everyday entrepreneurialism that bridges the gaps between global discourses such as 'Fair Trade' and local labour union politics.

Taken together, these 11 chapters revisit Darjeeling from new and provocative perspectives. Each article speaks in some way to every one of the others; we encourage readers to dive into all sections equally, even if you come to the collection with an existing interest in one theme or another. We cannot understand resource management without understanding cultural politics; or contemporary electoral politics without understanding histories of territorialization. These are just a few examples of connections that emerge across these chapters, revealing Darjeeling as a multi-faceted locale that is at once old and new, remote and central, rural and urban, a site of relaxation and exploitation, and so forth. Darjeeling's complexities exceed what any single author or book can offer, but we hope that reconsidering this place in detail will prove a timely and productive endeavour for scholars, policymakers, and citizens alike.

Section I
Histories of Exception

1 *Unwritten Histories*

Difference, Capital, and the Darjeeling Exception

Townsend Middleton*

On 18 July 2011 India's central government, the state of West Bengal, and Darjeeling's ruling party (the Gorkha Janamukti Morcha or GJM) signed an agreement to establish the Gorkhaland Territorial Administration (GTA)—a semi-autonomous governing body for the Darjeeling Hills. The GTA was to put an end

* I owe considerable thanks to editor Sara Shneiderman, the fellow authors in this volume, and the book's two reviewers for their helpful feedback on this chapter. Eklavya Pradhan and Jason Cons have also been instrumental to this work—as, of course, have been my friends and collaborators in the hills and archives. Various portions of this work were supported by the American Council of Learned Societies, Duke University, IIE-Fulbright, and The University of North Carolina at Chapel Hill. All shortcomings remain my own.

to a subnationalist agitation that had been raging since 2008—the second movement for a separate state of Gorkhaland in as many generations. Since its inception in 2012, the makeshift GTA has largely failed to answer the Gorkhas' longstanding desires for autonomy in India. Politically, it has functioned as a one-party adhocracy, where the policies and jurisdictions of self-governance have been constantly renegotiated and manipulated by local, state, and federal governments alike. This state of *adhocracy*—to borrow Elizabeth Dunn's useful term[1]—is nothing new in the hills. Improvised and exceptional forms of governance extend deep into the region's past. Beginning in the 1830s with the *carte blanche* authority vested to British administrators to transform Darjeeling into the consummate hill station sanatorium, the region has periodically been treated as separate—and largely 'above' the fray of India writ large. During the colonial period, Darjeeling was consistently exempted from the standard rule of governance, being first governed as an Non-Regulated Area, then made a Scheduled District in 1874, a Backward Tract in 1919, and a Partially Excluded Area in 1935. This legacy of exceptionality has been subsequently extended in a range of postcolonial configurations, including: the Darjeeling Gorkha Hill Council (in place from 1988 to 2012); the failed attempt to make Darjeeling a Sixth Schedule 'tribal area' (2005–7); and the recently created GTA (2012–present). Ad hoc set-ups and special arrangements have been a hallmark of governance in the hills, making Darjeeling's history exceptions 'all the way down'.

In this essay, I step back to ask how this history of exceptionality has both *marked* Darjeeling and *made* it a place apart. To be sure: Darjeeling's colonial history fits a broader pattern of exception that extended to other 'frontier', 'backward', and/or ethnically distinct regions—including the tea-growing areas of the North-East. Yet even within this greater pattern of colonial exception, the historical production of Darjeeling as an exceptional space is distinct in particular ways. The proximity to Nepal, Bhutan, and Sikkim was part of Darjeeling's unique profile, as was its proximity to Calcutta. As Bennike and Sharma discuss in the ensuing chapters (this volume), these geographic circumstances rendered Darjeeling at once: a geopolitically strategic 'frontier'; a hub of Himalayan cosmopolitanism; and a key site of the tourist gaze and colonial travel. These elements were part of the constellation of historical forces that made Darjeeling an exceptional space—at once similar

[1] Dunn develops this concept in the context of humanitarian aid in Georgia. See Dunn (2012: 2).

to and distinct from other exceptional spaces in colonial India. But there were other factors as well. My analysis focuses on the interplays of three key elements of the region's history: colonial governance, planter capital, and labour. Throughout the colonial era, relations between the British Indian government and Darjeeling's tea industry were anything but stable—shaped, as they were, by periods of palpable collusion, tension, and renegotiation. But they were formative of life in Darjeeling and what made the hills exceptional. Rethinking the Darjeeling exception, this chapter draws on nineteenth century colonial archives to interrogate the shifting arrangements of governance, capital, and labour that enabled the region to become a bastion of imperial capitalism, and a place that in mind, if not matter, has forever stood apart from the rest of India.

There is no doubt that Darjeeling's exceptional status owes much to its geopolitical position, its Himalayan landscape with its cool, misty climes, and its fertile land. But in indulging these romantic framings, we should not underestimate the strategic practices through which British officials and planters *made* Darjeeling different for their own personal gain and that of the British Empire more generally. Reading against the grain of prevailing historiography in the hills, here I explore Darjeeling's exceptionality not as a 'natural' outcome of its Himalayan setting, but instead the endgame of a particular calculus of difference and capital that forever transformed life in the hills.

Darjeeling, in this regard, offers an acute site through which to study broader paradigms of imperial capitalist expansion across the Indian subcontinent. Of particular interest are the strategies through which British actors—particularly planters—leveraged difference (ethnic, geographic, administrative, and otherwise) to advance the interests of capital. At times, this was accomplished in concert with the colonial government. In other instances, however, the aims of planter capital were clearly at odds with those of the British Empire. Keeping these registers distinct is therefore crucial if we are to understand the interplays of governance and capital that shaped this and other colonial spaces. It is likewise critically important if we are to venture a deeper reading of how labourers negotiated—and perhaps manipulated—Darjeeling's exceptional terrain of capital and difference to their own ends.

Darjeeling, in these dynamics, both epitomizes broader imperial patterns and demands analysis on its own terms. Here it is worth evaluating Darjeeling's development in relation to—and contrast with—other 'aboriginal', 'frontier', 'backward' and/or tea-growing regions in India's North-East and beyond. In terms of how these regions were governed, how labour was brought to market, how business was regulated, and how it was not, the continuities and contrasts between Darjeeling and places like Assam, Cachar, and Sylhet afford critical bearings for locating Darjeeling within the broader context of British imperialism. These comparisons demonstrate telling similarities with other 'frontier', 'hill station', and tea-growing regions, but they also reveal notable differences that throw Darjeeling into its own kind of historical relief.

Interrogating Darjeeling's perennial exceptionality marks an important first step in this endeavour. The question to be asked is not whether Darjeeling is special, but rather what—and who—made the region so ostensibly different, unique, or exceptional. Towards that end, the historical critique that follows aims to shed some light on the untold processes through which Darjeeling has become such an exceptional figure—and figment—of the postcolonial imagination. This requires thinking through Darjeeling's historical similarities with other exceptional spaces, as well as its formative differences. Confronting this legacy of exceptionality in this way is indispensable for understanding Darjeeling's past and present—and perhaps too, for reimagining its future.

The Origins of Adhocracy

The British 'discovery' of Darjeeling is an oft-repeated history. The story of Captain George Lloyd and J. W. Grant arriving to 'Dorje-ling' and declaring the crescent shaped ridge an ideal perch for a colonial hill station sanatorium teems with the trappings of a classic discovery narrative: the intrepid traveller stumbling upon a wild, uninhabited land; the staking of a territorial claim; the winning over of the shy, 'backward' natives; and the victorious transformation of a land and people as per the colonizers' civilizational designs. This 'discovery' of Darjeeling needs no further celebration here. Such victorious histories do, however, raise questions about how exactly Darjeeling became the lauded 'queen of the hills'. What, for instance, were the conditions of governance, capital, and labour that enabled the actualization of these Victorian designs? The issue is not *that* Darjeeling became something of a colonial utopia for the British, but rather *how*. The answer, I believe, lies in the special—that is, exceptional—status Darjeeling was granted from the start.

Shortly after the British acquired Darjeeling by the controversial Deed of Grant from Sikkim in 1835, the task of transforming Darjeeling into a hill station sanatorium was handed to Dr A. Campbell. Campbell had earlier served as Assistant to the British Resident of Nepal, so he was no stranger to the Himalayas. In 1838, Campbell was put in charge of the fledgling hill station, becoming Darjeeling's first Superintendent in 1839—a post he held for the next two decades.[2] The powers vested in Campbell and his assistant Lieutenant Napier were remarkable. Technically, Darjeeling was a 'Non-Regulated Area', meaning it could be administered in accordance with its special needs and circumstances.[3] Guidelines drafted in 1839 vaguely instructed Campbell to follow the 'spirit of the laws and regulations of government'.[4] But in reality, the arrangement granted Campbell virtual carte blanche authority to develop Darjeeling as he saw fit. In this role, Campbell assumed wide-ranging responsibilities, including: land distribution, foreign relations with neighbouring countries, labour acquisition, revenue collection, management of law and police, presiding over criminal and civil courts, and overseeing the region's infrastructure and development. Campbell's capacities did not go unnoticed. An official report in 1854 explained:

> The entire management of this district has, from the first cession in 1838, been in the hands of the present superintendent, Dr. Campbell. When he took charge of it, there were not twenty families in the whole tract of hills; there is now a population of 10,000 persons in this portion.... The Superintendent has no assistance whatsoever; the whole progress of the Station, and the success which has attended the establishment of the sanitarium, is attributable solely and exclusively to his exertions.[5]

That one man could wield such wide-ranging authority signals the governmental circumstances that enabled Darjeeling's rapid transformation. What is notable is not the sophisticated administrative apparatus

[2] Campbell took over from Captain Lloyd. On Campbell's early activities, see (India, *Foreign*, 18 September, 1839, 167–8 PC), (India, *Foreign*, 9 October, 1839, 97–98 PC); (India, *Foreign*, 26 October, 1840, 113–5FC), (Hodgson Collection, Vol. 9/9/47). For brevity and to facilitate further enquiry, I have referenced archival sources by their call number.

[3] See also Besky (2013: 43); Subba (1989a, 1992); Warner (2014).

[4] 'Rules for Regulating the Assignment of Building Locations and Grants of Land in the Hill Tract Attached to the Station of Darjeeling, and For the Administration of Said Tract, Passed on 4th September 1839, To Be in Force From the Date of Promulgation' available in (India, IOR, 1854, v/23/94, [17]). The quoted phrase comes from Commissioner of Cooch Behar's 1869 review of Darjeeling from 1839–69. (Bengal, Judicial, Proc 1–13 December 1870).

[5] (India, IOR, 1854, v/23/94[17]).

applied to Darjeeling, but precisely the *lack* thereof. Throughout the 1840s and 1850s, official reports lauded Campbell's achievements under this special arrangement—even likening Darjeeling's governing structures to 'the superintendence of a private estate' with the added benefit of revenue collection.[6] The legality of Campbell's power was dubious. And indeed, questions were raised about its basis. An 1854 report framed the concern as follows: 'It is certain that complicated questions of right will arise and the legality of the Superintendent's jurisdiction will form the subject of legal discussion: it is therefore desirable that an Act of Legislation should pass, defining the powers of the Superintendent.'[7] Per this review, the grounds of Campbell's rule were tenuous and in need of shoring up. Such bureaucratic concerns, however, were easily swept beneath the rug of his impressive achievements.

By all accounts, the transformations of the 1840s and 1850s were profound. As roads and bungalows were built, British colonials began recognizing the hill station's restorative qualities and economic potential.[8] Investors acquired large tracts of land. By the mid-1850s, planters were busily establishing the tea plantations that would become Darjeeling's signature. When documenting these developments, the colonial archive offers little insight into the native peoples whose lands and lives were subject to these changes. What the official record does illustrate, however, are the origins of a laissez faire adhocracy laying the groundwork for significant capitalist expansion.

The collusions between governance and private capital became especially conspicuous around the issue of land distribution. Wielding the power to title and distribute land, Campbell singlehandedly converted massive tracts of native and common land into the private property of European investors.[9] This means of primitive accumulation presaged Lord Canning's 1861 'Resolution on the Sale of Wastelands', which established legal procedures across India for converting designated 'wastelands' into private property.[10] Colonial law defined 'wastelands' as uninhabited,

[6] (India, IOR, 1854, v/23/94[17]).

[7] (India, IOR, 1854, v/23/94[17]).

[8] Kennedy (1996: 184).

[9] Policy set in 1839 established Campbell's power to assign land titles and administer 30-year agricultural leases for tracts of 10 acres or more. While technically these holdings were 'leased', the de facto reality was that they were private property. See 1839 'Rules for Regulating ...' cited in Note 6 above.

[10] See Marx's *Capital*, Chapters 26 & 32 (1978). On land distribution, see also Besky (2013: 43).

uncultivated, and thus non-revenue producing lands. Once designated 'wastelands', the colonial state could then sell or lease the given territory into private use. The practice was used widely throughout British India and its function was particularly acute in Darjeeling.[11] By considering massive tracts of the hills uninhabited, Superintendent Campbell and his successor B.W. Morton effectively sold off much of Darjeeling. For British interests, the benefits of this primitive accumulation were two-fold: First, privatization subjected these lands to taxation, enabling Darjeeling to generate revenue to fund its own development. Second, the creation of large chunks of private property set the stage for budding capitalism—most notably, the plantation-driven economy of tea.

The selling of 'wastelands' dovetailed nicely with the discovery narrative of 'uninhabited' Darjeeling—both of which conveniently dismissed the presence of native cultivators (*ryots*) living and working in the hills. In all the records surrounding the lease and purchase of land in the 1850s and 1860s, there is notably little said of ryots.[12] The presence of these native communities and the expropriation of their lands, it seems, were inconvenient truths amid the capitalist free-for-all unfolding in the hills. With officials and planters privatizing Darjeeling—and excluding native inhabitants from the historical record—expropriation and primitive accumulation thereby generated their requisite forms of subalternity.

Subsequent reviews of land distribution (conducted in the 1870s, after Campbell's tenure) revealed rampant abuse of the 'wastelands' designation. Many of the tracts that Campbell and his successor, B.W. Morton, declared 'uncultivated' had in fact been inhabited by native cultivators. The reviews subsequently concluded that much of Darjeeling had 'been sold over the heads of ryots', a process that involved dispossessing local peoples of their lands and rights.[13] The abuses were so severe that a

[11] ('Annual Report on the Police of the Darjeeling Division', India, IOR, 1861, V/24/525).

[12] When and where land was sold over the heads of native cultivators, ryots were given the option of either moving off the sold land, submitting to rent, or in certain cases, becoming labourers on the gardens. ('Lands Sold Over the Heads of Ryots in the Darjeeling District', Bengal, Revenue, Head, WL, Coll. 6, Proc 14–15 August 1873). On ryots' pre-colonial systems of shifting cultivation in the area, see Warner (2014).

[13] An 1873 Resolution by the Government of Bengal titled 'The Irregular Sale of Waste Lands in the Darjeeling District', for instance explains, 'It is the fashion in the Darjeeling district to say in regard to old grants that the people came there "after the grants were made". But Hooker's Journal and other papers

moratorium was subsequently placed on any further 'wasteland' sales in Darjeeling. By then though, the damage was largely done. The majority of Darjeeling's prime lands were now in the hands of the planters.

The privatization of land—and in particular 'wastelands'—thus became a mechanism through which Campbell and a small coterie of British interests effectively transferred Darjeeling into the hands of an emergent planter class, with whom they shared palpable interests. This land distribution system marked an historic collusion between colonial governance and planter capital that would dictate Darjeeling's fate for decades to come. Importantly, this was a collusion made possible not by the heroic discovery and taming of a wild land, but rather by the special administrative arrangements that afforded Darjeeling's early leaders—namely Campbell—sweeping authority to realize British imperial designs. As would become increasingly clear, making a colonial utopia required a host of unwritten rules and unwritten lives.

Labour Recruitment and Strategic Informality

Making Darjeeling a hill station required immense amounts of labour—far more than the indigenous populations could provide. Deeming the Darjeeling tract 'almost uninhabited' when the British arrived, Campbell turned to neighbouring Sikkim, Bhutan, and Nepal to secure the needed labourers.[14] Campbell saw in these neighbouring countries conditions that might work to the British's advantage—among them slavery, forced (*begari*) labour regimes, and oppressive taxation schemes.[15] These push factors, coupled with the pull of wage labour and freedom in Darjeeling, facilitated a massive influx of labour. But this labour migration brought with it a host of legal problems. Unlike the tea industry of the North-East, which drew the majority of its labour from within India itself, the transnational components of Darjeeling's labour pool raised a suite

---

make mention of thriving villages existing in places now the property of tea planters; and the Lieutenant-Governor has little doubt that while the cultivators have been treated as squatters without rights, occupied lands in Darjeeling have all along been sold or leased under the wasteland rules' (Bengal, Revenue, Head, WL, Coll. 6, Proc 14–15 August 1873).

[14] (India, *Foreign*, 28 June, 1841, 135–6FC).

[15] On these push-pull factors, see Chatterjee (2001: 65–80); Holmberg et al. (1999); Hutt (1997: 109–13); Shneiderman (2015: 110–15); Subba (1989, 1992: 39–44); Subba and Sinha (2003: 14–17); Whelpton (2005: 50–5).

of alternative concerns. Neighbouring governments refused to sanction migration to Darjeeling. In nineteenth-century Nepal, Sikkim, and Bhutan, subjects were considered property of the sovereign and consequently subject to taxation and mandatory state labour.[16] British Darjeeling therefore figured as a competitor not only for national loyalty and revenue, but also—and crucially—for labour. In 1841, Campbell wrote to the Governor General explaining:

> It will readily appear to the Governor General in Council that almost all the hill people who have settled at Darjeeling are by usage of our neighbors claimable from us. It will also be evident that in admitting the propriety of such claims, the British government would in many cases be directly countenancing slavery, and in such cases ... it would be unjustly interfering with the right that all men should have in peace and good faith to adopt new laws as their own.[17]

Campbell's letter charts a peculiar liberal quandary: either meet Darjeeling's labour needs by encouraging a politically problematic pattern of migration, or acquiesce to oppressive regimes and countenance slavery. Heeding his liberal persuasions and need for labour, Campbell tacitly encouraged labourers to migrate from Sikkim, Bhutan, and Nepal throughout the 1840s and 1850s, doling out, in his words, 'a great deal of relief and assistance to many newcomers and to settlers.'[18]

With the advent of Darjeeling's tea industry in the 1850s, the demands for labour grew considerably. The tea gardens drew labourers from communities across the region. But Nepal soon emerged as a primary source, from whence thousands proved ready and willing to set out for a new life in Darjeeling. For the British, Nepal proved optimal not only for the quantity of labourers it produced, but also the quality.[19] The Gurungs, Rais, Tamangs, and other ethnicities that poured across the border were deemed uniquely suited to the mountainous climes of Darjeeling. The British had found an ideal labour pool.

[16] (India, *Foreign*, 28 June 1841, 135–6FC); (India, *Foreign*, 31 December 1858, 2522–6FC). On *begari* labour, Warner (2014). On taxation, Shneiderman (2015: 111–12).

[17] (India, Foreign, 28 June, 1841, 135–6FC) (India, Foreign, Indian Political Dispatch 50 of 1841).

[18] (India, Foreign, 1 August, 1851, 149–50FC).

[19] (India, Foreign, August, 1837, 139–40) (India, Foreign, 28 June, 1841, 135–6FC) (India, Foreign, 27 April, 1855, 63FC).

Problems arose, however, when the Nepali government refused to consent to this migration. Campbell wrote in the late 1850s of the 'bad feelings on the part of the Nipal Durbar towards the British government' and the Nepali government's repeated orders 'directed against the increase of our own labourers'.[20] The Nepali government's disapproval of the migration to Darjeeling raised innumerable problems for the British and the Nepali settlers. For the British, the flow of labour from Nepal created political tensions with the Nepali state. Campbell and the planters accordingly provided wages, shelter, and freedom to the settlers, but refused to legally recognize the Nepali coolies as British subjects. The coolie labourers consequently had little legal protection. As I have elaborated elsewhere, this created an enduring sense of precarity and anxiety on the plantations.[21] The archive tells harrowing tales of escaped slaves being kidnapped from Darjeeling and returned to Nepal under the dark of night.[22] Repeatedly in the 1850s, rumours circulated through the estates that an invasion by Nepal was imminent, sparking coolies to flee in large numbers out of fear of being forcibly returned to Nepal.[23] There was also the lingering threat of extradition. And although extradition cases were rare, they clearly illustrated the British's unwillingness to claim the Nepali coolies as British subjects.[24] These legal considerations notwithstanding, the British nevertheless considered Nepali coolies integral to Darjeeling's development. 'They are the best tea coolies known,' an

[20] (India, Foreign, 31 December 1858, 2522–6FC). The Nepali government allowed Gurkha military recruitment elsewhere in Nepal, but disapproved of migration to Darjeeling. In fact, the Nepali state demanded the immediate return of emigrants, promising amnesty to refugee slaves or else the denial of future entry and citizenship in Nepal.

[21] Middleton (2013a, 2013c).

[22] (Bengal, Judicial, Proc 200, August, 1868); (India, Foreign, August, 1868, 219–20, Political, A).

[23] (India, Foreign, 29 December 1854, 22–34SC); (India, Foreign, 21 December 1858, 2522–6FC); (India, Foreign, 30 December, 1859, 1431–1446FC/SUP); (Bengal, Political, November, 1864, 27–8). As historian Catherine Warner (2014) reminds us, the borders between Nepal, Sikkim, and India were nebulous prior to British rule. The British, however, 'territorialized' the region, creating starker borders.

[24] (India, Foreign, August 1868, 219–20, 404–5, Political, A); (India, Foreign, February, 1869, 9, Political, A); (India, Foreign, March, 1878, 1–8, Political, A); (India, Foreign, January, 1864, 222–3, Political, A); (India, Foreign, July, 1866, 63, Political, A); (Bengal, Judicial, August 1868, 206–9).

1873 government report noted, 'the growth of the Nepalese population is the best surety that planters can have for labour in the future.'[25] If this were true, how then did the British get around the legal quandaries of migration to satisfy their demand for this ideal labour?

The British relied on informal labour recruiters known as *sardars* to bring labour to Darjeeling. This was largely in keeping with labour recruitment patterns throughout colonial India, wherein informal recruiters (sardars) were integral to various industries, plantation and otherwise. Yet Darjeeling's *sardari* system took distinct forms, particularly in relation to questions of transnational migration, legality, and regulation (a point I develop later). Similar to sardars operating elsewhere on the subcontinent, these native recruiters mobilized their ethnic ties, local knowledge, and cultural familiarity to spread the word of a better life and therein lure labour.[26] To this day, one can still hear folksongs about the gold growing on the tea bushes of Mugalan (the Nepali term for India at the time).[27] Generally speaking, sardars organized bands of coolies, ushering them across the border and to the particular estates where labour was needed. Their role entailed more than just delivering labour to market, however. The sardars came to occupy a key position in the plantation system. Working closely with planters, these native agents both supplied and managed labour.[28] For coolies, sardars served as liaisons to the planters and as community leaders within the gardens, brokering the workers' material and cultural needs. As intermediaries between labour and management, sardars were lynchpins of the entire system.

The sardari system remains a largely untold chapter of Darjeeling's history. Sardars were not only responsible for the tens of thousands of labourers who made their way to Darjeeling during the nineteenth century, they also helped shape a nascent cultural landscape. Recognizing the value of a good sardar, planters deputized favourite sardars to issue housing and small parcels of land to labourers within their estates. Soon small village communities began developing around sardars, who acted as the de facto headman of these coolie villages.

[25] (Bengal, Revenue, Head, WL, Coll. 6, Proc 14–15, August, 1873).

[26] On *sardari* labour recruitment, see also Besky (2013: 56, 74–7); Bhowmik (2016); Middleton (2013a: 612), (2013c: 17); (2015: 36).

[27] Hutt (1998); Shneiderman (2015: 113).

[28] The sardari system, as Warner argues, resembled pre-existing headman and client–patron relationships of the region (2014: 27–31).

Because sardars tended to recruit from within their own ethnic group, these coolie villages were often ethnically distinct—earning them names like Gurung Busti and Tamang Busti. The sardars were thus largely responsible for the patchwork ethnic geography that can still be seen across Darjeeling's plantations. To this day, the tea gardens contain rich oral histories of the formative roles that sardars played in shaping everyday life in the hills.

For the British, the sardars served other purposes. Relegating the dirty work of moving bodies across borders to these native actors, planters and colonial officials washed their hands off the dubious legality of this labour migration. Moreover, the sardari system effectively ran itself, requiring little to no capital investment. With informal recruiters supplying and managing labour, governmental oversight was neither needed nor wanted. Regulation would only bring attention to a labour recruitment system that was vital to their interests, but legally problematic at best. The entire system accordingly operated in a realm of quasi-legality, which obviated the need for formal papers, documentation, and formal oversight. In sum: the system worked *precisely because it was off-the-record.* So long as it stayed that way, sardari labour recruitment would remain a lynchpin of capitalism in the hills—and a strategically unwritten chapter of its history.[29] Like with land, here again with labour, Darjeeling's administrative arrangement—involving, as it did, an operative *lack* of regulation—afforded fertile grounds for planter capital.

Assam by Comparison

The situation looked similar but also different elsewhere in India. Sardari labour recruitment played a vital role to industries throughout British India—particularly in the tea-growing regions of the North-East.[30] However, unlike in Darjeeling, where the sardari system remained strategically informal and unregulated, sardari recruitment in places like Assam, Cachar, and Sylhet became the subject of growing regulatory concern. By the early 1860s, abuses associated with informal recruitment were endemic to labour migration across India. The inland areas of Chota Nagpur and Santal-Parganas were key sources of coolie labour

[29] This explains the relative paucity of colonial archival information on plantation labour in Darjeeling, especially in comparison with other tea districts like Assam, Cachar, and Sylhet.

[30] Ghosh (1999); Sen (2010); Sharma (2011).

for not just the North-East, but also for distant colonies of Mauritius, British Guiana, Trinidad, and beyond. Serving multiple industries, sardars were instrumental in bringing *adivasi* (indigenous) peoples from their interior homelands to the gardens of Assam and to the ports of Calcutta where they were packed onto ships bound for indentured servitude in colonies throughout the British Empire. Without regulation though, sardari labour was prone to abuse. Sardars frequently misled coolies about the terms of their employment and even their destination. For coolies making their way to the North-East, transit was perilous, as bands of coolies were handed from one sardar to another, finally making their way to their place of employment. Identification, bona fides, and safeguards were lacking, as were formal contracts between coolies and planters.

The sardars' cunning cut both ways. The violation of coolies' rights and well-being were obvious. But unregulated recruitment also posed problems for planters. These capitalists demanded particular kinds of bodies for particular kinds of labour. In this *market for aboriginality*—as Kaushik Ghosh has framed it—adivasi labourers fetched a higher price than the average plainsman.[31] Adivasi labourers were consequently a prized commodity for sardars. Taking advantage of the high demand for adivasi bodies, recruiters and labourers could easily dupe planters by passing non-adivasis off as adivasis. With no regulation in place to ensure the quantity and quality of labour arriving in the tea districts—much less the rights and well-being of the coolies—something needed to change.

Noting the 'reckless misdealings' of informal recruiters in the early 1860s, the British Raj kicked into gear to create a Protector of Immigrants, responsible for overseeing the well-being of coolies migrating within India, as well as to other parts of the British Empire.[32] Notably, the Protector's jurisdiction did not cover Darjeeling.[33] By contrast, the

[31] Ghosh (1999: 34).

[32] The full title was 'Protector of Immigrants, Medical Inspector, and Emigrants and Colonial Emigration'. See (Bengal, General, Emigration, Proc 20, April 1861), ('Rules for the Guidance of Protector of... Under ACT XIII of 1864), (Bengal, Emigration, Proc 18–29, December, 1864), (Bengal, Financial, Emigration, Proc 69–73, August, 1865).

[33] Though intervention in Nepal was impossible, the Protector did recognize Nepal as a source of inland and foreign labour migration (Bengal, Financial, Emigration, Proc, 40–61, June 1865).

Protector travelled extensively throughout Assam inspecting plantations to ensure: that coolies were being properly paid; that they had migrated on their own volition; that working and living conditions were humane; and that planters and labourers were fulfilling their obligations to one another. Per these responsibilities, the Protector functioned as an advocate for coolie rights. However, the creation of the post also served planter capital by stabilizing the quantity and quality of labour coming to the market. Articulating a broader trajectory of regulation, laws were subsequently put in place to formally license recruiters—thereby bringing their work squarely under the purview of the colonial state. Bills to standardize the contracts between planters and labourers in Assam, Cachar, and Sylhet soon followed.[34]

As the government took a growing interest in the shadowy underworld of labour recruitment, two themes became especially prominent: identification and health.[35] Identification of coolies in transit would help secure and protect coolies' individual rights. Medical care along the way would ensure their physical well-being. But these regulatory interests in the epistemology and medicalization of the coolie body served collateral purposes. They answered two questions of great value to the British: (a) How were the planters and other capitalists to know *who* they were hiring? (b) How could they guarantee the fitness—and thus labour capacity—of their coolies?

Regulatory measures passed throughout the next two decades (1860s–80s) elaborated these concerns with coolie identification and health.[36] Checkpoints and depots were instituted along labour migration routes to establish coolies' identities. When coolies arrived at these outposts, their anthropological particulars (caste/tribe, native district, etc.) were recorded in official ledgers and they were given bona fides documenting their identity and rendering them able to enter into formal

[34] (Bengal, Financial, Emigration, Proc 13–20, February, 1865); Contract in (Bengal, Financial, Emigration, Proc 40–61, June 1865).

[35] (Bengal, Financial, Emigration, Proc 72, August 1865).

[36] See, generally, Proceedings from the General Department—Inland Migration during this period. More specifically, see the Parliamentary Report on the coolie trade in Assam (India, Parliamentary Papers, IOR, V/50/357, 1867); (Bengal, Financial, Emigration, Proc 34, April, 1868); (Bengal, Financial, Emigration, Proc 21–3, November, 1870); (Bengal, General, Emigration, Proc, B63, November 1871); (Bengal, General, Emigration, Proc 58–9, December 1871); (Bengal, General, Emigration, Proc, B90–3, February, 1876).

contracts with planters once they arrived at their destination.[37] These identification measures were complemented by health checks, wherein government medical inspectors determined whether or not individuals were 'fit for labour'.[38] Those rendered physically unfit were retained at the depot. Those deemed able-bodied were allowed to proceed.

These regulatory mechanisms naturally slowed the supply of labour. And it was not long before the planters of Assam began to complain.[39] Planters called the Protector's regulatory interventions 'a powerful discouragement and opposition to the supply of labour for the tea districts.'[40] Planters further opined that regulatory hassles along the migration routes would relay back to the adivasi hinterlands and thereby 'NOT tend to make emigration to the tea provinces more favourably entertained in the district from whence they [coolies] came'.[41] The planters' complaints demonstrate the two-sided nature of regulation. On the one hand, the regulations assured workers' rights and a stable labour supply for the capitalists. Proper identification of particular kinds of coolies and their physical health was deemed of paramount importance to the tea industry. As one planter reflected during the 1880s, some years after these regulatory mechanisms were in place: 'Of course, I do not look for coolies such as we used to get in the old days, but provided you send me healthy black skins, with good chests, and no tendency to dropsy, I shall be satisfied.'[42] On the other hand, the regulatory constraints

[37] (Bengal, Financial, Emigration, Proc 13–20, February 1865); (Bengal, Financial, Emigration, Proc 69–73, August 1865); (Bengal, General, Emigration, File 43, Proc 34–6, March 1878); (Bengal, General, Emigration, File 43, Proc 10–22, April 1878); (Bengal, General, Emigration, File 93, Proc 1–6, September 1878); (Bengal, General, Inland Emigration, File 29, Proc 1, April 1879); (Bengal, General, Inland Emigration, ProcAll, November 1880); ('The Labour Districts Emigration Act', Bengal, General, Inland Emigration, ProcAll, February 1881); (Bengal, General, Inland Emigration, File 36, Proc 1, December 1885).

[38] (Bengal, Financial, Emigration, Proc 34, April 1868).

[39] (Bengal, Financial, Inland Emigration, Proc 103–4, November 1865).

[40] ('Letter from Jardine, Skinner and Co' in Bengal, Financial, Inland Emigration, Proc 103–4, November 1865); other complaints in (Bengal, General, Emigration, Proc, B63 November 1871); (Bengal, General, Emigration, Proc 58–9, December 1871).

[41] (Bengal, General, Emigration, Proc 103–4, November 1865).

[42] ('Letter from James Bining to Government of Bengal', Bengal, General, Inland Emigration, 36, Proc 1, December 1885).

hindered the functioning of planter capital itself. They did so by formalizing a labour supply chain that thrived on informality. Reading these complaints, one gets the sense of a capitalist elite wanting to have its cake and eat it too. This paradoxical call for—but resistance to—regulation became a signature of the planters' ambivalent dealings with government throughout this time. Thus were the tensions between planter capital and colonial governance in the North-East.

Territories of Exception

What did these increasingly regulated relations between governance, planter capital, and labour in Assam have to do with Darjeeling? Very little. And this is precisely where we can see interesting differences between Darjeeling and tea-producing areas of the North-East. On the surface, the tea industry in Assam shared much in common with Darjeeling.[43] In both regions, the plantation economy introduced significant environmental and cultural changes in the nineteenth century. The high demands for labour induced migrations that profoundly altered both regions' demography. And sardari labour recruitment proved vital to these transformations. However, when it came to regulation, the similarities between Assam and Darjeeling ended.

Unlike Assam and other regions of the North-East, Darjeeling's sardari system remained conveniently excluded from regulatory oversight. When it came to labour recruitment, Darjeeling was literally off the regulatory map. (See Figure 1.1, where Darjeeling does not figure at all. Were it to appear, it would be located behind the title in the top-right quadrant.)

This was not accidental. This territory of exception was instead the outcome of longstanding collusions between government and Darjeeling's planters—and, increasingly, an active fending off of regulatory incursions into the hills.

Given Darjeeling's proximity to Assam, there was an inevitable overlap in the geographies of labour recruitment and regulation. The Dooars, Jalpaiguri, and the Terai more generally became natural gray zones. As labour recruiters and regulation policies from Assam moved into these areas and towards the actual Darjeeling Hills, Darjeeling's planters

[43] The scholarship on Assam's Tea industry is extensive. See, in particular, Behal (2006); Sharma (2009; 2011). On Darjeeling tea, see Besky (2013); Bhowmik (1981); Chatterjee (2001); Nag (2000); Subba (1989a).

Figure 1.1 Government of India's 'The Districts in Which Inland Emigrants Were Registered, 1894'
Source: 'Report on Inland Emigration for Year 1894' (Bengal, General Emigration, 5r/11-1, Proc 11–12, July 1895).

defended their unregulated territory from recruitment and regulatory creep. The issue came to the fore in 1872 following a cholera outbreak in the region, when the government proposed extending laws into the Darjeeling district that would require planters to provide hospitals for labourers.[44] The planters stridently opposed the extension of this regulatory mechanism into their territory, arguing that their labourers were far better off than those in other tea districts like Assam and Cachar. The planters insisted that they themselves would develop medical arrangements for their special labour pool. The issue arose again in 1875 when a small contingent of planters in the plains below Darjeeling (the Terai) called for an extension of Act VIII of 1873, which would provide formal contracts between gardens and labourers, into the area.[45] Tellingly,

[44] Government proposed extension of Sec 76 of Act II of 1870. (Bengal, General, Emigration, Proc, B90–3, February 1876). On health and plantations in colonial Darjeeling, see Bhattacharya (2012).

[45] (Bengal, General, Emigration, Proc, B90–3, February 1876).

the planters from the hills successfully resisted this proposal. In doing so, they drew important climatic and labour distinctions between the Terai—where workers were prone to abscond to other agricultural ventures (such as rice cultivation)—and the hills, 'where the labour [was] plentiful'.[46] Per these topographic logics, the need to contractually regulate the relationship between workers and employers did not apply to the Darjeeling hills proper. Regulation, they argued, was therefore not warranted in the district. Drawing lines as they did, both these instances from the 1870s are indicative of the planters' broader agenda to defend Darjeeling from regulatory incursion.

Managing the reach of government was one thing, corralling the unruly networks of labourers and recruiters was another. Unbound by formal contracts, tea coolies strategically pursued better-paying alternatives, both in local sectors like Darjeeling's government-run cinchona plantations, and in military, police, and other services outside the region. Seen from the side of labour, the lack of regulation offered its own set of opportunities, which the coolies of Darjeeling duly capitalized on—much to the chagrin of the planters. Compounding the planters' troubles, recruiters gathering men for Assam's tea gardens and for indentured labour in the colonies were increasingly venturing into Darjeeling in search of recruits. Darjeeling had always been a labour-importing district, but now it faced becoming the opposite. The prospect of coolies being recruited away from Darjeeling's plantations was unacceptable to the planters. In 1881 and again in 1888, the planters sternly rejected the opening of Darjeeling to labour recruitment for the colonies. Their 1888 memorandum articulated their proprietary claims to labour in the hills, underscoring their arguments with a sense of the industry's vulnerability: viz, 'This current year gardens are short of their full compliment, the supply being no way sufficient for demand ... I trust for the above reasons that Government will refuse the application [for recruitment to the colonies], which if granted would cause serious damage.'[47]

The planters' contradictory dealings with government were telling. At the same time that they resisted regulation, they also demanded governmental protection of their ideal labour pool. The stakes escalated

[46] Words of Albert Smallwood of Lloyd and Company (planters) in (Bengal, General, Emigration, Proc, B90–3, February 1876).

[47] (Bengal, General, Colonial Emigration, B, 1–4, July 1888); Regarding 1881, Bengal, General, Colonial Emigration, File 20, Proc 17–18, August 1883).

throughout the latter decades of the nineteenth century. The British Empire's labour requirements in the North-East, Burma, Mauritius, the Caribbean colonies, and elsewhere were forcing the opening of new labour recruitment fields. Now, with recruiters creeping into their prized territory, Darjeeling was increasingly 'on the map'.

The planters' bid to stave off competition for their labour eventually met an unassailable force—the British Indian government itself. For decades, the British Indian army had recruited men out of Nepal to fill the ranks of the famed Gurkha regiments. In the wake of the Revolt of 1857 when Nepal's 'brave' 'martial races' proved their mettle and loyalty, the British expanded the Gurkha regiments significantly.[48] This put added strain on the Gurkha regiments' traditional recruiting fields in central and western Nepal. With the homelands of the Gurungs, Magars, and others drying up of able and willing recruits, recruiters moved eastward into the territory of the Rais, Limbus, and others—in other words, towards Darjeeling and into the recruiting grounds of the planters.[49] Further competition came from the Assamese and Burma police, who were also keen to fill their ranks with Nepalis from these regions.[50] To facilitate immigration out of Nepal (and perhaps to tap local sources), a Gurkha recruiting centre was opened in Darjeeling in the early 1890s.[51] This meant that potential and actual tea coolies could, much more easily than before, become soldiers and police.[52]

The planters made desperate pleas to government to stop this incursion and preserve the unique labour conditions that had allowed Darjeeling's tea industry to thrive. A planter's memorandum from 1890

[48] Besky (2013: 76); Des Chene (1991: 123); Hunter (1896 [1991]: 259–60).

[49] (India, Foreign, Political, A, Proc 141–158, July 1880); (India, Foreign, July, 1886, 818–43, Sec E).

[50] See Imdad Hussain's (2003) work on the recruitment of Gorkha soldiers and police to India's North–East.

[51] Onta (1996b). This was an alternative to the recruitment depot in Gorakhpur. See (India, Foreign, Political, A, Proc 141–158, July 1880); (India, Foreign, September 1887, 113–20, Sec E); (India, Foreign, August 1893, 52, Part B, Ext l).

[52] The recruitment of police through the Darjeeling military depot was stopped in 1893. (India, Foreign, August 1893, 52, PartB, Extl) British preferences for Nepal's 'martial races' meant that not all Nepalis qualified for Gurkha service—those that the British classified as belonging to 'martial races' (c.f. Shneiderman 2015: 12).

framed the industry's dependence on proprietary labour in almost existential terms:

> It is of vital importance to this district of Darjeeling that we should retain all the local labour for the development of our gardens ... Imported labour from the plains does not thrive and will not remain here. We are dependent wholly on indigenous labour of these hills. This has been interfered with of late by recruiting from Cachar and if it continues, the tea industry of these hills will be a thing of the past.[53]

By all accounts, the recruitment of civilian and military labour away from Darjeeling was taking a toll. The Deputy Commissioner of Darjeeling confirmed that in a space of two months that same year, more than 1,000 labourers had been recruited away for service in Burma alone, and that he was trying his best to stop recruitment from the gardens.[54] This was perhaps a futile endeavour.

The planters elaborated their cause repeatedly in the 1890s. Railing against the 'predatory recruiters' at work in the hills, the planters argued that the recruitment of their coolies for police and army service, as well as coolie work in the North-East, was depopulating their labour pool to deleterious effects.[55] Invoking difference in the interest of capital, they called upon the government to recognize and protect Darjeeling's unique labour market. This required a careful negotiation of exceptionality, wherein the planters necessarily framed Darjeeling as both similar yet operatively different from the North-East—an exception, if you will, within a broader pattern of exceptional spaces. Tellingly, Assam afforded a productive point of contrasts in these bids for protection:

> It may hence be argued that the only difference between the positions of the Assam and the Darjeeling planter is that the former pays a little more for his imported coolie and has the protection of a definite law, and that though the latter is not protected by a labour law, the labour population on his private garden for which he has paid *is his own*, and does *not provide an open market* for any recruiter to frequent.[56]

[53] (Bengal, General, Inland Emig, 1r/1, Proc B, December 1891).

[54] (Bengal, General, Inland Emig, 1r/1, Proc B, December 1891).

[55] (Bengal, General, Emigration, 1r/2, 1898, 1 October 1898); (Bengal, General, Emigration, 1r/2, Proc B, 29–31, November 1899); (Bengal, General, Emigration, 1r/2/1, Proc 15–20, November 1899).

[56] (Bengal, General, Inland Emigration, 1r/1, Proc B, December 1891).

Note how the planters frame their estates essentially as private fiefdoms, wherein labour had no rights or protection but instead was owned, not unlike chattel. As private estates, so the logic went, the tea gardens were neither open nor free markets for labourers or recruiters.

The planters' pleas brought mixed results. Colonial administrators conceded that the 'Darjeeling district suffered very much from the promiscuous recruiting that had taken place.'[57] The District Recruiting Officer for the army, Captain Eden Vansittart, even assured the planters that he had their interests in mind:

> I am positive that any good man who has served as a coolie in a tea garden is not likely to turn out such a good soldier as a lad imported direct from his own village in Nepal, and therefore independent of the fact that I should be sorry to injure the private interests of the planter community in the interest of the State I strongly object to enlisting coolies, and have done and will do all I can to put a stop to this and I intend to get all my recruits from Nepal.[58]

The solution was not so simple. Recruits from Darjeeling could—and did—pass as subjects of Nepal. Moreover, recruiters could easily enlist tea garden coolies and then quickly sneak them out of the district, unbeknownst to planters. How then were planters or recruiters (official and otherwise) to know *who* the recruits were? The question of coolie identification (that we saw emerge in the Assam context) here became a pointed concern in Darjeeling.

To forestall subterfuge, the planters and government recruiters called for all enlisted recruits to be held in a depot for two weeks in order to give planters and garden sardars ample time to account for their coolies. For identification purposes, each week the recruits were to be paraded in front of planters in Darjeeling, so that they could visually confirm that none of the recruits were actually their own coolies. Recruits who passed this identity test on two consecutive parade days would then be given certificates and allowed to proceed.[59]

[57] (India, Foreign, August 1893, 52, PartB, Extl).

[58] (India, Foreign, August 1893, 52, PartB, Extl). On this topic, I am indebted to Pratyoush Onta's excellent article 'Gurkhas as Coolies and Soldiers', which draws from many of the same archival sources. (Onta, *Kathmandu Post*, 22 September 1996, p. II).

[59] (Bengal, Judicial, 17 February 1891/17–25 October 1892).

These measures seem to have done little to stem the tide of coolie labour out of the hills. Throughout the 1890s, the planters filed repeated grievances over the loss of coolies. They further claimed that the industry could not afford to compete with the higher wages being offered elsewhere. The Government of Bengal acknowledged their concerns, but also called attention to the alternative: full blown regulation of the Darjeeling tea industry. A.W. Paul raised this threat/option in his report to the Chief Minister:

> But on this subject of protection against losing their coolies, it might be as well ... to enquire into their [planters] Association, whether as they practically wish for all the benefits of the Assam Coolie Acts, they are prepared to accept the responsibilities entailed thereby; in other words, whether they wish the Assam Acts to be introduced in the Darjeeling and Julpaiguri districts ... I do not think they will.[60]

Paul's inclinations were, as we have seen, historically grounded. Darjeeling planters had, to date, largely evaded the regulations in place in Assam. But now, with the government taking a stand, the planters' cunning had been called out. They could not have it both ways. If the planters wanted the government to secure their labour supply, they would have to assume the responsibilities for the coolies' well-being that went along with regulation.

The collusions between government and planter capital that defined the early period of colonial rule in Darjeeling were now morphing into overt tensions. Over the next decade, colonial administrators increasingly rebuked the privileged exceptionality claimed by the planters. Evoking the logic of free-market capitalism, the government in 1899 opined:

> They [the Darjeeling planters] find that they suffer from the competition of the government and of private persons in their local labour market, and naturally desire to keep it to themselves. They know very well that the high wages offered by their rivals are the real attraction, and operate with precisely the same effect whether used in a legitimate way or otherwise.[61]

It bears remembering that the government itself—primarily through its recruitment for military and police service—now had a competitive

[60] (Bengal, Judicial, 17 February 1891/17–25 October 1892).

[61] (Bengal, General, Emigration, 1r/2/1, Proc 15–20, November 1899).

interest in Darjeeling's labour pool. In this pitched battle between government and private capital, the exceptional status enjoyed by the planters could only go so far. By the end of the nineteenth century, the message was clear: planter capital was not above the broader needs of the Empire. Whereas earlier collusions of planter capital and colonial governance had shaped Darjeeling in formative ways, now the government was putting the planters in their place.

Recognizing that their success hinged on keeping Darjeeling different, the planters continued to lobby for Darjeeling's exceptional status. The ensuing decades would see them be largely successful in this endeavour. Nevertheless, the grounds of Darjeeling's exceptionality—and its constitutive relations of difference and capital—had shifted in profound ways by the century's end.

The Exception Reconsidered

Tracking Darjeeling's exceptionality through the colonial era shows that relations between governance and capital were formative, but not stable. A brief review of the administrative arrangements in Darjeeling illustrates broader shifts in the rationales of colonial rule throughout the subcontinent. As various historians have demonstrated, the Revolt of 1857/8 marked a pivotal turn in the structures and technologies of British rule in India.[62] With the British government assuming control from the East India Company, strengthening and standardizing the rule of law throughout the colony became a top priority. The first step was to take stock of what rules and regulations were actually in force in the various corners of British territory. Darjeeling's adhocracy soon became a source of concern. Campbell's laissez faire administration had enabled impressive transformations to the hills, so much so that by 1864 Darjeeling had been crowned the summer capital of the Bengal Presidency. But the arbitrary terms by which the hills were—and were not—being governed, ran counter to the British Raj's imperatives of standardization. Up until the 1870s, Darjeeling was variously governed as an 'Non-Regulated Area', marking the hills as a place removed from the standard operating procedures of colonial law.[63] Darjeeling was not alone in this regard. The territorial holdings of British India were a

62 See, for example, Dirks (2001), Mehta (1999), Metcalf (1995).

63 See Besky (2013: 188); Samanta (2000: 77); Warner (2014: 24).

patchwork of differently administrated zones, many of which shared the ad hoc designs of Darjeeling. That said the 1870s would see the British Raj work to standardize its forms of exception—eventually developing the legislation of the Scheduled Districts Act of 1874. The Act delineated special regions that, because of their geopolitical, economic, and/or ethnic conditions, were to be governed differently than the rest of India.[64]

As government officials weighed the potential application of the 1874 Act to various frontier and alternatively administered regions, the question arose as to whether Darjeeling should be brought under this official ambit of exception. At the request of the government, local officials scrambled to reconstruct the administrative genealogy of the hills. Their queries produced a telling picture of Darjeeling's extant adhocracy. Local officials maintained that any attempt to document the list of acts that were actually in force would be necessarily 'uncertain and badly inaccurate'—even 'guesswork'.[65] In the end, Darjeeling was officially made a Scheduled District in 1874. However, significant confusions remained as to what acts and legislation had actually been applied in Darjeeling. Confusions aside, Darjeeling's exceptional status had now been institutionalized and thus brought under a broader ambit of colonial governance and sovereignty. Darjeeling would no longer operate unto itself. Instead—to invoke the logic of political philosopher Carl Schmitt—the terms of its exceptionality now would be determined by the sovereign power of the British India government.[66]

The Scheduled District Act of 1874 set the precedent for Darjeeling's subsequent designation as a Backward Tract in 1919 and Partially Excluded Area in 1935. Major negotiations attended each of these classificatory moments—first through the reviews associated with the Montague–Chelmsford Reforms that produced the Backward Tract

[64] On the 1874 Act and Darjeeling (Bengal, Judicial, Proc 1–3, February 1873), (Bengal, Judicial, File 151, Proc 32–41, August 1874); (Bengal, Judicial, File 144, Proc 34, February, 1875); (Bengal, Judicial, File 25, Proc 6–49, April 1878); (Bengal, Judicial, File 421, Proc 64–65, May 1879).

[65] Wording from Commissioner of the Rajshahye and Cooch Behar Division's report to the Officiating Secretary of the Government of Bengal (8 December 1876), available in (Bengal, Judicial, 25, Proc 6–49, April 1878).

[66] For Schmitt (1985), the sovereign is that which sets the terms of the state of exception.

designation of 1919 and, second, through the reviews associated with the Simon Commission a decade later.[67] Amid these deliberations, the question of Darjeeling's *ethnic* difference increasingly took centre stage—as the Hillmen's Association and the Darjeeling Planters Association together argued that Darjeeling was sufficiently different to warrant special status.[68] For the Hillmen's Association, the ultimate goal was an autonomous government of their own. The planters had other designs. Maintaining Darjeeling's exceptional status promised the planters continued freedom from regulation and a circumscribed political territory within which to wield their power. Keeping Darjeeling a place apart was—and would remain—good for business. Mobilizing their fiscal and political capital, the planters got their way. Darjeeling was declared a Backward Tract in 1919 and a Partially Excluded Tract in 1935. As had so often been the case throughout Darjeeling's history, the call of the natives—in this case, for autonomy—was conveniently elided amid these exceptional configurations.

The legacy of the colonial exception has extended into the postcolonial present. And it has benefited the planters throughout. Tracking Darjeeling's exceptionality from the origins of adhocracy, through its special administrative statuses, and into the postcolonial set-ups of the Darjeeling Gorkha Hill Council (1988–2012) and the Gorkhaland Territorial Administration (2012–present), the influence of planter capital mustn't be overlooked. Crucially, at no point in Darjeeling's history—and this includes the most recent movements for subnational autonomy—has the power and property of this capitalist elite been truly challenged.[69] Given the historical patterns at hand, perhaps the time is now for a renewed interrogation of the planters' extant powers and collusive influences.

[67] I have written about these negotiations elsewhere. Middleton (2013c, 2015). See also Chhetri, this volume.

[68] As I have argued elsewhere, while colonial designations like Scheduled Districts (1874), Backward Tracts (1919), and Partially Excluded Areas (1935) were meant to recognize geographic and ethnic differences of particular areas, they also helped produce these and other forms of difference. See Middleton (2013: 17, 2015: 37).

[69] Today, Darjeeling's planter elites are no longer European, but they remain 'foreign' to the hills insofar as they are businessmen and conglomerates from the plains. Sarah Besky details these dynamics in *The Darjeeling Distinction* (2013). See also Besky and Sen, this volume.

Lessons for the Present

The nineteenth century history of governance, planter capital, and labour holds important lessons for understanding Darjeeling today. First, it challenges us to recognize what is unique about Darjeeling, but to always also appreciate its exceptionality in context. The production of Darjeeling as an exceptional space was part and parcel of a broader colonial pattern of exception. The comparison of Darjeeling with India's North-East, in this regard, reveals important similarities, but also notable differences that can help us modulate between various states of exception and their lingering effects on the present. The continuities with other hill stations and other tea-growing regions such as Assam are critically instructive. Yet the comparison with Assam—especially on the registers of labour and regulation—also reveals the actors and circumstances that made Darjeeling strategically different from other exceptional spaces. As we have seen, difference and capital found a special and precarious balance in the hills. By the century's end, Darjeeling's planters were staving off a litany of competing interests, none more formidable than the British Indian government and the army. The encroachment of recruiters and regulation into their hallowed territory, and the government's increased unwillingness to acquiesce to the planters' privileged demands, made it clear: Darjeeling was not—and had never been—'above' the needs of the Empire and the hard realities of imperialism. Despite narratives telling otherwise, Darjeeling was, from the start, inextricably bound up in broader networks of capital and colonial domination. Amid this milieu, its difference became both its signature and operative advantage.

Second, and along similar lines: the nineteenth century history of governance, capital, and labour begs a more critical reading of Darjeeling's discovery, development, and distinction. Undergirding the romance with this 'queen of the hills' has always been a deeper set of material and political forces at work. Re-examining these material histories provides a way to think beyond the 'natural' explanations of what makes Darjeeling so special and to thereby raise a more grounded set of questions about what—and *who*—made Darjeeling different. This is, of course, a question with many answers.

Of late, the question of *who* made Darjeeling different has become both an historiographic and political issue. And here we arrive at a third and final set of lessons that the nineteenth century history of Darjeeling puts to the present. This concerns the subaltern histories of the Gorkhas themselves. Whatever may be said of the most recent Gorkhaland agitations, the Gorkha Janamukti Morcha deserves credit for reinstating the primacy of the Gorkhas' labour in the history of the hills. At the end of the day, it was *their* labour, *their* hands, and *their* bodies that made Darjeeling. Anthropologist Sarah Besky has cogently shown how the Gorkhas' affective labour has fuelled powerful claims to belonging and territory—manifest most viscerally in the demands for a separate state of Gorkhaland.[70] Posing a timely challenge to prevailing histories of the hills, these subaltern voices offer a promising way of re-engaging Darjeeling on its own terms.

Any such histories from below, however, can ill-afford to eschew the broader capitalist contexts within which labour was brought to market and made to produce value for a particular class of colonial elites. A subaltern history of plantation labour, in this regard, begs a corresponding critique of planter capital. While the latter has clearly been my project in this essay, I venture this analysis in the hope that it too may help clear a space for the histories—and voices—of the Gorkha labourers who have been so conveniently elided from Darjeeling's history. In the offing then is a historiographic synthesis of political import. Combining the attentions of subaltern history and more orthodox Marxian approaches, we may ask anew: What were the forces that made Darjeeling? In what way? To whose long-term advantage? And to what enduring effects and affects? To venture these questions is to forge a critical understanding of how the legacy of the exception continues to condition the possibilities and impossibilities of life and politics in the hills. Taken up in this spirit, revisiting the history of governance, planter capital, and labour in the nineteenth century may be an important step for rethinking the prospects of meaningful autonomy in the years ahead.

[70] Besky (2013).

2 *'A Summer Place'*

Darjeeling in the Tourist Gaze

Rune Bennike*

21 May 2011, my final day of doctoral fieldwork in Darjeeling, was also the one-year anniversary of Madan Tamang's murder in one of Darjeeling's central public spaces. Tamang was an outspoken critic of the ruling GJM and the commemoration taking place that day was a reminder of the brutal politics of place and belonging to which Darjeeling is home. The Madan Tamang memorial is an unimposing structure. During the past month in Darjeeling I had not even noticed

* The author would like to thank Ursula Rao, Emilija Zabiliute, Ravinder Kaur, Sara Shneiderman, and Townsend Middleton as well as two anonymous reviewers for excellent comments and suggestions to many different drafts of this chapter. Research for the chapter was supported by the Asian Dynamics Initiative at Copenhagen University.

it, but today it was bedecked in flower garlands and Buddhist scarfs. A small crowd of 20 to 30 people had gathered around: friends and relatives, journalists, and quite a few police officers. Among the crowd the profile of a single, blond tourist stood out. He gazed timidly at the spectacle. To me, his presence that day illustrated the puzzling quality of Darjeeling that this chapter explores: the coexistence—with reference to the same place—of leisurely touristic commodification and violent political contestation.

The following year, while I was working on my fieldwork material from Darjeeling, the Bollywood box office success *Barfi!* premiered across the world.[1] Acclaimed as the 'brand ambassador' for Darjeeling, this movie is set in the 1970s, well before the eruption of the violent Gorkhaland Movement.[2] As the backdrop to its humorous love story, the movie makes extensive use of the touristic heritage sites of Darjeeling: the Darjeeling Himalayan Railway, the old Planter's Club, and so on. In the words of director Anurag Basu, *Barfi!* 'has been able to capture *the true spirit of Darjeeling*'.[3] In a historic summersault, this massively successful movie thus situates the 'true spirit' of Darjeeling before the Gorkhaland Movement broke the spell of colonial romanticism and forced Darjeeling 'into the post–independence national consciousness of India'.[4]

In this chapter, it is the history of this commodified form that interests me. Whereas the preceding chapter circumvents the romantic framings of Darjeeling to explore the histories of governance, capital, and labour that built Darjeeling, this chapter takes the romantic framings themselves as an object of investigation. Here, *Barfi!* is just one contemporary example. As a major early tourist destination and a reference point for globally marketed luxury tea, commodified Darjeeling has been observed, represented, and circulated far and wide since the mid-nineteenth century. But what does this mean to the production of Darjeeling as a place? How has Darjeeling historically emerged as 'a summer place': a landscape defined more by its scenery than by its inhabitants; a place you visit rather than a place of belonging; a consumable good, if you like. What becomes of Darjeeling as a place when its commodified avatars—tea and

[1] IMDB (2012).

[2] Banerjee (2012).

[3] Banerjee (2012), emphasis mine.

[4] Lama (2006).

tourism—take over the global imagination of the area? And how does commodification condition the politics of belonging and autonomy that also takes Darjeeling as its stage?

Pursuing these questions, the remainder of this chapter explores the colonial origins and historical persistence of the 'tourist gaze' in producing Darjeeling—even in the context of violent political contestation. The chapter is primarily based on textual analysis of a broad range of colonial and contemporary documents, supplemented with a month of fieldwork in Darjeeling during state elections in 2011. On this basis, it investigates the picturesque sensibility and classed, relational character of the tourist gaze, and provides circumstantial evidence as to the consequences of this gaze for the politics of belonging.

Darjeeling in the Tourist Gaze

Darjeeling was—globally speaking—an early tourist destination. John Urry's seminal book *The Tourist Gaze* points to the year 1840 as a watershed in the development of modern tourism. Counting, among other things, the invention of the camera, the organization of the first packaged holiday, and the introduction of the first national railway table, Urry argues that: 'This is the moment when the "tourist gaze", that peculiar combining together of the means of collective travel, the desire for travel and the techniques of photographic reproduction, becomes a core component of western modernity.'[5] If this was indeed 'western modernity', it did not exclude the colonies. Darjeeling was, in fact, at the forefront of modern tourism development at the time. The Darjeeling Himalayan Railway that was to become the quintessential means of accessing Darjeeling in the late nineteenth and early twentieth century was opened in 1881, post-dating the first European mountain railway (the Vitznau–Rigi in Switzerland) by only a decade;[6] already in the 1870s Darjeeling became the object of Samuel Bourne's famed photographs, deeply inscribing the hill station in the visual archive of the British Empire;[7] and, like various early tourist destinations across nineteenth century Europe, Darjeeling quickly inspired a large body of guidebooks and other 'guiding' material.

[5] Urry (2001: 148).

[6] Gyr (2010).

[7] Rayner (2009); Banerjee (2014).

Mediated through picturesque paintings, tourist guides and even governmental documents, narratives and images of Darjeeling began to circulate shortly after Darjeeling's 'discovery'. Like its European counterparts, this guiding material 'defined a style of travel' and selected 'which tourist attractions were worth visiting'.[8] Intermeshed with historical, geological, and ethnographic descriptions of the area, the Darjeeling guides are full of advice to the traveller on transportation, food, and accommodation. And, as guides do, they point out to the reader what there is to see. This material was, in other words, central to a *disciplining of the gaze* with which Darjeeling was approached and experienced.[9]

In this chapter, I argue that such touristic observation is not only a way to consume places, but also—in its generalized, globally mediated form—a distanced form of *place production*.[10] Inspired by Foucault's notion of the medical gaze, Urry conceptualizes the tourist gaze as a specific *way of seeing* whose emergence is tightly related to the development of modern tourism.[11] Just as the empirical, scientific gaze of the clinic, the tourist gaze is ocular—a social practice that is primarily organized visually. From the early-nineteenth century onwards, tourism in general, and sightseeing in particular, thus joins science in situating the visual sense at the core of its practice.[12] In terms of place production, this is important. The visual character of modern tourism practice enables an increasingly 'omnivorous production and "consuming [of] places" around the globe' not only through corporeal travel, but also through more distanced and mediated forms of virtual and imaginary tourism.[13]

If we recognize that touristic consumption is part of the modern production of places, what—then—becomes of such places? If the 'tourist gaze' played a central role in the 'reflexive process' by which Darjeeling 'came to enter the global order', what does this mean for Darjeeling? In his 'introduction to supermodernity', Marc Augé argues that modern, distanced observation creates a 'false familiarity' with certain places, an image-mediated sense of place that is global rather than local.[14] With reference to Darjeeling, I suggest a different perspective. In contrast to

8 Gyr (2010).
9 Urry (2001: 148); see also Rojek (1997).
10 Lefebvre (1991); Cresswell (2004); Rojek (1997).
11 Urry (2001: 145).
12 Urry (2001: 145, 4); Adler (1989).
13 Urry (2001: 141).
14 Augé (2008: 26).

Augé, I propose that distanced, mediated senses of place are not necessarily to be seen as *false* familiarity.

Firstly, the falseness that Augé emphasizes relies on a distinction between distanced observing of places and what he calls 'anthropological place'—the proximate experience of places that arise from being there. Informed by the Heideggerian notion of 'dwelling', this latter sense of place is eloquently elaborated in the phenomenological literature, but its clear distinction from a 'false' sense of place seems problematic, especially when dealing with a globally branded tourist destination. Studies of tourism have, in fact, documented significant effects of prior, mediated senses of place on the actual experience of places visited. One study of tourists in Queensland Australia, for example, documents that 'actual experience of place [did] not significantly affect' tourists' already established sense of that place mediated by the tourist industry.[15] While experiencing a place as a tourist obviously differs from long-term dwelling, the notion of a fully unmediated experience of place seems unlikely.

Secondly, as the present chapter is ultimately concerned with collective political struggles over place, I argue that even 'false' senses of place can be politically significant. As political struggles such as the Gorkhaland Movement operate beyond the sphere of personal experience, they necessarily involve generalized representations or ways of seeing. Here, widely shared senses of place become all the more important *despite* their potential dissonances with proximate experience of the place. In fact, globalized, 'tourist' senses of place might trump local experiences in creating a sphere for politics of place that is detached to a certain extent from the locality. As I describe in detail below, the history of Darjeeling illustrates this.

Disciplining the Gaze: Darjeeling As 'A Summer Place'

I take the main title of this chapter from a republication of the 1907 District Gazetteer for Darjeeling.[16] Although the Gazetteers were an administrative cornerstone of British domination in India, providing centralized 'state legibility' of the dominated areas,[17] its republication

[15] Young (1999).

[16] O'Malley (2001 [1907]).

[17] Cohn (1996), (1987: 224–54); Ludden (1993); Breckenridge and van der Veer (1993); Dirks (2001); Scott (1998).

frames the document very differently. The title page of the republication likens the Gazetteer to 'good wine', presenting it as the 'fruits' of the colonial official, L.S.S. O'Malley's, 'labour of love'. The reprint also adds an introduction to the Gazetteer with the title 'A Summer Place'. In this, the author describes Darjeeling exactly as a tourist place: 'a precious summer place' where one can 'take a break' and 'get away from the insane world' where people are 'obsessed with money and the material goods that can be bought and consumed to satisfy our endless appetite'.[18] Although a visit to Darjeeling is thus framed as a departure from materialist obsession, the place itself appears exactly as an object of touristic consumption: 'the land of that magic potion' that can be gobbled down by the visitor just like the tea for which the area has become famous.[19]

Albeit striking, this intrusion of commodified touristic leisure into a governmental document is not at all unprecedented. Darjeeling became, from the mid-nineteenth century onwards, the object of a range of governmental documents, historical tracts, and touristic guides. The overlap between these different documents is quite remarkable. Sections are often copied verbatim between the sources; the colonial bureaucracy's minute categorizations of land and people are repeatedly coupled with suggestions for the traveller on what to see and where to eat. These documents, in other words, repeatedly represent a merger between the tourist gaze and the gaze of centralized government—be it colonial or national. The result of this merger is an authoritative disciplining of a gaze that is *relational* and *classed*, constituting Darjeeling as a picturesque place for leisurely visits rather than one of belonging. In the following, I analyse this gaze in detail.

Scenic Landscapes, Picturesque People

It is already well-known how the hill stations that the British established in India from the 1830s onwards provided ostensibly 'familiar' and 'empty' spaces in which the picturesque aesthetic of contemporary Europe could be transplanted.[20] Substantially informed by comparison to the homely landscapes of the British hills, the British residents of the hill stations represented the landscape—graphically and discursively—in a nostalgic

[18] Biswas (2001: xii, xv).

[19] Biswas (2001 : xviii).

[20] Kennedy (1996); Talukdar (2010); Dowler, Carubia, and Szczygiel (2005); Rose (1994); Banerjee (2014).

and romantic light. A range of physical interventions, from the felling of forest to the construction of European style cottages, further moulded the landscape to fit this image.[21] In Darjeeling, large swathes of forest were cut down giving way to 'tea gardens'.[22] The 10,000 acres under tea cultivation in 1866 had, by 1905, been expanded to more than 50,000 acres.[23] A combination of the hard labour of Nepali migrants and British ways of seeing the landscape—structured around the contemporary aesthetic categories of the picturesque and sublime—turned the 'jungle' into 'gardens' and 'mountains' into 'hills'.[24]

Supported by these material interventions, the tourist gaze was directed insistently at this scenic landscape rather than Darjeeling's inhabitants. For example, *Picturesque India* states that: 'Darjiling lives under the shadow of Kinchinjanga, in the heart of the great Himalyan Range. The giant mountain fills the window of the comfortable English Hotel, the "Woodlands", perched on the summit of a little hill, which is only twice the height of Snowdon or Ben Lomond.'[25] Drawing parallels to the homely hills of the Welsh and Scottish countryside, Darjeeling is here situated in clear contradistinction to the greatness of Kanchenjunga—a sublime presence to be taken in only as viewed through the window of 'the comfortable English Hotel'.

This preference for picturesque scenery overshadows notions of inhabitation. Guidebooks and governmental documents repeatedly display this preference in their layout. Ubiquitously, sections on the geology, flora, and fauna precede sections on people. Furthermore, when the inhabitants of Darjeeling are described, they are themselves treated as a part of the scenic landscape. The guides tend to locate their description of the Darjeeling inhabitants in the noisy commotion of the bazaar or the commodified space of the tea garden. *Picturesque India*, published in 1891, describes the Darjeeling bazaar as 'the most interesting and amusing in India', a place where one can watch 'throngs of Hill people and tea-coolies come into town' and bargain so loudly that the 'noise of the Bazaar at noon can be heard for a mile'.[26] *Newman's Guide*, published in 1900, similarly notes that 'it is both interesting and amusing

[21] Kennedy, (1996): Kenny (1995).
[22] Hunter (1876: 19); Kennedy (1996: 53).
[23] Hunter, (1876: 165); O'Malley (1907: 94).
[24] Sharma (2011).
[25] Caine (1891: 348).
[26] Caine (1891: 350, 52).

to watch the coolies as they flock to and fro'—drunk and noisy—concluding that 'they are, even in their dirt, picturesque'.[27] And, as Avery's guide from 1878 suggests: 'all who visit Darjeeling should pay a visit to a Tea Garden, it is interesting not only from seeing the tea in all its stages, but also for the study it affords of the picturesque hill men and women.'[28] Thus, although the inhabitants are not removed from the landscape—as in European landscape painting—they are relegated to the delimited space of the bazaar and tea garden.[29] Here, they are treated as passive components of the landscape rather than active inhabitants; rendered 'picturesque' and suitable for the visual consumption of the tourist gaze.

While this dimension of the tourist gaze on Darjeeling conforms largely to the literature on hill station landscapes across India and beyond, this is not the only thing the tourist gaze does. As I describe below, the tourist gaze furthermore presents a Darjeeling that is seen in a fundamentally relational and classed light—dimensions that just as the focus on the picturesque scenery—carries over from the colonial period to the contemporary.

Relationality

> The traveller leaves Calcutta at four o'clock in the afternoon, in the thinnest clothing he possesses. Next morning he is glad of a winter's suit, and before his arrival ulsters, fur cloaks, and rugs are more than welcome. The world cannot furnish a stranger railway journey than that from Calcutta to Darjiling.
>
> —William Sproston Caine, *Picturesque India: A Handbook for European Travellers*

The narratives of the various guiding documents consistently situate Darjeeling relationally; not as a place in and of itself, but as a place seen and approached from Calcutta. This relational gaze goes a long way back. The very establishment of Darjeeling as a British hill station was itself a product of 'visits' from the (then) colonial capital in Calcutta. One of the first British 'visitors' to the area was the Deputy Surveyor General of India Captain J.D. Herbert. Herbert travelled around Darjeeling in February and March 1830, in order to survey the area as a

27 Newman and Co. (1900: 24–5).

28 Cited in Sharma (2016a: 90).

29 Cosgrove (1984).

potential place for a hill station and sanatorium for the British in India. Upon his return to Calcutta he submitted a report that is telling of an early tourist gaze. Like the majority of later narratives, Herbert's report is structured as a diary that follows his itinerary through the area. Rather than presenting a synoptic mapping of the area, the tour structure of his narrative plays up a sense of exploration, discovery and proto–tourism.[30] Intermeshed with scientific observations on the environment he passes through, Herbert comments, annoyed, on the 'total insensibility of the natives of the plains to the charms of rural scenery' and laments how the entourage is invariably 'passing by or stopping short of scenes of the greatest natural beauty'.[31] Even in an official governmental report predating Darjeeling's annexation, we thus see the contours of a *classed, scenery-oriented, and relational tourist gaze* that soon became a quintessential way of seeing Darjeeling.

As illustrated in the above quote, taken from the popular London-produced guide *Picturesque India*, this 'tour' structure is repeated over and over again in subsequent guides to Darjeeling. It goes without question that Darjeeling is a place one reaches from Calcutta. After the opening of the Darjeeling Himalayan Railway, histories and guidebooks for Darjeeling ubiquitously open with a train journey from Calcutta to Darjeeling. The very first lines of *Newman's Guide* to Darjeeling state unambiguously that 'the traveller to Darjeeling, whether in search of health or pleasure, leave the Sealdah terminus of the Eastern Bengal State Railway at about 4 p.m.'.[32] Similarly, E.C. Dozey's *A Concise History of the Darjeeling District* commences with a description of the advances in accessibility of Darjeeling from Calcutta cutting down travel time from 'the best part of a fortnight' to 'nineteen short hours' followed by a lengthy review of "The Journey'.[33]

Through such accounts, Darjeeling is repeatedly constituted through its accessibility from and relation to Calcutta and—via Calcutta—the wider world. Rather than constituting a place in its own right, Darjeeling is framed in terms of accessibility from the outside. While this might be explained away as a functional consequence of the audience the guiding material addresses (travellers need to know how to get there), the

[30] For a distinction between 'map' and 'tour' narratives, see de Certeau (1984: 118–22).

[31] Herbert (2000 [1830]: 5).

[32] Newman and Co. (1900).

[33] Dozey (1922).

relationality of the gaze runs deeper than this. The multiple territorial decisions regarding Darjeeling that were made in the context of India's partition and the ensuing restructuring of Indian states repeatedly situated Darjeeling relationally *vis-à-vis* Calcutta, thereby reproducing the relationality of the tourist gaze in administrative practice.

During Partition, Darjeeling residents were all but isolated from the negotiation process, although a host of proposals for territorial re-alignment and various forms of local autonomy came out of Darjeeling in this period.[34] The British partition plan for the region was based on a (severely limited) Indian participation through the Bengal legislative assembly. Here, out of the 250 members, only two were elected from Darjeeling.[35] Thus, while the major parties were scrambling to secure their core constituencies—uncertain about where the border line would eventually be drawn—the role of Darjeeling was reduced to that of 'a glittering prize': an area equated with its production of 'practically all of India's finest teas' and therefore 'a significant source of revenue for the new state' rather than a part of the negotiations in its own right.[36] As Darjeeling was claimed by six out of seven 'non-Muslim' proposals, as well as by the Muslim League, who even had the Pakistani flag raised over Darjeeling town hall from 14–18 August 1947, it was thus reconstituted as Calcutta's backyard.

Following Partition, Darjeeling ended up as administratively part of West Bengal, but, territorially, was largely cut off from the rest of the state.[37] Thus, in 1956 when the States Reorganisation Commission considered the future status of the Darjeeling area, accessibility from Calcutta was once again central to the administrative gaze, itself reproducing the relationality of the tourist gaze.[38] Overall, the issue of reorganization was cast as a question of negotiating territorial demands

[34] Subba (1992).

[35] Dasgupta (1999: 61). One of the Darjeeling MLAs, Damber Singh Gurung of the All India Gorkha League, went on to become the only 'Gorkha' in the Constituent Assembly. The other MLA, Rantalal Brahmin, was among the first Gorkha communists and was eventually elected to the Lok Sabha (1971–7) for the CPI(M). However, by the time of first Gorkhaland Movement, the conflict between the GNLF and the communists led to a tacit erasure of the communist influence from the history of the Gorkhaland Movement.

[36] Chatterji (1999: 197–200: (2007: 48–51); van Schendel (2005: 27, 52).

[37] Chatterji (2007: 51–2); van Schendel (2005: 43–4).

[38] States Reorganisation Commission (1955: 172, 75).

between the existing states of Bihar and West Bengal so as to allow 'mainland' West Bengal access to, and control over, the northern districts that were included in the state after Partition. The main problem of making the state 'a compact and integrated unit' was a problem clearly approached from the relational perspective of Calcutta. Since 'the northern districts of the Presidency division [had] become *less accessible from Calcutta*' after Partition, the solution should enable 'West Bengal ... to control road traffic with Darjeeling and other places in the North'.[39] Thus, with the dry statement that, 'the continued isolation of the northern districts from the rest of West Bengal will tend to foster and accentuate separatist trends in these districts' the States Reorganisation Commission reinforced a relational gaze on Darjeeling.[40]

Class: Labour and Leisure

> Tourism is a leisure activity, which presupposes its opposite, namely regulated and organised work. It is one manifestation of how work and leisure are organised as separate and regulated spheres of social practice in 'modern' societies. Indeed, acting as a tourist is one of the defining characteristics of being 'modern'....
>
> —John Urry, *The Tourist Gaze*

The relationality involved in seeing and visiting Darjeeling was not a neutral one. If the tourist gaze, as Urry suggests in the quote above, relies on the 'modern' distinction between labour and leisure, it is clear on which side of this distinction Darjeeling falls. In the tourist gaze of the guidebook material, Darjeeling emerges as a 'landscape of privilege' *par excellence*: a place reserved for the wealthy visitor from the plains.[41] The first lines of E.C. Dozey's 1922 *A Concise History of the Darjeeling District*, for example, state that: 'In these strenuous days when the struggle for existence shackles men to their desks, or keeps them tied to counters in the sweltering heat of the plains, the very mention of Darjeeling recalls memories of the last but too short week-end during which as much pleasure as possible was pressed into it.'[42] The audience Dozey addresses is here represented by a privileged male tied to his white-collar employment

39 States Reorganisation Commission (1955: 172, 75), my emphasis.

40 States Reorganisation Commission (1955: 175).

41 Duncan and Duncan (2001, 2004).

42 Dozey (1922: 1).

at a desk or counter in the plains of Bengal. This man has the economic wherewithal to visit Darjeeling—if only for a weekend—with the sole objective of seeking pleasure. The voyage that he undertakes is thus clearly distinct from that of the Nepali labour migrants who today call Darjeeling their home:[43] he is travelling for leisure rather than travelling for labour, thus perfectly illustrating the classed inequalities of the modern, colonial 'paradigm of movement' where the former type of mobility is advertised while the latter is made invisible.[44]

While this classed gaze could easily be written off as an outdated remnant from colonial times it is, in fact, reproduced extensively after Indian independence. The introduction to the 2001 republication of the Darjeeling Gazetteer, mentioned above, is a case in point. Recommending a visit to Darjeeling, the author here reminds the reader that 'life is not all work, there should also be some time to play' and criticizes how we 'tie ourselves down to desks whose wood imperceptibly enters into our souls.'[45] Eerily reminiscent of Dozey's phrasing, we again find the white-collar worker rising from his desk to visit Darjeeling and carve out 'some time to play' from his busy schedule. What is also important here is that this gaze is *classed more than it is racial*. Colonial discourse on the hill stations in general had a substantial racial dimension and colonial notions of labour were particularly racialized.[46] Nonetheless, the overriding classed organization of the tourist gaze on Darjeeling enabled, it seems, an adoption of the gaze that crossed racial boundaries.

Following Banerjee and Basu's recent analysis of representations of the Himalaya in Bengali travelogues, we might connect this recurring gaze to the particular class anxieties of an emerging class of Anglo-vernacular elites in colonial and post-independence Bengal—the *bhadralok*.[47] Not unlike Benedict Anderson's creole pioneers, this emergent middle class employed cultural techniques such as travel writing to set themselves aside as 'the principal claimants of [an] emergent nation-space.'[48] In their writings, they negotiated 'Hindu notions of sacred geography, pre-colonial patriae, and colonial territoriality' to create a novel, secular

[43] See Besky (2013: 55–6); Middleton in this volume and Middleton (2013a); Sharma (2016a); Shneiderman (2015: 98–127).

[44] Goswami (2004); Aguiar (2011); Clifford (1997); Kaplan (1996).

[45] Biswas (2011: xiv).

[46] Sharma (2016a); Kenny (1995).

[47] Banerjee and Basu (2015).

[48] Banerjee and Basu (2015 : 635).

sense of nation-space.[49] Hitherto considered a sacred space for religious pilgrimage, the Himalayas were, in their writings, recast in terms of natural beauty rather than supernatural power. And much like the colonial British, the bhadralok fashioned themselves as 'secular sojourners' visiting the Himalayas for leisure. As a result, their class anxieties fuelled a reproduction of the possessive 'quasi-orientalist' gaze of the colonial rulers in post-independence Bengal.[50] While the racial difference between British colonialists and Bengali bhadralok was overcome, the class hierarchy of the colonial setting was maintained.

Politics of Belonging in a Summer Place

With its emphasis on Darjeeling as a tourist destination suitable for leisurely visits and visual consumption, the tourist gaze leaves notions of inhabitation and belonging obscured. Organized around notions of travel for leisure rather than labour, the gaze overlooks the large number of Nepali labour migrants who provided the physical input that transformed Darjeeling from the 'forested spur', described by its first colonial visitors, into a landscape that is both picturesque and productive.[51] The tourist gaze thus reinforces the complicated political situation of the 'Indian Nepalis'.[52] At a time when claims for belonging are routinely legitimized through notions of indigenous rooting in place, the migration history of most Darjeeling inhabitants can quickly be seen as a liability.[53] Consequently, as Townsend Middleton has argued, the politics of belonging in Darjeeling are fuelled by a persistent, underlying anxiety and unfold in episodic spurts across multiple, shifting incarnations.[54]

Rather than looking directly at these episodic spurts, the final section of this chapter traces the notion of 'normality' that is repeatedly pitched as their background: the picturesque and harmonious Darjeeling of the tourist gaze that provides a basis upon which the fierce political agitation of the Gorkhaland Movement's multiple incarnations can be discounted as exceptional—that is, out of character of the Darjeeling that we know.

[49] Banerjee and Basu (2015: 649).

[50] Sharma (2016a: 95).

[51] Bennike (2017).

[52] Sinha and Subba (2003); Subba et al. (2009).

[53] Baviskar (2006); Li (2000); Middleton (2013a, 2015); Rycroft and Dasgupta (2011); Shneiderman (2009, 2015); Shneiderman and Turin (2006).

[54] Middleton (2013a).

In the mid-1980s, an 'information document' published by the Government of West Bengal and widely circulated in the hills during the peak of the first Gorkhaland Movement, claims that: 'The peaceful Himalayan region of West Bengal, with a Nepalese majority, is largely known for its tea gardens and scenic beauty and is a major tourist attraction in the country.'[55] Later, the same publication goes on to emphasize how 'until the recent happenings' everyone 'lived peacefully and amicably' and that 'the atmosphere in the hills of Darjeeling was in keeping with the excellent tradition of communal harmony in the rest of the state'.[56] In line with this insistence that Darjeeling was, even in the midst of subnational agitation, a place of harmony and scenic beauty, other government documents repeatedly describe the violence taking place as something external to Darjeeling as a place, fuelled simply by the 'anti-nationalist' and 'secessionist' agitation of the Gorkhaland National Liberation Front (GNLF) and incited by the 'invisible hand' of 'foreign influence'.[57] Just like *Barfi!*, these documents thus situate the 'real' Darjeeling in the touristic image, discounting the ongoing agitation as exceptional.

News reports from the period similarly dramatize the ongoing events on the background of a 'normality' of scenic beauty and harmony. One article—aptly titled 'Darjeeling Disquiet'—commences with the following paragraph:

> The Nepalese in their inimitable manner, have given themselves an absolute gem of a word–'Kunni', which means; 'I don't know, and I couldn't be bothered to find out.' This writer will wager his finest silk kurta that were one to descend (due to the GNLF roadblocks) on any one of the tea bushes in Darjeeling's 45-plus tea estates, and ask the astute Nepalese there what all the fuss and fury was about, out would come a succinct 'Kunni'. So, how an extremely breathtaking and tranquil mountainscape has turned truculent is surely a complex, contradictory story.[58]

Whereas the West Bengal government's 'information document' conveniently sought to erase class differences in its insistence on communal

[55] Government of West Bengal Director of Information (1986: 1).

[56] Government of West Bengal Director of Information (1986: 6).

[57] Government of West Bengal Director of Information (1986): v, 30; Ranadive (1986).

[58] The Sunday Observer (1986). 'Gorkhaland Imbroglio.' *The Sunday Observer*, August 3.

harmony, here, the classed notion of the reporter waging 'his finest silk kurta' and 'descending' to the Nepali labourer in the tea bushes is hard to miss. Much like the colonial guides, the news report reinforces the difference between the labouring inhabitant of Darjeeling and the leisure class visiting the area while situating the latter's sense of Darjeeling as 'an extremely breathtaking and tranquil mountainscape' as defining for its 'normality'. Once again, the mobile gaze of the leisure–class tourist is privileged over and above the experiences of inhabitation.

Even the Gorkhaland Movement's own narratives and visuals don't go very far in presenting an alternative sense of Darjeeling. Ghisingh's speeches, interviews, and orchestrated practices seem directed more, as Middleton argues, towards nourishing an anxiety of belonging and harnessing its energy rather than at presenting and promoting an alternative 'Gorkhaland' vision of Darjeeling.[59] In an important speech widely circulated on cassette tapes, Ghisingh instead combines a confusing historical sketch of the area—vaguely alluding to some kings in the twelfth century and the late-eighteenth century Gorkha conquest—with a complex and convoluted analysis of the legal situation of the 'Gorkhas' in India. Stray mentions of the recent expulsion of Nepalis from Assam, of being 'orphaned', 'not bona fide citizens of India' and 'hired tenants' dot the speech along with familiar notions of the brave Gorkhas. What emerges from Ghisingh's speech is an unclear but insistent emphasis on the area's unsettled position within the political landscape of the borderland. Mixing historical and legal complications, Ghisingh indicates that the area was left dangling between Nepal and India when the British left the subcontinent. Did the British propose the area to the Gorkhas only to have the All India Gorkha League reject the proposal? Was it given to Nepal as a 'buffer province'? Should there have been a 'plebiscite'? Was the Sugauli treaty nullified when the British left the subcontinent? And does the Indo-Nepalese Treaty of 1950 stand 'rejected and nullified' as Nepal is declared a 'Zone of Peace'?[60] The speech alludes to all these options suggesting that 'the proper settlement of Darjeeling and Teesta has not come so far, not the settlement of our fate'.[61] To this situation, the only solution is Gorkhaland—but what this means remains opaque. Gorkhaland is not represented as a place, not even a place-to-be, but

[59] Middleton (2010: 150–5), (2013a). Many of Ghisingh's speeches and interviews are collected in Lama (1996).

[60] Lama (1996: 25–6).

[61] Lama (1996: 26).

more like a *fata morgana* simmering in the horizon—fuelling desires but essentially ungraspable.

Searching for Gorkhaland: GJM and the Second Movement

When I began doctoral fieldwork in Darjeeling in 2011, local politics of belonging had gone through a range of transformations. Following a long period of semi-autocratic reign by Ghisingh under the auspices of the Darjeeling Gorkha Hill Council (DGHC), culminating in attempts at establishing Darjeeling as a tribal area according to the Sixth Schedule of the Indian Constitution, the Gorkhaland Movement was revived in 2007 under the renewed leadership of Bimal Gurung and his GJM.[62] Once again, the hills were shut down by strikes in an intense, sometimes violent, agitation. On 21 May 2010, Madan Tamang—whose memorial anniversary introduced this chapter—was killed in public in Darjeeling town. In February 2011, two GJM supporters were killed by the police further adding to the tension in the hills as well as to the demand for Gorkhaland. With a research imagination shaped by earlier fieldwork on the movement for a Limbuwan state on the other side of the border in Nepal, as well as readings on the politics of belonging across South Asia, I was searching for discursive and practical outlines of what this Gorkhaland-to-be looked like. 'What is Gorkhaland', I kept asking myself. To my frustration, answers were hard to come by.

It all seemed quite paradoxical. I had arrived just around the time of what was to be a historic state election—an election where Mamata Bannerjee's Trinamool Congress ended 34 consecutive years of rule by the Communist Party of India-led Left Front, and where the GJM swept all three hill constituencies in Darjeeling. At this time, the renewed demand for a Gorkhaland state that propelled Gurung and the GJM into power was forcefully written and performed across Darjeeling's public space. The urban space of Darjeeling presented itself as a virtual canvas for slogans and symbols. While one would occasionally meet election posters from other parties, the GJM was massively represented on walls, shop fronts, and vehicles. The green, white, and yellow colours of the GJM flag provided a ubiquitous background to most of the Gorkhaland inscriptions around town, visually fusing the GJM party and the Gorkhaland agenda. The colours of the GJM flag were also repeated ubiquitously

[62] Middleton (2015).

on light-posts, benches, hand-rails, and wall decorations throughout the centre of the town. These numerous signs on wall and shop fronts clearly signalled that Gorkhaland was now spelled GJM.

However, while there was a clear concern about situating GJM and the Gorkhaland agenda for everyone to see—as something tangible—within the public space of Darjeeling town, Gorkhaland remained elusive. The political agenda was first and foremost focused on *who* represented Gorkhaland, and secondly, on *why* Gorkhaland was a legitimate demand. *What* Gorkhaland is remained unaddressed. Much like the Asad cult analysed by Lisa Wedeen, the public spectacle that was played out across Darjeeling at this time seemed thoroughly directed towards the production of compliance.[63] Although the GJM appeared ubiquitous, newspaper reports and public speeches were full of anxious attempts to exorcize the ghost of the old leader, Subash Ghisingh, from the hills. The day before the election results were announced, Bimal Gurung used a newspaper interview to emphasize that Ghisingh's 'visa to the hills' would expire after the elections.[64] The threat of repercussions was only slightly veiled. As Gurung had stated in an earlier interview, 'the common people would not allow him to stay even a single day in the hills. The security would definitely be relaxed after the electoral process is completed. Then we would see.'[65] Even during the victory rallies—after GJM had won with large margins, and Ghisingh left the hills—the slogans shouted across town were still about Ghisingh, how he was 'rotten' and how he 'should be thrown into the dam'.

While the public spectacle of Gorkhaland in spring 2011 was all about *who* was in control, GJM publications were intensely focused on the *why*. In this sense, the GJM discourse does not differ much from Ghisingh's—it's all about the uncertainty of an identity denied recognition. A core GJM publication, the pamphlet *Why Gorkhaland*, in fact reuses the title of a 1986 GNLF publication. The pamphlet presents

[63] Lisa Wedeen describes the 'Asad cult' as 'a strategy of domination based on compliance rather than legitimacy'. This compliance is brought about largely through the visual orchestration of symbols and visceral orchestration of public rituals in a grand 'spectacle' that discipline participants in a way that 'both symbolizes and prepares for political obedience' dramatizing 'power by providing occasions to enforce obedience, thereby creating a politics of pretense in which all participate but few actually believe. Wedeen (1999: 6, 19).

[64] Chhetri (2011).

[65] Bagchi (2012).

a shortened and revised version of a document named *The Case for Gorkhaland* submitted to the Home Secretary of India in September 2008 in preparation for 'tripartite talks' between GJM, and the West Bengal and Union Governments. Reading for what Gorkhaland is in these publications results in a curious backward argument. Gorkhaland is posed largely as a pragmatic political solution to a problem of national recognition rather than a problem of local belonging and autonomy. *The Case for Gorkhaland* argues that 'Gorkhaland is the dream of over a crore of Indian Gorkhas living all over India' whose 'demand has perforce been located in present-day West Bengal for historical and geographical reasons.'[66] It is, in other words, not the specific character of the Darjeeling area as a place that motivates the Gorkhaland Movement, as it is presented here, but broader questions of national recognition that might—due to somewhat arbitrary historical reasons—be solved through territorial intervention in this area. Against this backdrop, Gorkhaland is plainly described as an 'area'—a generic administrative space—rather than a place. *Why Gorkhaland?* simply states that:

> 'The total area of the proposed State of Gorkhaland comprising the present Darjeeling District and the contiguous area of Dooars in North Jalpaiguri district is approximately 6459 square kilometres. The Total population of the proposed State of Gorkhaland is approximately 30 lakhs as per 2001 census ... the district of Darjeeling lies between 26°31' and 27°13' North latitude and between 87°89' and 88°53' East longitude.[67]

Finally, when this space is occasionally described in more detail, the GJM publications once again recycle the existing touristic image of Darjeeling. *Why Gorkhaland* states that: 'Darjeeling is popular[ly] known as "Queen of Hills", a tourist paradise. Darjeeling produces world famous tea known as the "Champagne of Tea", which fetches sizeable foreign exchange for the country... Darjeeling is also famous for its "Toy Train" which has been accorded the status of International Heritage by UNESCO.'[68] Here, even a core document of the Gorkhaland Movement taps rather uncritically into the readily available repertoire of touristic phrases to describe Darjeeling. Visually, we find the same resonances. The front

[66] GJM (2008: 10).
[67] GJM (2009: 16).
[68] GJM (2009: 16).

cover of the pamphlet draw extensively from the archive of commodified signs related to Darjeeling as a tourist destination. As background to a large question-mark, the cover presents a collage of images pertaining to Darjeeling: the scenic view of a snow-clad Kanchenjunga, brave Gurkha soldiers, lush green tea gardens undergoing peaceful plucking, and the heritage Toy Train. Neither text nor image gives any substantial clue to what a 'Gorkhaland' Darjeeling might look like.

Conclusion: Commodification and the Politics of Belonging

> In certain cases becoming a tourist destination is part of a reflexive process by which societies and places come to enter the global order.
>
> —John Urry, *The Tourist Gaze*

Unfortunately, I never got a chance to interview the lone tourist who observed Madan Tamang's memorial session in Darjeeling. What did he think of the spectacle? How did it impact his perception of Darjeeling? Did this coincidental experience set him apart from tourists visiting Darjeeling any other day when reminders of Darjeeling's violent politics were not so obviously on display?

In this chapter, I have tried to make sense of the 'reflexive process' by which Darjeeling entered the global order as 'a summer place': a tourist destination related to classed notions of pleasure and holiday visits rather than hard labour and uncertain belonging. I have also attempted to account for some of the consequences of this process for the politics of place and belonging in Darjeeling. In a recent essay, Sarah Besky notes that 'to make claims to belonging in a place that was built for someone else' is 'complicated' and argues that understanding these claims in Darjeeling 'requires a historical view of the hill station as a built environment.'[69] While she convincingly substantiates the significance of material legacies in her book, I have argued, in this chapter, that material matters are not the only factor circumscribing belonging.[70] Although 'material' Darjeeling is today water–scarce and polluted, presenting a fearful scenario for the future of the tourism industry, the 'false' sense of Darjeeling induced by the tourist gaze, largely persists—fuelled by

69 Besky (2015).
70 Besky (2013).

recurring fantasies of capitalist consumption.[71] This sense of Darjeeling fills the lulls between recurring waves of anxiety-ridden claims for belonging and provides an—equally 'false'—sense of normality on the basis of which these episodes are evaluated.

Today, there are even signs that the commodified avatars of Darjeeling themselves are becoming political battlefields. As presented above, rather than pushing a different Gorkhaland image of Darjeeling, the GJM continues to recycle existing touristic narratives and signs. Following the agreement between the GJM and the West Bengal government in 2011, the responsibility for promoting Darjeeling tourism has been given to the new Gorkhaland Territorial Administration (GTA), which is strongly dominated by the GJM. The GTA has made a new Darjeeling Tourism logo, website, and promotional video, and is currently investing heavily in tourism development (especially in the Jamuney area)—claiming to work towards 'tourism the Darjeeling way'.[72] As for tea, the other great commodified avatar, the GJM demanded in 2009 that the existing geographical indications branding and logo should be supplemented with the label: 'Darjeeling Tea—The Flavour of Gorkhaland'.[73]

[71] See Drew and Rai, this volume; Mell and Sturzaker (2014); Ganguly-Scrase and Scrase (2015).

[72] See Off Road Adventure (2016). 'Official Video of Department of Tourism, Gorkhaland Territorial Administration.' Youtube Video, 3:59. Posted May 3. https://www.youtube.com/watch?v=20kMQ2rdtZs; See also GTA (2012). 'Darjeeling Tourism'http://www.gtatourism.com/. GTA Tourism Policy and investment figures are available at http://www.gta-darjeeling.org/node/165.

[73] Gupta, Aparajita (2009). 'Darjeeling Tea: Now Savour the Flavour of Gorkhaland.' *Hindustan Times*, February 3.

3 *Himalayan Darjeeling and Mountain Histories of Labour and Mobility*

Jayeeta Sharma*

Darjeeling, the hill station, was meant to provide a colonial, high-altitude equivalent of the English spa towns and Alpine resorts that metropolitan elites patronized for leisured recuperation. The establishment of an imperial settlement in the mountain habitat of the Eastern Himalayan borderlands created numerous—

* I wish to thank editors Townsend Middleton and Sara Shneiderman, the fellow authors and reviewers of this volume, and the many people in Darjeeling, Kalimpong, and those connected to those places who gave generously of their hospitality, time, and personal histories. Various portions of this research were supported by the Social Science and Humanities Research Council of Canada, the Connaught Fund, the Vice-President's Research Fund, and the Historical and Cultural Studies Department at the University of Toronto. All shortcomings remain my own.

often unanticipated—opportunities that absorbed newcomers into plantation, missionary, military, commercial, domestic, and exploration ventures, creating new modernistic and mobile possibilities for livelihoods and cultural change. This chapter interrogates the historical trajectories and social actions of labouring subjects who played a crucial role in the constitution of Darjeeling as a vibrant space for circulation and enterprise on the mountain frontiers of the British Indian Empire. Through an exploration of how Darjeeling's lived histories of labour transcended its colonial origins as a place where indigenous people were envisioned as mere auxiliaries to European needs, this chapter pursues the agency that its labouring subjects achieved through and beyond their encounters with imperial institutions such as plantations, schools, missions, and expeditions. Despite the challenge of interpreting the largely opaque processes through which such subaltern actors negotiated their lives, this chapter seeks to problematize and recover fragments of the labour transcripts of the Himalayan subjects whose voices, names, and visages appear only fleetingly, if at all, in the conventional archives of colonial urbanism and mobility.

Colonial Settlement and Lepcha Nature

In 1830, Captain J.D. Herbert, dispatched from Calcutta to Sikkim to assess a remote Himalayan hamlet's potential as a colonial hill station for the East India Company, wrote appreciatively of the local guides on whom he depended to reach his mountain destination. His guides were the Rong, a people whose preferred name originated in the phrase *mutanchi rong kup rum kup*, children of snowy peaks, or the Lepcha. The mightiest of those peaks was Kanchenjunga (a transliteration of the Tibetan name, Kangs–chen–mdzod–lnga), also known as Kongchen Kongchlo (big stone), whose snows gave birth to the Rong ancestors, Fudongthing and Nazong Nyu.[1] The name Lepcha, in the colonial archive, was originally a pejorative term bestowed by their neighbours from Nepal. Unconcerned with its negative connotations, Herbert lauded Lepchas as a unique mountain people, 'a totally different race, morally and physically, from the people in the plains ... they allow themselves to be originally the same people with the Bhoteeas or inhabitants of Tibet ... in every thing the reverse of the Hindoostanee.'[2] In his view,

[1] Hermanns (1954: 29).

[2] Herbert (2000 [1830]: 11).

the moral and physical traits that constituted Lepcha 'difference' were what suited them to service colonial needs. Herbert declared, 'the character of these people particularly fits them to cooperate with Europeans in improving the country ... without those prejudices which obstruct our efforts at improvement every step we take in the plains.'[3] The key trait here was their versatile command over Nature's bounty. 'With nothing but a long straight knife, the Lepcha will in an incredibly short period of time, house himself. If we were thirsty on the road, a Lepcha was immediately ready with a drinking cup fashioned out of a bamboo ... or a large leaf.'[4]

In tune with their intimate ties to Nature, Lepchas aspired to live and die within view of the snow-topped Kanchenjunga peak that abutted their mythical land of happiness, Mayel Lyang.[5] British Darjeeling enjoyed this same sublime view, but for its colonial functionaries, Kanchenjunga inspired very different sentiments. Unlike most Himalayan inhabitants, the post-Romantic ethos of Euro-American belief valued mountains not for symbolic or devotional associations, but for beauty or size. For the majority of the Euro-Americans who flocked to the new hill station, this Himalayan settlement served as a potent symbol of human triumph over Nature. They looked for similar triumphs over the denizens of those mountains. On their part, those denizens often had other ideas and desires, which they sought to realize within the strictures of the colonial establishment and Darjeeling's urban morphology.

During Darjeeling's early years, the British faced the challenge of successfully mobilizing urban infrastructure and human power in a high-altitude space that reputedly had fewer than a hundred residents at the start of the colonial settlement. Captain Herbert attributed the locality's near-desolation to the prior flight of a thousand Lepchas who fled the Sikkim king's suzerainty for refuge in Nepal.

> With their chief, Eklatok, whose brother [is] Barrajeet Kazee, whose wife and children have been murdered by the Raja of Sikkim, they have sought protection within the Goorkhalee territory, where they have obtained a settlement. Like all mountaineers, however, they sigh to return to their native glens.... The first step towards establishing a sanatorium at Darjeeling would be to invite these men to return to their homes.[6]

[3] Herbert (2000 [1830]: 11).
[4] Herbert (2000 [1830]: 11).
[5] Denjongpa (2002: 5–37).
[6] Herbert (2000 [1830]: 11).

He anticipated that those Lepchas would return once news circulated about the security that British Darjeeling afforded. During 1839, such Lepcha inhabitants included Pattho, Leeboo, and Sunam Dorji who settled at Tukvar, Dongdo at Sintam, and Benjoree at Malbaus, individuals who with their families had left the suzerainty of the Sikkim king, his Dewan, and chief Lama, for Darjeeling.[7] The British official in charge dolefully reported that only 51 males and 37 females had responded to colonial overtures, despite a warm official welcome for the chief's son and cash advances for his followers.[8]

Unlike Herbert's sanguine predictions, the majority of Lepchas, even when they were amenable about seeking work around Darjeeling, proved unenthusiastic about the arduous manual labour that building urban infrastructure entailed.[9] Their preferred lifestyle was to combine foraging, hunting, and shifting cultivation, moving from one spot to another as they deemed fit. Such moves allowed the soil to regain fertility, and allowed cultivators to evade the increased dues that the Sikkim ruler levied after three years on a site.[10] However, an increasingly monetized colonial economy gradually made it a challenge to sustain a viable livelihood solely from shifting cultivation and foraged commons. This was a major reason why numerous Lepchas sought out temporary wage-earning tasks, as when the British botanist Joseph Hooker journeyed to Darjeeling to advance his quest for scientific fame and success.

Between 1848 and 1851, Sir William Hooker, the Director of the Royal Botanical Gardens at Kew received from his son Joseph 21 baskets of orchids, rhododendrons, and other Himalayan plant specimens that survived a three-month long voyage from India. Those were prizes from a collecting expedition for which the British government, with a little

[7] National Archives of India (1839). Correspondence between J. Princep, Secretary to the Government of India, Fort William and Archibald Campbell, Officer on Special Duty, Darjeeling, Foreign Department, Political Consultations, 10 July, Nos. 72–4. New Delhi.

[8] National Archives of India (1839). Correspondence between J. Princep, Secretary to the Government of India, Fort William and Archibald Campbell, Officer on Special Duty, Darjeeling, Foreign Department, Political Consultations, 10 July, Nos. 72–4. New Delhi.

[9] National Archives of India (1840). *Miscellaneous Files on Road-making; Foreign Department Consultations of 5 February 1840, Nos. 91–2; 9 November 1840,* Nos. 91–2; 24 May 1841, Nos. 59–62; and 4 October 1841, Nos. 118–20. New Delhi: National Archives of India.

[10] Hooker (2002 [1854]).

prodding from Sir William, had funded Hooker junior. Jim Endersby points out that expeditions to distant lands served as a successful and quick strategy for aspiring men of science to publish unusual observations and gain a professional reputation that surpassed stay-at-home peers.[11] This opportunity was particularly important for Joseph Hooker who lacked the private means that many of his contemporaries enjoyed, while he aspired for a quick route to scientific prestige that might enhance his case to become the next Director of Kew.

No less a personage than Lord Auckland, the Governor-General of India, advised Hooker on his itinerary through India and Nepal, as did Hugh Falconer, the Director of the Calcutta Botanical Gardens. Both advised that the new hill station was an essential halt, 'ground untrodden by traveller or naturalist'.[12] On 4 March 1848, Hooker wrote to his friend Charles Darwin to whom he was providing invaluable observations for his forthcoming *Origin of Species*, 'Darjeeling is in the Sikim Himalayah, between Nepaul & Bootan, a rainy rich Botanical Station, where I shall stay for several months I hope.'[13] Hooker was struck by the grand landscape, dominated by what was then supposed to be the world's loftiest mountain, Kanchenjunga. He rhapsodized on the view from Bryanstone, the retirement abode of his host, administrator-ethnologist Brian Hodgson.

> Kinchinjunga (forty-five miles distant) is the prominent object, rising 21,000 feet above the level of the observer out of a sea of intervening wooded hills; whilst, on a line with its snows, the eye descends below the horizon, to a narrow gulf 7000 feet deep in the mountains, where the Great Rungeet, white with foam, threads a tropical forest with a silver line.[14]

Later, an artist etched this view into a lithographic frontispiece for his 1854 magnum opus, the *Himalayan Journals*. It depicted, against a backdrop of snowy peaks, the figures of several Lepchas, whom Hooker called 'the prominent characters in Dorjiling, where (they) undertake all sorts of out-door employment ... conspicuous for their honesty, their power as carriers and mountaineers, and their skill as woodsmen' (Figure 3.1).[15]

[11] Endersby (2008a, 2008b).

[12] Hooker (2002 [1854]: 3).

[13] Hooker, J.D. 1848. J.D. Hooker to Charles Darwin, 4 March. Letter From University of Cambridge, Darwin Correspondence Project. http://www.darwinproject.ac.uk/entry–1158 (accessed 30 April 2013).

[14] Hooker (2002 [1854]: 52).

[15] Hooker (2002 [1854]: 54).

Figure 3.1 'View of Kinchinjunga from Mr Hodgson's Bungalow', from a Sketch by W. Taylor
Source: *Himalayan Journal*, 1. Available at https://archive.org/details/darwin-online_1854_Himalayan_A945.1 (accessed March 19, 2018).

With the assistance of Superintendent Archibald Campbell, Hooker hired Lepchas to collect and preserve botanical specimens from the forested slopes around Darjeeling, at wages that varied from 8 to 20 shillings a month, roughly Rs 3–5.[16] The indefatigable botanist exemplified the ironic appellation that the Lepchas coined for Euro–American employers—*mik thuk*, 'those who poke with their eyes'.[17] Hooker's eyes surveyed his Lepcha employees as he did his botanical specimens and the topography. Felix Driver writes of how Victorian narratives of exploration enhanced credibility with their Victorian readers with copious descriptions of the efficacy of local collectors, albeit solely as human instruments for the collection of natural knowledge.[18] Hooker thus wrote: 'These (collectors) either accompanied me on my excursions, or went by themselves into the jungles to collect plants, which I occupied

[16] From the Great Re-coinage of 1816 all the way up until the First World War, the Indian rupee was pegged to the British pound at a rate of Rs. 4.80 to £1, or 10 shillings to Rs. 1. Since 20 shillings made £1, the best–paid among these collectors earned roughly the same amount as a porter.

[17] Foning (1987: 71).

[18] Driver (2015: 13).

myself in drawing, dissecting, and ticketing: while the preserving of them fell to the Lepchas, who, after a little training, became, with constant superintendence, good plant-driers.'[19] Like Herbert before him, Hooker appreciated how Lepcha skills enhanced his journey with 'the simple resource of a plain knife (as he) makes his house and furnishes yours, with speed, alacrity, and ingenuity.'[20]

Lepcha knowledge of Nature's bounty proved vital to amass the 150,000 botanical specimens that Hooker dispatched to Kew. Two major books resulted: *Himalayan Journals* and the *Rhododendrons of the Sikkim Himalaya*, as well as a considerable oeuvre of letters. Across these writings, Hooker named nearly all the 2,000 plant species that he acquired. Several were named after friends and benefactors such as *R. Campbelliae, R. Hodgsoni*, and *R. Dalhousiae*.[21] The Tibetan mastiff he acquired on the expedition received a local name Kinchin. We read of Meepo, a high-born Lepcha emissary sent to accompany him into Sikkim territory. But Hooker's Lepcha collectors remain un-named, despite many pages on the forest talents they brought to his purpose. Hooker's appreciation of such local intermediaries in his writings is heartfelt, but it is inseparable from the scientific explorer's strategy that simultaneously displayed triumph over mountain Nature, and locals as instruments. However, the very existence of those writings allows the postcolonial historian to interrogate this colonial archive for some hint of the labouring transcripts that might allow her to find the otherwise elided, nameless subaltern actors.

Circulating Labour

Hooker was amazed to find Darjeeling as busy as 'an Australian colony, not only in (the) amount of building, but in the accession of native families from the surrounding countries.'[22] Rough mountain arteries for Himalayan circulation were improved via the District Commissioner's office that renamed them as Local Fund roads. Linking to the newly built Darjeeling Cart Road that connected the hill station to the plains, those paths were busy with carts and pack animals that conveyed oranges

[19] Hooker (2002 [1854]: 49).
[20] Hooker (2002 [1854]: 72).
[21] Hooker (1849).
[22] Hooker (2002 [1854]: 50).

and potatoes from Nepal, wool and salt from Tibet, as well as numerous groups of labouring newcomers.

It is pertinent here to recollect the Marxist philosopher Henri Lefebvre's declaration that 'social space contains a great diversity of objects, both natural and social, including the networks and pathways which facilitate the exchange of materials, things, and information. Such 'objects' are not only things but also relations.'[23] Following his call to examine space in light of the labour that constitutes it, we can problematize Darjeeling as a circulatory social space where seasonal, temporary, and permanent labouring migrations into a colonial high-altitude setting produced complex networks of classed, raced, and gendered relationships between, for, and by constituent subjects.

On steep Darjeeling streets, everyday conveyance of everything from people to goods depended on subaltern human bodies, in the virtual absence of wheeled and animal transport. European women and children, and sometimes men, rode in a type of sedan chair called a *dandee*. A pioneering missionary wife described her journey in such a vehicle (Figure 3.2): 'In those days this was a simple chair, to each side of which a porter's pole was affixed and a board was contrived as a foot-rest.

Figure 3.2 Missionary Carried up the Mountains by Porters
Source: C. 1890. Photographer, unknown. Available at http://digitallibrary.usc.edu/cdm/singleitem/collection/p15799coll123/id/78892/rec/25. Licensed with a Creative Commons license from the National Library of Scotland; USC Digital Library; accessed 10 June 2016.

[23] Lefebvre (1991: 77).

The men had to go on foot but we ladies were carried up the 8600 feet to Darjeeling.'[24] As late as 1895, when the World Transportation Commission surveyed Darjeeling, its photographer William Henry Jackson documented the dandee chairs that carried elites around Darjeeling, alongside the novel 'toy train' whose engines conveyed them up the mountains. Himalayan labouring migrants aspired to work for the mountain railway, but in their first years, often settled for carrying the dandee.

During the 1860s and 1870s, when new transport infrastructure of roads and rail improved hill station access to the plains, labouring men were able to move into domestic openings for cooks, major-domos, grooms, bearers, and watchmen that provided better wages and less onerous work than porterage. Guidebooks list wages for household jobs at approximately Rs 8 a month in Darjeeling's early years, rising to Rs 10–12 by 1862–78. But these opportunities were almost entirely limited to men. Women had a narrower range of jobs available as sweepers and ayah nursemaids whose wages ranged between Rs 5–8 a month.[25] Labouring female remuneration changed little over the years, compared to the higher-end domestic jobs that went to men over whose skills households might compete. A matter of shocking titillation for many Euro-American visitors was the high visibility of female load-carriers on Darjeeling's streets. Such images as the stereoscopic views of labouring women porters by the American globetrotter James Ricalton, served to underline the alienness of these frontier people, and the exoticism of the imperial space, which their labour constituted (Figure 3.3).

Race became as crucial a determinant as gender since employers sought to differentiate and discipline a floating subaltern proletariat on the basis of reified cultural and biological traits that rested on ascribed racial and national origins. Hooker's second collecting expedition, a three-month stint across Sikkim and eastern Nepal to the Tibet frontier, forms an early test case. In a letter, he described to Sir William how 'preliminaries towards my trip to the snows' involved interviews with a 'motley group of natives—of various tribes, colours & callings such as one rarely sees any of & still more rarely all together.'[26] For prior sorties

[24] 'The Wernicke Stölke Story: A History of a Family of Darjeeling Planters', Mss. Eur Photo Eur 421, British Library: Asian and African Collection.

[25] Hathorn (1863: 56) and Avery (1878: 37) list wages for these decades.

[26] Hooker, Sir Joseph Dalton (1848). Sir Joseph Dalton Hooker to Sir William Jackson Hooker from Darjeeling, India, 20 October. Letter. From The Royal Botanical Gardens, Kew, Indian Letters 1847–1851, JDH/1/10

Figure 3.3 Nepalese Porter Girls Who Carry Luggage Many Miles for a Twopence
Source: Ricalton (1900: 127). Available at https://archive.org/details/indiathroughste00ricagoog/ (accessed June 1, 2016).

around Darjeeling that went until the Rungeet River, he employed Lepcha collectors who lived off their familiar environs, with little need for heavy loads. But for his next trip, Hooker required supplies for the entire party for as long as three months to travel up to the eastern flank of Kanchenjunga.

From the motley group who vied for employment, Campbell advised him not to hire Nepali migrants as porters, lest such 'runaway' labourers find trouble in their erstwhile homeland. It was out of the question to hire labourers who hailed from lower altitudes. Lepchas, he was told, 'disliked employment out of Sikkim, especially in so warlike a country as Nepal, and (were) unfit for the snowy regions.'[27] Finally, Campbell mustered on his behalf 14 hefty 'Bhotan run-aways domiciled in Dorjiling, who are accustomed to travel at all elevations, and fear nothing but a return to the country which they have abandoned as slaves, or as culprits: they are immensely powerful, and though intractable to the last degree, will generally work and behave well for money.'[28] Led by Nimbu, their headman, Hooker was assured that this team would easily carry

f.115–17. http://www.kew.org/learn/library–art–archives/joseph–hooker/letter–hooker–sir–joseph–dalton–hooker–sir–william–jacks–73 (accessed 1 January 2016).

[27] Hooker (2002 [1854]: 73).

[28] Hooker (2002 [1854]: 73).

80-pound loads over mountain terrain in return for cash wages and rice rations.

It is important to analyse how and why colonial ethnography characterized these 'Bhutan' labourers, the people, whom the archive otherwise terms as Bhootea, Bhotiya, Bhotia, or Bhutia. In a study of Tibetan border worlds, Wim van Spengen describes them as cross-cultural traders who combined transhumance herding of yak and sheep with summer cultivation.[29] During winter migrations, these Tibetan-dialect speakers carried loads of wool, hides, butter, iron, and salt to barter for plains peoples' grain and sugar at periodic open-air markets all over the Himalayas.[30] Hooker's hiring them at Campbell's urging shows how after a few years of Himalayan rule, colonial officials had become convinced that Bhutia readiness to travel and familiarity with carrying loads made them the most desirable recruits for outdoor labouring jobs as sedan bearers, seasonal road-builders, load carriers, pony and mule operators. An important contributing factor was that Bhutia unfamiliarity with a settled lifestyle and urbanism made them more likely to accept low wages than Lepchas. This is borne out by the evidence from observers such as the guidebook authors Hathorn and Avery that outdoor wages were at the lowest end of labouring remuneration, and tended to remain stagnant.[31]

Colonial descriptions, especially those in official publications, emphasized that Lepchas were a shy and reserved children of Nature. Postcards and other visual depictions established them as picturesque representatives of the Himalayan exoticism that attracted visitors from around the world to Darjeeling.[32] The reluctance of many Lepchas to permanently forego a semi-sedentary agrarian habitus was taken to mean that they were inferior to other Himalayan people for physical endurance and cultural adaptability. Hooker marvelled at a nimble Lepcha 'carrying 140 pounds on his back (as he) crosses (a narrow rope bridge over water).'[33] But that praise was juxtaposed with his opinion that 'indolence, when left to themselves, is their besetting sin; they detest any fixed employment.'[34]

[29] van Spengen (1992).
[30] van Spengen (1992).
[31] Hathorn (1863); Avery (1878).
[32] Sharma (2016a); Harris et al. (2016).
[33] Hooker (2002 [1854]: 62).
[34] Hooker (2002 [1854]: 54).

Evidence that challenged the stereotypical primitive Lepcha seldom emerged out of the archive. Take, for instance, the expedition contributions made by Hooker's treasurer-scribe whose 'fine, clear hand' maintained his accounts.[35] It is astonishing that Hooker's copious writings omit even a single mention of this employee. Only when the linguist Dr R.K. Sprigg discovered a Lepcha-language document that enumerated Hooker's expedition expenses among his Kew papers, did this Lepcha scribe emerge out of the shadows. The image of a Himalayan people unable to cope with a changing world, solidified into an official orthodoxy even as Lepchas worked alongside Nepalis in urban indoor jobs and alongside Bhutias on expeditions. When the Schlagintweit brothers undertook scientific explorations in 1854–8, in their company was Dablong, a Bhutia who had travelled with Hooker, alongside Chagi, a Lepcha, both hired at Darjeeling.[36] Ironically, the first printed book in the English language published by a Lepcha writer, Arthur Foning, accepted his people as 'a dying race' even as he sought to assert their unique heritage with Nature.[37]

Hill Station Labour

Just a few years after Joseph Hooker's visit, the forested slopes where Lepcha collectors foraged for orchids and rhododendrons were being transformed into romantically named tea gardens. Captain Hathorn, a military officer who returned to Darjeeling as a civilian planter, described how, in 1863, nine years after his first cantonment stay, 'fire and axe have swept away the tree and creeper to make way for tea'.[38] Hooker had glimpsed tea-plants growing on 'the fine, wooded spur of Leebong' and Campbell's garden, offspring of China seeds that plant-hunters such as Robert Fortune smuggled into British territory.[39] The descendants of those China plants laid the foundation of the first commercial plantation in 1856.[40] Some decades later, a planter noted, 'The China leaf makes pretty and flavoury teas and the gardens, which get the best prices

35 Sprigg (1982, 1998: 5).
36 Driver (2015: 12).
37 See Foning (1987).
38 Hathorn (1863: 13).
39 Hooker (2002 [1854]: 60).
40 Fielder (1868–9).

up here, are (with one exception) all China gardens.'[41] That China leaf when transplanted to Darjeeling terroir and nurtured by Himalayan labour became the famed Darjeeling tea.[42]

A combination of push and pull factors encouraged labour circulation along porous Himalayan frontiers once the possibilities of wage-work in and around Darjeeling became known. Many migrants spoke Tibeto-Burman languages and were unlettered villagers who fled a difficult agrarian economy and semi-feudal exploitation in the hilly tracts of eastern Nepal. The topography of their homeland earned them the label Pahari (from *pahar*, or hills). Michael Hutt describes how Nepali peasants, enslaved, or landless, or over-taxed, or indebted, long sought better prospects in 'Mugalan' (meaning India, literally, land of Mughals).[43] By the 1870s, William Hunter estimated that 34.1 per cent of the Darjeeling district's population was born in Nepal.[44] The magnitude of the push and pull situation is apparent when we read about the difficulties that attended such moves. One migrant recollected, 'You do not run across the wild country of eastern Nepal. You creep up and down, out and about, over steep ridges, through jungle valleys, across rushing rivers, on trails that you can hardly see.'[45]

From the 1860s, labour needs on tea plantations expanded rapidly under the demands of clearing forests, and the demands of growing, picking, and harvesting the crop. In 1895, the Darjeeling Tea Company's co-chairman, the Scottish planter George Christison estimated that the region's 175 tea gardens employed 70,000 workers, the majority from Nepal.[46] Undoubtedly, many had heard sentiments such as this folk saying that went: 'Darjeeling will take care of me.'[47] However, this was not yet a permanent or even a settled workforce. Tea managers unhappy with such patterns of movement accused tea workers of running away to Nepal so as to default on moneylender debts.[48] In reality, their workforce included many peasants eager to earn tea wages during winter when their fields were fallow, but had no compunction when they deserted

[41] *Notes on Tea in Darjeeling by a Planter* (1888: 8).

[42] Besky (2013).

[43] Hutt (1998).

[44] Hunter (1876: 85).

[45] Norgay and Ullman (1955: 17).

[46] Christison (1895–6).

[47] Gibbs (1943).

[48] *Notes on Tea in Darjeeling by a Planter* (1888: 70–2).

at springtime to plant back home. Even when tea workers moved more or less permanently across the border, they often were inspired to do so by the lure of another colonial enterprise, the Gurkha regiments of the British Indian army.

Sir S.C. Bayley, former Lieutenant-Governor of Bengal, remarked that when he spent summers in Darjeeling, he constantly had to handle planter distress that workers abandoned them in favour of a military career. The Gurkha recruitment station that opened at Darjeeling in 1890, recruited no fewer than 27,428 Gurkhas until 1904 to serve in battle and to perform peacetime tasks such as border road building.[49] Plantations faced a constant problem of desertion, despite state attempts to impose strict checks so that army recruiters might sift out deserting tea labourers.[50]

Colonial Darjeeling's attractiveness for Nepal's subaltern population was popularly perceived via its tea enterprise, with a popular Nepali saying that translates as 'money grows on tea bushes.'[51] But once they joined the plantation, workers realized the limited character of social and economic mobility that it offered since promotions were limited to a handful of overseer jobs. By contrast, a Gurkha soldier's job was more or less permanent, it held the prospect of land grants, it offered pensions and benefits, and it held relatively high status. A top major-domo in a household might earn more than a soldier but did not enjoy the same retirement benefits and access to land grants. However, there were two important caveats that limited the mobile possibilities offered by the military.

First, the fact that only men could become soldiers reinforced the stark gendered reality that the better types of labouring opportunities excluded women. Rather than some intrinsic gendered predisposition, subaltern women's seeming allegiance to plantation employment largely stemmed from lack of choice, their given relative immobility due to child-rearing responsibilities, as well as female exclusion from upper-end domestic jobs. Second, successful Gurkha applicants were supposed to belong to those groups whom the British considered as naturally 'martial races,' the Magar, Gurung, Limbu, and Rai, from the mountain tracts of Nepal. Originally theorized by Hooker's host, Brian Hodgson, the

[49] Morris (1933: 130–1).

[50] Bayley (1895–6: 645). See also Middleton, this volume.

[51] Golay (2006); Shneiderman (2015: 98).

traits that constituted such a martial race were comprehensively revised and tabulated in Lieutenant-Colonel Eden Vansittart's army handbook *Notes on Goorkhas*.[52] Vansittart's handbook was published in 1890, the same year that the Gurkha recruitment station opened at Darjeeling. Recruits were required to have arrived directly from Nepal, rather than be living in British India.

Nonetheless, the ability of colonial recruiters and officials to enforce this type of ethnographic orthodoxy was severely limited. Even as the identity of a Gurkha soldier was restricted to certain ethnicities among freshly arrived Nepali men, diverse Darjeeling recruits who belonged to excluded groups such as Lepchas and Newars, successfully became Gurkhas. To a great extent, this was possible because army recruiters relied on the appearance, testimony, and documents of applicants, as well as the mediation of local translator-intermediaries. Residents of Darjeeling and Kalimpong took advantage of shared Himalayan physiognomy, knowledge of the Nepali vernacular, and labouring networks to hoodwink British recruiters, with the full knowledge of local society. For instance, family lore recalls Dak Singh, a member of a Gurkha regiment, who adopted the Nepali sounding name Singh for official use when he was accepted into the army, although his family knew him as Dak Singh Lepcha.[53]

Paths to Labouring Mobility

Many Himalayan newcomers to Darjeeling followed a trajectory of chain migration in the wake of relatives or village brethren, spurred on by success stories, some of which were real, others imagined. In a handful of cases, oral histories and family memories allow us to reconstruct some such success stories, which are often tied to the opportunities that a new settlement offered. In some instances, mobile Himalayan individuals chose to take advantage of such opportunities and move back to their homelands. This was the case for the founders of the first Sherpa monastery in Nepal who earned most of their wealth during a sojourn as labour contractors in Darjeeling.[54] One success story whose family treasures his humble origins was Gopal Singh Pradhan, who moved as a

[52] See Vansittart (1890); Hodgson (1847, 1880); Des Chene (1999).

[53] Foning (2012), pers. comm.

[54] Ortner (1989).

youth from Bhatgaon to Fikkal, close to the Indo-Nepal border. He subsequently journeyed with family members to labour on the Darjeeling race course being built at Lebong. We know little of Gopal's subsequent years except of his steady rise through labouring ranks to become a petty contractor who employed other labourers and successfully carried out government contracts. His services towards infrastructure construction earned him a state grant of land at 12th Mile, near Kalimpong, on territory newly annexed from Bhutan. His family talks of the decisive shift in status that they achieved when the government promoted his eldest son, Bhim Bahadur, to a first-class contractor qualified to handle jobs over Rs 50,000, followed by the award of a Rai Bahadur title.[55] From labourer to Rai Bahadur was an impressive and rare journey, rarer still to find a genteel South Asian family willing to acknowledge a labouring past.

Literacy as social capital played a transformative role in the journeys of those labouring migrants who encountered the Eastern Himalayan Mission of the Church of Scotland. The Reverend William Macfarlane, previously working at Gaya in Bihar, moved to the Darjeeling region in 1870 at the invitation of tea planters, many of whom were fellow Scottish Presbyterians. One planter, Captain Jorden, had sponsored several Lepcha and Nepali students at Macfarlane's Gaya school, aiming to employ them as plantation clerks.[56] At Darjeeling, Macfarlane obtained state funding for a normal school that every year trained 30 Himalayan male students as primary schoolteachers, each receiving a full scholarship from public funds. Unlike other hill station missionary schools that charged high fees and aimed to educate domiciled Europeans, the Normal School aimed to educate adult students from humble backgrounds, for whom this financial support was crucial. One such student was Gangaprasad Pradhan, born in 1853, who moved from Chainpur as a lad to work as a labourer on a plantation at Ging village. At some point, he enrolled at the Normal School, where he later became a teacher and acted as a Nepali translator of Christian printed works. After the establishment of a Scandinavian Mission at nearby Ghoom, an informal local division arose whereby the new missionaries focused on Tibetan ethnics while the Scottish Presbyterians from their Lochnagar headquarter concentrated on a congregation of Nepalis and Lepchas. While Christian belief was not required for Normal School students, Macfarlane held

[55] Kushal Pradhan and Laval Pradhan (2012), pers. comm.

[56] *Darjeeling Kalimpong and Sikkim News* (1895).

regular Bible sessions that inspired several graduates to convert, despite heavy opposition from kin and caste-fellows. The first Nepali convert was a Normal School graduate Bhimdal Dewan, later a Sub-Inspector of police at the border town of Sukhia Pokhari. Another early convert was Sukhman Limbu who became a catechist at Kalimpong, volunteering to lead a pioneering mission into Bhutan before his untimely death.

The most prominent Normal School graduate and convert was Gangaprasad Pradhan. A Newar from the Kathmandu valley, his knowledge of the Nepali vernacular surpassed that of most labouring contemporaries who after their Normal School education, settled into modest jobs via missionary patronage as teachers or village catechists. Gangaprasad possessed enough social capital that, after working as a teacher, a Bible translator, and then a catechist, he was selected in 1901 for the high honour of ordination as the first pastor from a Himalayan community. Gangaprasad made a mark in the emerging world of Nepali print through his long commitment to the Gorkha Press at Darjeeling, for which he wrote and published numerous books and tracts, including a co-translation of the Bible.[57]

The urban mobility that men such as Gangaprasad and Sukhman personified was a new attractive model for Paharis and Lepchas willing to consider the potential gains from missionary patronage, modern education, and print culture against the risk of alienation from one's familial and caste networks. However, its scope should not be overestimated. The vast majority of Darjeeling's converts made a modest living within local educational and church structures, acting as teachers, catechists, and when a medical division was added, health workers. Christian affiliation could not bridge the raced, classed, and cultural divide with white or mixed-race society, even as it separated them from their Buddhist, Hindu, and animist counterparts. Missionary patronage allowed for a modest livelihood and some degree of class mobility but did not suffice to enter more than the lowest clerical rungs of the colonial bureaucracy.

As elsewhere in Darjeeling's political economy, men were the principal beneficiaries of missionary mobility, even though the Scottish Presbyterians placed considerable emphasis on the promotion of female education. Inspiration came from the Scottish parishes of their own upbringing where subaltern women (and men) received better

[57] 'Reports of the Darjeeling Mission, Letter to Supporters 22 February 1876: iii.' Adam Matthew Publishers, *Eastern Himalayan Mission Papers*, Reel 26.

opportunities for basic schooling than in England. However, missionary efforts for female education were shaped by the era's gendered expectations, and its aim was to train future wives and mothers for local congregations, especially suitable helpmeets for mission-trained young men. At the mission girls' school established at Darjeeling in 1873, prizes were awarded solely for prowess in knitting, sewing, conduct, and cooking, rather than for literacy and numeracy as in the boys' schools. Only after the early twentieth century did a handful of female catechists and teachers emerge from the Darjeeling Christian community, which grew as a whole from 130 in 1880, to 2,500 in 1900, and to over 14,000 by 1945.[58]

Climbing Labour and Mountain Mobility

During the mid-nineteenth century, Joseph Hooker was a rare British visitor who, thanks to his host Brian Hodgson's contacts in Nepal, enjoyed royal permission to travel to eastern Nepal in search of botanical finds. This was a special privilege as until European powers compelled them otherwise, Himalayan rulers deemed it best to close their frontiers to the former's representatives. This acted greatly to Darjeeling's benefit, until it became the main embarkation point for sports aficionados who discovered that their Alpine climbing pursuits transferred well to the Himalayan peaks surrounding the hill station.

In addition to normative explorer requirements for collectors, cooks, major-domos, and porters, the new type of expedition created a burgeoning demand for high-altitude porters and mountain guides at Darjeeling. Initially, British climbers hired Swiss and Italian Alpine professionals to facilitate their Himalayan expeditions, but they were expensive and lacked local knowledge.[59] Instead, the mountaineering enthusiasts who coalesced around the Royal Geographical Society at London and later, the Himalayan Club at Darjeeling, experimented with home-grown versions of Alpine labour, even as new imperial and nationalistic fervour around mountaineering shifted Euro-American mountain interest to the newly discovered highest peak in the world, Everest. They surveyed the ranks of Himalayan migrants for those who could meet the labouring

[58] Perry (1997); Nepal Church History Project Archives (1896–2007). Yale University Library, *Yale Divinity School Library*, Record Group No. 215.

[59] Hansen (1999).

expectations of expeditions that aspired to triumph over the highest peaks in the world.

Since many climbers were British military officers, it was natural for them to first look at Himalayan recruits for talent. Vansittart's revised edition of the army handbook contributed the information that sporting talent was as intrinsic a trait of the Gurkha soldier as his aptitude for battle.[60] One man who took credit for that discovery was General, the Hon. Charles Bruce, who took pride in his Gurkha soldiers and commanded them in fluent Nepali. In his memoir *Himalayan Wanderer*, Bruce recounted his strategies to transform 'fresh caught recruits' of the 5th Gurkha Regiment into modern sportsmen.[61] Bruce portrayed himself as the pioneer who had discovered Gurkha sporting potential when he recruited Parbir and Harkbir Thapa into competitive hill racing and track running and showcased their talent in British races.[62] But Bruce later concluded that climbing was the one sport where Gurkhas were outshone by 'Bhutia Nepalese'.[63] The first mention of these climbing auxiliaries was from two Norwegian climbers, Rubenson and Monrad Aas, who praised the willingness and bravery of their 'coolies, especially Nepalese Sherpas' after a failed 1907 summit attempt. They noted that 'we could not persuade them to be roped when loaded, but by making good steps, fixing in pegs and ropes, and helping them over difficult places there seems to be no limit to what they will surmount.'[64]

Such an opinion received much more credibility, especially among the British imperial establishment, when a British climber-cum-scientist offered similar sentiments in the journal of the Royal Geographical Society (RGS). This was Alexander Kellas, lecturer in Chemistry at the Middlesex Hospital Medical School in London. Kellas began his climbing career in his Scottish homeland's Grampians, followed by the Alps and Himalayas. From 1907 until his untimely death in 1921, Kellas climbed a number of peaks across the Kashmir, Garhwal, and Sikkim Himalaya. In his 1917 article, he recommended, based on his own experience, 'a solitary traveller, anxious to do a little easy climbing, might find it worth his while to take a few carefully selected Bhutia Nepalese with him as personal servants to any mountain region. They can be engaged

60 Vansittart (1890).

61 Bruce (1934: 32).

62 Bruce (1934: 32).

63 Kellas (1917).

64 Cameron (1984: 154).

at Darjeeling.'[65] Kellas' stature as a scientist who united his medical and climbing interests in researching the impact of high-altitudes upon human physiology, as well as the imprimatur of the RGS as the apex body of imperial mountaineering, was crucial. It influenced Bruce and other military men who sought climbing auxiliaries to shift their focus from Gurkha soldiers to those Darjeeling Bhutia labourers whom they now identified as Sherpas, seeing them as the closest Himalayan equivalent to the sturdy Alpine peasant.

Sherpas were relatively recent entrants into the Darjeeling economy, who for centuries worked as seasonal load carriers in Nepal and Tibet to supplement the meagre subsistence that their home environs provided. Legend placed them as having migrated from eastern Tibet to the Solu–Khumbu border region of Nepal in the seventeenth century.[66] There they grew barley and buckwheat and pastured yaks at 11,000–12,500 feet. At the time of Kellas's untimely death in 1921, he had just finished an attempt on the Kabru peak in Sikkim aiming to train Sherpas in modern Euro–American mountaineering techniques before the forthcoming Everest reconnaissance.[67] Whether it was the training or their much-vaunted biological adaptation to high altitudes, Sherpa porters acquitted themselves famously on the much-publicised 1921 Everest expedition, the first in a series of British and European attempts to conquer the top of the world.[68]

After 1921, it became an accepted colonial precept that the skilled, risky, and relatively lucrative labouring jobs on Himalayan climbing expeditions went to Sherpa men.[69] The widespread press publicity along the lines of 'such is a Sherpa porter' that high-profile Everest climbers provided, served to make a British public almost as familiar with the name Sherpa as they were with Gurkha. This soon transformed the labouring lives of many Sherpa migrants to Darjeeling.[70] Sherry Ortner writes of the importance of the Darjeeling wage-work

[65] Cameron (1984: 154).

[66] Oppitz (1974: 1–2).

[67] West (1989).

[68] 'Mount Everest Expedition' (1921).

[69] See Ortner (1999).

[70] *The Scotsman* (1924). 'Expedition. General Bruce Reports All Well.' Edinburgh: Johnston Publishing, Apr 16. From ProQuest Historical Newspapers, The Scotsman (1817–1950) accessed 1 July 2016.

situation in empowering 'small' Sherpas in their Solu–Khumbu subsistence economy.[71] It allowed the fortunate ones among them to use cash earned seasonally at Darjeeling to cement a solid economic basis and respectable social status with land and yak ownership, buttressed by religious patronage.[72] Until these climbing labour opportunities arose, Sherpas were indistinguishable to employers from other Bhutia groups, or even from other Nepali labourers. Now they were sought out by name. Sherpa children such as the young Tenzing Norgay grew up in Solu–Khumbu watching adults carry salt and wool loads as far as Darjeeling, inspired by tales of the 'chilingna' white men whom Sherpas accompanied to mountains that reached the sky.[73]

On the one hand, the 'discovery' of the Sherpa male as an exalted high-altitude labourer did serve to disadvantage other Himalayan groups, whether Lepchas, Nepalis, or other Bhutias. The mountain establishment's biological logic, which fetishized the Sherpa male body on the highest peaks, meant that others were relegated to less lucrative, less risky jobs lower down the mountain, as were Sherpa women. On the other hand, it can be argued that the popularity of climbing meant that there were many more waged opportunities for expedition labour from Darjeeling.

Among Sherpa men, colonial institutions consciously fostered differentiation. The Himalayan Club, the colonial institution that acted as the official gatekeeper of Himalayan mountaineering, created an elite category of Tigers when it awarded a coveted badge and stipend to porters who distinguished themselves on expeditions. One such Tiger, Sherpa Tenzing Norgay, went on to become Darjeeling's most famous citizen when he climbed the world's highest mountain in 1953. Before this, he had spent decades as an ordinary labouring migrant in Darjeeling. Norgay had journeyed as an 18 year old with 12 other boys and girls from his village over perilous mountain terrain to the promised land of Darjeeling. There he exchanged his rags for Nepali-style clothes gifted by his milkman employer and cut his Sherpa-style braid so as not to appear rustic. However, he did not realize that cutting his hair was a misstep towards his ambition to work as a climbing porter. Norgay later recollected, 'This was all right for Darjeeling, but bad with the expedition, for

[71] Ortner (1999: 30, 90).

[72] Ortner (1989: 160).

[73] Norgay and Ullman (1955: 17); see also Hansen (2013).

they thought I was a Nepali, and they wanted only Sherpas.'[74] Since his appearance was no longer that of a Sherpa, the Himalayan Club rejected him when he applied to the 1933 British Everest expedition.

After his 1933 rejection, Norgay returned to mundane labouring work, travelling back to Solu–Khumbu to carry salt loads to Tibet, and joining the labour gang that rebuilt the St. Paul's School chapel. Two years later, when he applied to join Eric Shipton's new Everest expedition, he made sure that he conformed to the British recruiters' image of a genuine Sherpa. Ironically, this involved wearing a western-style suit.[75] Norgay was overjoyed when he was hired, since 'the wages on the expedition were 12 annas a day, which would be raised to one rupee a day for every day above snowline; so if I went, I would make more money than I ever did before.'[76] Norgay and his climbing Sherpa community settled in the Toong Soong and Bhutia Busti neighbourhoods of Darjeeling, alongside other Himalayan neighbours. For successful Sherpa climbers, ambitions began to centre around schooling their children on the one hand, and saving for yak and land purchases in Solu–Khumbu on the other. Living in the urban and colonial space of Darjeeling, everyday cultural norms changed; for instance, Indian tea with milk and sugar became their daily staple, while Tibetan tea was reserved for special, ceremonial occasions. Norgay recollected how living in Darjeeling, Sherpa households like his could afford their beloved momo dumplings filled with pork many more times than once a year at the Tibetan New Year celebration, and how they frequently supplemented this delicacy with Indian-style meat curries. With newly acquired Indian citizenship, these climbing Sherpas joined fellow Himalayan denizens who came to claim the Nepali language, a multi-ethnic Pahari identity, and the space of Darjeeling as their own.

An expanding and diversifying colonial economy accentuated the Darjeeling region's historical and geographical connections to

[74] Norgay and Ullman (1955: 19).

[75] The Royal Geographical Society's Online Picture Library owns a photograph that shows Eric Shipton, the expedition leader, interviewing Sherpas, including Tenzing Norgay, at Darjeeling in 1935. http://images.rgs.org/imageDetails.aspx?barcode=3682.

[76] Norgay and Ullman (1955: 24).

surrounding Himalayan borderlands and greatly increased numbers of labouring newcomers who were attracted to the hill station and its agrarian hinterlands. This chapter explored how the British imperial hill station of Darjeeling was constituted through the mobile passages, livelihood strategies, social relationships, and cultural yearnings of such subjects who became known as Lepchas, Bhutias, Gurkhas, and Sherpas. Colonial institutions such as plantations, expeditions, schools, and missions facilitated those passages, yet it was the tenacity and creativity of those Himalayan citizens who gradually carved out new identities for themselves as Pahari people, who would subsequently strive for greater control over that space and its institutions. These endeavours often aligned themselves against postcolonial regimes whose nationalistic ambitions proved antithetical to the borderland crossings that had catalyzed prosperity and vitality for Darjeeling in its colonial incarnation.

Section II
Politics and Social Movements

4 *Electoral Competition and the Gorkhaland Movement*

Bethany Lacina*

Nepali-speakers in the state of West Bengal have a longstanding demand that the Darjeeling district be converted into Gorkhaland, which would be a new state within the Indian federation. In the 1980s, these demands sparked a law and order crisis large enough to draw the central government's intervention. The creation of the Darjeeling Gorkha Hill Council quieted demands for Gorkhaland until 2007, when the movement again became a political flashpoint.

* Thank you to Sara Shneiderman and Townsend Middleton, who hosted the excellent conference that lead to this edited volume and are committed to nurturing scholarly interest in Darjeeling. I thank Miriam Wenner and Bengt Karlsson for their comments on this chapter and Matthew Hoddie, Caroline A. Hartzell, and Philip G. Roeder for help with similar earlier pieces.

Thus, mass mobilization pressuring the state and central governments to concede Gorkhaland has waxed and waned over the years.

This essay highlights the electoral incentives of Gorkha politicians to explain the variable intensity of mass autonomy movements.[1] I point out the parallels in the careers of three major Darjeeling political figures, whose careers span decades: Deoprakash Rai, Subash Ghisingh, and Bimal Gurung. Each of these leaders de-escalated his movement for Darjeeling autonomy as his personal power and electoral dominance was consolidated. In less competitive periods of Darjeeling politics, these leaders were able to maintain a tacit bargain with the state and national governments, receiving resources in return for quiescence on the issue of local autonomy.

Reconsidering the Gorkhaland Movements in light of electoral competition provides institutional and political context for ethnographic and sociological accounts of Darjeeling. The popular anxieties animating calls for Darjeeling's autonomy only reach the national stage via political organizations. These organizations and their leaders produce disconnects between Darjeeling's social realities and the varied career of the Gorkhaland demand in national politics.

The First Calls for Autonomy

The first major Gorkha political party was a response to European mobilization for an autonomous Darjeeling dominated by the white settler community. Darjeeling's European residents formed the Hillmen's Association and asked that a separate administrative unit be carved out for the Nepali, Bhutia, and Lepcha areas of British India.[2] Political mobilization in Darjeeling did not really pick up, however, until decolonization was imminent. At that point, the Hillmen's Association, emphasizing the pre-Gorkha, tribal populations of Darjeeling, asked for total autonomy from independent India and ethnic electorates within Darjeeling to ensure continued European control. A rival movement, the All India Gorkha League (AIGL) founded in Darjeeling in 1943, grew out of union and communist movements among tea garden workers. The AIGL's original demand was that Darjeeling become a part of the neighbouring state of Assam, where Gorkhas would have a larger

[1] See Lacina (2014).
[2] Chakrabarty (2005).

population share than in Bengal.[3] The AIGL also flirted with the notion that Darjeeling, Sikkim, and perhaps even Assam should become part of Nepal. Neither the AIGL's nor the Hillmen's Association's vision was brought to fruition, however, and at Independence Darjeeling was included in the state of West Bengal without any special autonomy.

The Hillmen's Association quickly faded as many Europeans left Darjeeling after Independence. During nationwide reorganization of Indian states in 1956, the AIGL requested that Darjeeling become a separate state or a centrally administered unit.[4] The AIGL aligned with the Communist Party of India (CPI) in making these demands. The parties had shared roots in the trade union movement and the CPI's platform supported nationalist movements on the grounds that they were part of the progression from feudal to bourgeois to socialist society.[5] However, Darjeeling's demands were opposed by the state government of West Bengal, which was controlled by the India National Congress (INC) party, also the ruling party in New Delhi. Darjeeling was passed over during state reorganization.

The Era of Deoprakash Rai

Despite that setback, the AIGL continued to hold political sway as the voice of Gorkha politics. The leadership of the AIGL also consolidated in the late 1950s. A violent labour strike in 1955 split the party. The AIGL activist wing won the upper hand and expelled from the party its three representatives in the West Bengal state legislature. In the 1957 state legislative elections, the expelled members ran as independents and two lost their seats. In the most important of Darjeeling's three constituencies—that centred on Darjeeling town—Deoprakash Rai, the new AIGL candidate, narrowly defeated both the incumbent and a CPI candidate (see Table 4.1). He 'subsequently attained a stature of an indomitable regional leader of the All India Gorkha League from Darjeeling'.[6] Rai went on to win the next six elections for that seat with an average margin of victory of 17 per cent. Rai twice served as a state cabinet minister, as well.

[3] Thapa (1997).
[4] Sarkar and Bhaumik (2000: 27).
[5] Prakash (1973).
[6] Bomjan (2008: 112).

The era of Rai's political hegemony was a time of limited mobilization for autonomy in Darjeeling. After 1956, the AIGL's focus shifted to promoting the Nepali language throughout India.[7] The party also scaled back its demands regarding Darjeeling, passing resolutions for autonomy within West Bengal as opposed to prior demands for statehood or central administration. Little progress was made towards autonomy even under state governments in which Rai held a cabinet post. In 1976, a Darjeeling Hill Areas Development Council was formed but was only given an advisory role in development planning.[8] Despite the lack of autonomy concessions, the AIGL did not escalate its demands or tactics. Its mobilization consisted of little more than periodic memoranda to New Delhi or Kolkata. D.S. Bomjan argues that the AIGL also worked to marginalize upstart political formations that threatened to pursue Darjeeling's autonomy more forcefully. Within the AIGL, Rai likewise quashed dissent: 'the leaders who dared to challenge his style ... were made like a fish thrown on the sand'.[9]

Rai established a pattern for his successors: as his own stability in office consolidated, his party decreased its efforts at winning territorial autonomy for Darjeeling. That pattern became more obvious under the two later leaders—Subash Ghisingh and Bimal Gurung. Although this chapter is drawing a parallel between these three leaders, it is worth stressing that political life was more pluralistic under Rai's AIGL than subsequently thereafter. Opposition parties like the Communist Party of India (Marxist) (CPI[M]) and civil society organizations that operated in Darjeeling during the AIGL's tenure were largely purged from the hills in the 1980s.

Political Competition and Statehood Demands

In 1981, Deoprakash Rai passed away. After his death, the AIGL fell into internal disorder. The 1982 state legislative elections in the Darjeeling and Kurseong constituencies were each decided by less than 1 per cent of the vote, the most closely contested elections in these seats since Independence (Table 4.1). The AIGL's faltering created a political opening for a new champion of Darjeeling's autonomy. The political vacuum

[7] Bhandari (2003: 112); Chakrabarty (2005: 181).

[8] Chakrabarty (2005: 183).

[9] Bomjan (2008: 89).

was ultimately filled by the Gorkha National Liberation Front (GNLF), led by Subash Ghisingh, who had served in the military and was also a popular author. The GNLF won its struggle for ascendancy against the AIGL, other upstart Gorkha parties, and the Darjeeling chapter of West Bengal's ruling party at the time, the CPI(M). The struggle involved escalating demands for autonomy and confrontation with the Centre, as well as internecine violence.

In 1980–1, four local political parties, including the GNLF, called for Darjeeling to become a federal state, going beyond the AIGL's demand for autonomy within Bengal. The GNLF also won public attention by introducing a range of new issues into Gorkha mobilization. The party called for repeal of the 1950 Indo-Nepalese Peace and Friendship Treaty between Nepal and India, claiming (incorrectly) that the treaty undermined Gorkhas' legal standing as Indian citizens.[10] Ghisingh even talked of secession, claiming that Darjeeling was a no-man's land under arcane treaties of the British East India Company.[11]

The GNLF also escalated the movement for Darjeeling's autonomy on the tactical front with a blockade of timber industry shipments, general strikes, election and tax boycotts, and public burnings of copies of the Indo-Nepalese Treaty of 1950. Clashes between police and protestors motivated the Centre to deploy paramilitaries to Darjeeling.[12] However, the primary violence was between local political parties, which traded arsons, kidnappings, and killings, and fought for control of hospitals, food and commodity distribution, labour unions, and tea gardens.[13] One estimate of the toll from 1986–8 is 300 people killed and millions of dollars of property destroyed.[14]

By late 1986, the state government admitted that it had no authority in parts of Darjeeling. The majority of civil servants in the region had resigned from their posts in solidarity with the GNLF or in protest of the lack of protection they had from the state.[15] Other Gorkha political

[10] Sonntag (1999: 425).

[11] Dixit (2003: 323).

[12] Sarkar and Bhaumik (2000: 31).

[13] See, for example, the description of violent events in December 1981 found in Lal (1987: 158).

[14] See Crossette, Barbara (1989). 'Darjeeling Journal: For Gurkhas, Little Time to Stop and Sip the Tea.' *New York Times*, April 3. Also, Shrestha, Ananda (2003). 'Political Murders Rock Darjeeling.' *Nepali Times*, June 15–29.

[15] Sarkar and Bhaumik (2000: 33–4).

parties increasingly recognized the GNLF as the head of the Darjeeling movement.

Autonomy for Darjeeling

In January 1987, West Bengal's Chief Minister Jyoti Basu and the Indian Prime Minister Rajiv Gandhi began developing a plan for negotiations with the GNLF. The two leaders seemed to have little doubt Ghisingh would bargain. They offered Ghisingh an autonomous district council; he countered with demands for a larger geographic jurisdiction and control of more funds. The Centre prodded Kolkata to make more concessions, fearing that 'delay [would] ... trigger off [sic] large scale violence resulting in ouster of Mr. Ghisingh from leadership and his inability to carry all sections of hill people with him to the negotiation table.'[16] In 1988, a trilateral agreement set the terms for the Darjeeling Gorkha Hill Council (DGHC). The DGHC was an apex body for district, village, and municipal governments with authority for development funds and economic planning. The new council had no police or legislative powers but did come with a huge infusion of central development funds. In the 1988 accord the GNLF formally renounced the demand for Gorkhaland state and agreed to surrender its arms in exchange for rehabilitation of fighters.[17]

The terms of the settlement and the manner in which it was implemented seem designed to repress political competition in Darjeeling. DGHC elections were supervised by a political appointee rather than the state election commission. In the 1989 council elections the GNLF took 26 out of 28 seats.[18] In the second and third DGHC elections, GNLF intimidation of candidates and poll-irregularities went unchallenged. GNLF candidates also won all the state legislature seats from the Darjeeling hills between 1991 and 2006, by an average vote margin of about 30 per cent (see Table 4.1).

Ghisingh used the DGHC to develop a vast patronage network unhampered by New Delhi and Kolkata. Chakrabarty describes the tangible impact of the DGHC as visible power concentration in the GNLF:

> The Chairman [Ghisingh] and the Executive Councilors enjoy all the frills of cars/jeeps with red lights, etc., enjoyed by ministers in West

[16] Sarkar and Bhaumik (2000: 38).

[17] Bomjan (2008: 119).

[18] Sarkar and Bhaumik (2000: 121).

Table 4.1 Competitiveness of Elections for the West Bengal State Legislature from Gorkha Constituencies, 1951–2016

Darjeeling Bungalow/ Kurseong			Kalimpong		Jore	
Year	Winner	Margin (%)	Winner	Margin (%)	Winner	Margin (%)
1951	AIGL/INC	22	CPI	20	AIGL/INC	44
1957	AIGL	1.1	Independent	16	CPI	6.0
1962	AIGL	24	AIGL	20	CPI	0.60
1967	AIGL	19	INC	10	AIGL	6.7
1969	AIGL	15	AIGL	15	AIGL	17
1971	AIGL	18	AIGL	12	CPM	0.86
1972	AIGL	17	INC	5.1	AIGL	1.5
1977	AIGL	11	AIGL	15	INC	3.6
1982†	CPM	0.53	AIGL	32	CPM	0.47
1987†	CPM	84	CPI	84	CPM	55
1991	GNLF	14	GNLF	39	GNLF	15
1996	GNLF	25	GNLF	67	GNLF	17
2001	GNLF	43	GNLF	28	GNLF	30
2006	GNLF	20	GNLF	25	GNLF	28
2011	GJM	69	GJM	81	GJM	60
2016	GJM	31	GJM	8.3	GJM	21

†Boycotted by GNLF.
Source: Data from the Election Commission of India, *General Election Results and Statistics*, http://eci.nic.in/eci_main1/ElectionStatistics.aspx.

> Bengal and elsewhere. The Council is seen to be the governing agency in the district with control over most of the departments ... there has been a tendency to equate the DGHC with the GNLF.[19]

Such political dominance allowed the GNLF to concentrate all government resources under its own authority. The party dissolved or obviated levels of government below the DGHC and even horizontal regulatory institutions, such as the district's School Service Commission. The last external audit of the DGHC was performed in 1992, a failure that neither the state nor the Centre chose to press. The Council's

[19] Chakrabarty (2005: 188).

meetings were also suspended for years at a time, in violation of the law creating the DGHC, without central or state intervention.[20]

Defending Ghisingh's Power

Ghisingh did make periodic demands on the Centre and state governments, parrying criticism of the DGHC by pointing to gaps in its jurisdiction and budget. In 1994, Ghisingh petitioned the Supreme Court to review Darjeeling's status under the Indo-Nepalese Treaty of 1950; in 1998, he referred the treaty to the International Court of Justice.[21] These gestures combined rhetorical flourish with a minimal chance of alarming New Delhi or Kolkata. Ghisingh's threats of new popular agitations engendered minor expansions of the DGHC's functions and funding.[22]

While Ghisingh called for autonomy, he was, at the same time, committed to protecting his own political hegemony. That imperative meant eliminating political rivals who tried to outflank him with more aggressive demands for Darjeeling's self-rule. In 1989, after Ghisingh agreed to the creation of the DGHC in place of Gorkha statehood, leaders of rival political parties were murdered. Another challenger to Ghising's power, C.K. Pradhan, was killed in 2002 after threatening renewed statehood agitation. The state government worked in tandem to ensure Ghising's political dominance by arresting other upstart politicians.

New Delhi and Kolkata remained committed to Ghisingh's political survival, fearing anarchy or more extreme leadership if Ghisingh fell. A new Gorkha leadership would escalate demands for Darjeeling's self-rule.[23] The state government repeatedly acquiesced to Ghisingh's demand that the 2004 DGHC elections should be postponed. Ultimately, Kolkata allowed Ghisingh to take full control of the DGHC's resources, dissolving the council and appointing Ghisingh as its caretaker.

Ghisingh's rationale for the suspension of DGHC elections was that the council needed to be added to the Sixth Schedule of the Indian Constitution, a list of tribal councils. Both New Delhi and Kolkata were

[20] Chakrabarty (2005: 188).

[21] Express News Service (1998). 'Ghising Goes Global'. *The Indian Express*, February 1.

[22] Chakrabarty (2005: 189). Sonntag (1999: 432–3); Sarkar and Bhaumik (2000: 26).

[23] Shrestha (2003).

receptive. In 2005, a plan to include the council in the Sixth Schedule was announced, along with a central government promise of Rs. 1.5 billion in new funding for the revamped DGHC. However, Sixth Schedule status requires a constitutional amendment and so the new designation was not immediately effective.

The Fall of Subash Ghisingh

Rai's death was an obvious milestone in Darjeeling politics. It is harder to pinpoint the cause of Ghisingh's fall from power. One factor was the unpopularity of the GNLF's Sixth Schedule proposal. Many in Darjeeling considered the designation as 'tribal' to be contrived and even demeaning. The classification also had the potential to eliminate some of the special legal privileges of lower caste Gorkhas. Seizing an opportune political moment, Bimal Gurung, Ghisingh's second-in-command, broke from the GNLF in October 2007 to form the Gorkha Janamukti Morcha (GJM).[24]

Gurung promised the GJM would prevent Darjeeling from becoming a Sixth Schedule area and establish statehood instead. To put pressure on Ghisingh and his state and national allies, the GJM used general strikes, *gheraos* (sieges of government buildings), tax boycotts, and road blockades. GJM activists clashed with non-Gorkha protestors in the plains of Darjeeling and with GNLF members in the hills. New Delhi tried to assist Ghisingh. It pushed the national legislature to expedite Sixth Schedule status for Darjeeling. But that legislative manoeuvring did not proceed quickly enough. In March 2008, Ghisingh resigned and fled Darjeeling in face of massive GJM protests and interparty violence.

The GJM in Power

In 2011, GJM candidates for the West Bengal state legislature won in every Darjeeling constituency (see Table 4.1). Those elections signalled that the GJM was the new dominant political actor in Gorkha politics. Its electoral power was obvious again in the 2016 state assembly races. GJM candidates won with a margin of 8.3 per cent in Kalimpong, 21 per cent in Kurseong, and 31 per cent in Darjeeling. The GJM's elimination of its political rivals ran parallel with a ratcheting down of its demands.

[24] On this transition, see Middleton (2013a).

For example, in spring 2010, rumours that the GJM would accept a new hill council led to a revival of the AIGL, which pledged itself to continue the statehood movement. Months later, Madan Tamang, the leader of the AIGL, was murdered while in the company of state police escorts. Investigators have released cell phone recordings in which Bimal Gurung and other top GJM leaders seem to be plotting the assassination. Nicole Tamang, a GJM leader, was arrested for the murder and then escaped from state custody:

> The All India Gorkha League had already alleged that Nicole was allowed to flee as the state reached an understanding with the GJM after it dropped its demands to include [the areas of] Dooars and Terai in the proposed hill council. 'The theory sounds ridiculous,' said a senior official of the state police. 'But one thing is baffling. Nicole's escape was facilitated and [state police officer] Pahari could have a role in that. He was responsible for a serious lapse. It's intriguing that no action has been taken against him.'[25]

In July 2011, the GJM signed an agreement with New Delhi and Kolkata for autonomy arrangements well short of statehood. The GTA had legal control of more aspects of administration than the DGHC had, although the DGHC's de facto domain covered most GTA responsibilities. Like the DGHC, the GTA has no true legislative power and does not have jurisdiction over the police. In March 2012, the GJM dropped a demand for the territorial jurisdiction of the GTA to exceed that of the DGHC.

The summer 2012 GTA elections gave fresh evidence of the GJM's political hegemony in Darjeeling. The party won all 45 seats in the GTA, 28 of these in uncontested elections (Nicole Tamang was among those elected). Darjeeling-based parties, including those in favour of Gorkhaland, accused the GJM of suppressing competition:

> Representatives of the Communist Party of Revolutionary Marxists (CPRM) also accused the GJM of giving up the demand for Gorkhaland in the rush to get elected to the GTA … They said the polls were a complete farce where only the GJM candidates were allowed to contest—a contention also echoed by the leaders of the Communist Party of India

[25] Bandopadhyay, Sabyasachi (2010). 'State Silence on Pahari Baffles Hills,' *Indian Express*, August 27. On Tamang's assassination and its 'afterlives,' see Middleton (2018).

> (Marxist). 'There was no atmosphere to conduct elections in the hills. We were forced to withdraw our candidates because of the continuous threats of the GJM', said Jibesh Sarkar, acting secretary of the party in Darjeeling.[26]

The new ruling party in Kolkata, the Trinamool Congress (TMC), also withdrew its candidates. Despite alleged irregularities, both the chief minister of West Bengal and the national home minister attended the GTA swearing-in, with Bimal Gurung as the new chief executive. The home minister trumpeted the centre's promise of Rs. two billion of development funds to the GTA over the next three years, adding that 'if more money is needed for development, we will give you [sic]',[27] Chief minister Mamata Banerjee weighed in with promises of a university and hospital renovations.

Electoral Pressures and Faltering Alliances

The GJM's 2012 truce with the Trinamool Congress (TMC) had much the same character as the GNLF's tacit bargain with the CPI(M) in the 1990s. Gurung, like Ghisingh before him, has significant access to state and central financial resources, as well as forbearance in the face of anti-democratic and violent measures taken against Gorkha opponents. In exchange, the GJM accepted the GTA, shelving calls for Darjeeling's separation from West Bengal (at least temporarily).

On the other hand, cooperation between the GJM and TMC faltered over the course of TMC's first term in office, from 2011–6. In the 2014 national elections, the GJM backed the BJP's candidate to the national legislature rather than the TMC's pick. In advance of the 2016 state elections, Harka Bahadur Chettri, who had been elected MLA from Kurseong in 2011 on the GJM ticket, defected from the party. He announced the new Jana Andolan (People's Movement) Party, trumpeting a promise from the TMC to create a Kalimpong administrative district separate from Darjeeling. TMC, in addition to the alliance with Chettri, ran its own candidates in Darjeeling and Kalimpong. However, the GJM won decisively in all three assembly seats (see Table 4.1).

26 Singh, Shiv Sahay (2012). 'Non–GJM parties to Boycott GTA Swearing-in Ceremony Today,' *The Hindu*, August 4.

27 Indo–Asian News Service (2012). 'Gorkha Territorial Administration Members Sworn In,' *Times of India*, August 4.

As the TMC started its second term in the summer of 2016, the GJM/TMC relationship was rocky. The GJM's victory in the assembly elections rebuffed TMC's attempt to circumvent Gurung's party. However, the GJM's position is weakened by its continued dependence on the state government for releasing revenue to the GTA. Also, the BJP central government has signalled that it is not willing to create Gorkhaland state immediately, limiting the GJM's leverage against Kolkata.

It is worth remembering that Ghisingh's relationship with the CPI(M) combined mutual antagonism and grudging cooperation. It lurched from mini-crisis to mini-crisis as Ghisingh and the CPI(M) each tried to improve their end of the patronage–for–stability bargain. Nonetheless, that tacit alliance held together well enough to keep the GNLF in power for many years. The GJM and TMC may likewise be able to maintain an uneasy détente that both keeps the GJM in power and ensures mobilization for Darjeeling autonomy continues in abeyance. One challenge to that alliance is that the TMC does not (at this point) dominate West Bengal politics as clearly as the CPI(M) did when Ghisingh was in power. Other parties, including the CPI(M) and the BJP, are courting the GJM's support and can offer the GJM links to higher levels of government. The multiplicity of parties interested in an alliance with the GJM introduces instability into the GJM-TMC relationship. At the same time, statewide political competition means the TMC is motivated to compete directly in Darjeeling's electoral politics rather than abandoning the field to the GJM. To this end, the TMC has conferred development boards to a growing list of ethnic groups in the hills. The granting of these boards and the state resources that come with them have created direct lines of patronage to the TMC, which has helped the party make significant inroads into the hills. In keeping with this strategy, in 2016, the TMC announced development boards for three Nepali-speaking Scheduled Castes, the Kami, Damai, and Sarki. Like the plan to create a Kalimpong district, the development boards have the potential to be institutional counterweights to the GTA. By directing resources through the boards, the TMC can build alliances that circumvent the GJM. Predictably, the GJM responded by threatening to restart mobilization for statehood.[28] In 2017, GJM–TMC détente only looked more fragile when the TMC formed an alliance with

[28] Singh, Shiv Sahay (2016). 'In Darjeeling, Mamata Banks on Identity Politics,' *The Hindu*, July 19.

the GNLF for municipal elections. Further events have confirmed the fraught nature of the GJM's relationship to the TMC and West Bengal more generally. In summer 2017, the army was deployed to Darjeeling in response to GJM protests against the West Bengal chief minister Mamata Banerjee's visit. This proved an ominous development, which served as a stress test for Darjeeling's status quo, and any possibility of meaningful change in the near future.

Darjeeling Elites and the Gorkhaland Movement

This chapter describes a basic continuity to the structure of politics in Darjeeling. Autonomy demands have escalated after surprise events displaced political incumbents: Rai's death, Ghisingh's 2006–7 missteps, and so on. This kind of shock to the political system makes space available for challengers who try to build a following by rekindling demands for greater autonomy for Darjeeling. These challengers launch aggressive mass movements that clash with incumbent parties. Thus, electoral and partisan competition coincides with insecurity. By contrast, when incumbents are electorally secure, their incentive to press autonomy demands dwindles. They face no pressure from rivals in Darjeeling and no reason to disrupt the flow of resources from state and central coffers. Both the national and the state governments tolerate the anti-democratic features of Darjeeling's autonomous institutions precisely because periods of low political competition in Darjeeling have also been periods without aggressive autonomy movements.

Commentaries on Gorkhaland often emphasize the popular grievances that lend force to calls for autonomy: questions of identity, social and economic power, and insecurity within the Indian polity. The transformation of grievances into mass actions—*hartal*s, marches, tax boycotts, and even violence—have been dominated by political parties, notwithstanding the all–party alliances and civil society fronts that have periodically appeared and foundered.[29] Political parties offer tactical advantages, such as the ability to gain leverage in New Delhi by influencing parliamentary races. Yet, it is obvious that Gorkha parties have not achieved much material improvement in the lives of Nepali-speakers in and around Darjeeling.

Such failures prompt observers to denounce Darjeeling's political class. This verdict may be well–deserved but it suggests no solutions

[29] See Wenner, in this volume.

besides waiting for superior leadership or foregoing politics altogether. This chapter suggests that Darjeeling's political elite are less responsive to public sentiment when electoral competition slackens. In recent local elections, diminished electoral competition was not an organic outcome but the product of intimidation and irregularities. A priority for would-be reformers should be insistence on transparent, non-partisan oversight of GTA and other Darjeeling-level elections.

5 *Virtuous Movements and Dirty Politics*

The Art of Camouflage in Darjeeling

Miriam Wenner*

It feels like the beginning of a huge storm to come. It is 4 April 2012, and I sit in my friend's shop in a small bazaar along the road from Siliguri to Kurseong. The otherwise calm village is unusually busy with countless visitors attending a 'world peace puja', organized by the ruling party in Darjeeling, the Gorkha Janamukti Morcha (GJM). Despite the promising name of the event, my friends are aware that it has been organized to prevent a scheduled meeting of the Gorkha National

* I am very grateful to Townsend Middleton for his detailed and honest critique of the initial version of this paper that encouraged me to break free from earlier conceptual chains. Many thanks also go to Nicolas Martin for his important inputs, and to both Townsend and Sara Shneiderman for bringing this project to life.

Liberation Front (GNLF), the GJM's archenemy. The shiny new party flags symbolically underline the GJM's claim to the place.

My friends' fear of a clash between the two parties came to fruition the next day: when a small pick-up van carrying GNLF activists attempted to approach the scheduled venue, it was surrounded and stopped by a mob of men who hit and shook it, forcing the van to flee. Simultaneously, barely 200 metres away, a priest performed rituals under a tent at the peace-puja, while holy chants sounded over the field occupied by hundreds of attendants. When I confronted a sub-divisional GJM leader with the violent scene I had just observed, he insisted that the puja was intended 'to avoid unrest, to create peace in this area,' and blamed the GNLF for creating the disturbance. On the other hand, my friends Nirman and Sachin,[1] themselves local GJM leaders, expressed their disgust with the use of violence.

Both were founding members of the GJM, and had taken some risks to establish the GJM in their village. Sachin, an activist in his 20s, once participated in the weeks-long *pad yatra* (foot march) to the Assamese border in 2008. But while he initially strongly believed in the GJM's ability to achieve Gorkhaland, he now sadly concluded: 'Gorkhaland is not a movement for money, but the leaders make it a movement for money.' Nirman, the local leader, had even taken out a loan to meet the expenses of organizing a public GJM meeting. When asked why he stayed with the party despite his criticism, he hesitantly admitted that he was hoping for some kind of 'recovery'. A few months after the GJM 'peace-puja' succeeded in hindering the GNLF's scheduled programme, Sachin and Nirman indeed received small contract works through the GJM, indicating that their support had paid off.

Sachin and Nirman's statements left me puzzled. In conversations, both of them appeared to be strong believers in the redemptive vision of a separate state of Gorkhaland. Sachin, in particular, believed that only Gorkhaland could guarantee them an 'Indian identity', and bring development to the region. Both of them had been disgusted by the previous ruling party, the GNLF, and its leader Subash Ghisingh, whom they accused of exploiting the Gorkhaland demand for personal gain. In 2007, they had joined the GJM because they believed in the capacity and willingness of its president, Bimal Gurung, to make their dream of Gorkhaland come true. Such emotional enthusiasm, however, now seemed to be contrasted by rational and pragmatic expectations of

[1] For confidentiality, I use pseudonyms throughout this chapter.

patronage in return for their active support. Had Gorkhaland indeed become a movement for money, as Sachin claimed? Or, put more generally, had an 'all-pervasive instrumentalism'[2] displaced other moral values and issue-driven mobilization?[3] What are the implications of this for the meaning of the movement?

I propose to read Sachin's and Nirman's statements as expressions of deeper concerns about the relationships between virtue, immorality, and politics in South Asia. It is nothing new that in South Asia—as in other places—'labelling something as political amounts to discrediting it as a sly exercise in bargaining, trickery, elbowing aside, and outmanoeuvering others'.[4] Politics is often considered 'dirty',[5] a domain of the 'immoral' that is guided by selfishness, corruption, and manipulation, in contradistinction to socially held virtues such as participation, representation, and collective interest.[6]

But although several studies contend that in actual political practice many people compromise on their moral values in a sometimes 'cynical pursuit of self-interest'[7] or simply because they feel that criminal politicians are more able to get 'things done',[8] idealist imaginations of virtuous political conduct persist. This renders politics a domain of possibility and imagination that is evaluated along, and in tension, with moral values, and is embodied in powerful 'anti-political' visions.[9] For instance, in his oft-cited study of West Bengal villagers' perceptions of politics, Ruud

[2] Brass (1990: 19).

[3] It is not uncommon in India for political parties to emerge from, or initiate, movements for new states. Prominent examples are the Jharkhand Mukti Morcha, the Telugu Desam Party (Party for the Telugu land, Telangana), and the Dravida Munnetra Kazhagam (Dravidian Progress Federation; Tamil Nadu). Also Tillin's (2013) analysis on the creation of the states of Jharkhand, Chhattisgarh, and Uttarakhand in 2000 suggests that clear-cut distinctions between parties and movements are hard to make. The GJM was registered as a political party with the Election Commission in April 2008, only a few months after its foundation.

[4] Byrne and Klem (2015: 226); see also Banerjee (2011).

[5] Ruud (2000).

[6] Alm (2006); Banerjee (2011); Gooptu (2007); Piliavsky (2014); Price (2007); Ruud (2000). For the debate beyond South Asia, see Walzer (1973); Tillyris (2016).

[7] Gooptu (2007: 1927).

[8] Berenschot (2011); Chandra (2004); Michelutti (2010); Vaishnav (2012).

[9] Hansen (2001); Spencer (2007).

saw villagers' evaluations framed by the ambivalent logics of *dharma* and *artha*. When applying the higher religious principles of dharma, which ranks conduct based on notions of purity and impurity, the villagers saw 'politics' as immoral and dirty.[10] Yet, the pursuit of worldly interests and pragmatic needs (artha) justified a compromise on leaders' moral requirements as long as they delivered.[11] In a different approach, Parry found that people did not so much criticize the pursuit of private gain itself, but rather a conflation of this domain with the domain of public interest, becoming visible in corruption.[12] Kothari's distinction between social movements and political parties somewhat resembles this division between public and private domains.[13] He described 'grassroots movements' as ideologically driven alternatives to established, instrumentally driven party politics.[14]

Similar to Parry's distinction between public and private domains, and Kothari's idealistic take on 'grassroots movements', I propose that in Darjeeling, ideals of a virtuous politics are captured in the imagination of a 'true' movement for Gorkhaland as distinct from the domain of party politics and private pursuit. Importantly, in Darjeeling, commitment to Gorkhaland amounts to more than a moral question. Rather, the dream of Gorkhaland concerns existential issues like the belonging to the nation and the longing for a better life. Gorkhaland is a worldview, programme, and utopia alike.[15] Accordingly, many expect their leaders to *genuinely* fight for statehood. Their decision to participate in the struggle is, however, conditioned by the fear of being exploited for leaders' personal gain.[16] In this context, ascriptions of 'politics' concern allegations of 'selling' the statehood demand for personal benefits from

[10] Ruud (2000).

[11] Ruud drew on Dumont (1980) for this distinction. Ruud (2000: 130).

[12] Parry (2000); Parry drew on Khilnani (1997) to argue that ideas of virtuous political conduct were inspired by historically grown perceptions of the responsibilities of the state and the ideal picture of an impartial bureaucracy secured by the state as a guardian of public interest.

[13] Kothari (1985).

[14] See also Kumar (2011).

[15] Golay (2009); Middleton (2013a); Wenner (2013).

[16] Studies suggest how the GNLF leaders instrumentalized the statehood demand as a means to gain autonomy concessions from the government as part of regional elite construction [Chakrabarty (2005); Chettri (2015); Lacina (2009), this volume; Sarkar (2013)].

the government. At the same time, however, many also expect their leaders to share their presumed wealth, as was clear in Sachin's and Nirman's statements quoted at the beginning of this chapter.

Movement leaders are thus required to meet the double demands for distribution of welfare and the attainment of Gorkhaland—demands whose fulfilment can cause conflicts, as the former requires maintaining friendly relations with the government as the provider of development funds, and the latter requires a confrontation with the state to avoid the reputation of 'being bought'. Therefore, GJM leaders have to be involved in 'double-dealing',[17] a term Jeffrey used to describe the contradictory behaviour of student leaders in northern India who mobilized support by protesting against corruption while at the same time making money from their political influence.

But how do leaders go about this when their alleged longing for personal benefits and the need to deliver factual goods (such as patronage) requires their involvement in 'politics', making contradictions between moral and immoral principles visible? In Jeffrey's example, they justified their double-dealing through euphemism, denial, or obfuscation. Other studies show that 'bad' politicians try to appear 'good' by mobilizing moral principles as reference frames. For instance, Vaishnav, Jaffrelot, and Michelutti observed that *goondas* (thugs) in northern India portrayed themselves as 'Robin Hoods' who support the oppressed.[18] And often those involved in corruption present themselves as 'social workers'.[19] Following this, I argue that a main strategy to hide involvement in 'dirty' politics is what I call *the art of camouflage*, or the masking of politics as 'virtuous'. As such, camouflage is about obscuring the boundaries between what counts as 'political' and what does not.[20] Camouflage is about the work of representation and the (re)definition of meaning in

[17] Jeffrey (2010: 135).

[18] Jaffrelot (2002); Michelutti (2007); Vaishnav (2012).

[19] Berenschot (2011); Piliavsky (2014); Price and Ruud (2010).

[20] This resembles to some extent the way Povinelli introduced camouflage as 'practices of cloaking' or 'modes of concealment that allow otherwise visible [...] objects to remain indiscernible from the surrounding environment' (2011: 78). Povinelli identifies recognition, espionage, and camouflage as three modalities through which late liberalism governs difference and deals with its legitimacy crisis. In contrast to this, I am concerned with how political leaders manipulate the ways certain acts and practices are categorized as 'political' and how such attempts are perceived by their potential followers.

order to make events and conduct appear morally right. The 'peace-puja' described above, for instance, served to camouflage the violent repression of party rivals as an attempt to build peace, while at the same time avoiding confrontation with government authorities.

More specifically, I am concerned with how the GJM, after its foundation, established the boundaries between 'dirty politics' and the morally 'pure' Gorkhaland Movement, while constructing a reputation as dedicated and virtuous promoters of the statehood claim. As I will show, there are two different identities that political leaders refer to. These are (a) the identity of a radical social movement opposed to the state, and (b) the occasional promotion of the identity of a responsible political party interested in social welfare and development. Following Basu, who showed that political parties can switch between these at times contradicting identities as a strategy in electoral mobilization, I show that the GJM also utilizes both in response to certain situations.[21]

I want to complement the outlined discussion on the relations between morality and politics by exploring how ideals of virtue figure in the conduct of political leaders, and how the meanings of moral and immoral are employed and contested in struggles over political legitimacy within the statehood movement. The boundaries between moral and immoral are continuously contested. Blurring the line between the two is itself a political act.

To substantiate my argument, I draw on a selection of public speeches of GJM president Bimal Gurung between 2007 and 2013. I combine these with a description of shifting popular support bases and opinions about the GJM. In the final section, I draw some general conclusions on statehood movements as sites where both the ideals of virtue clash and intermingle with the perceived immoral domains of realpolitik, and the boundaries between the two are subsequently and continuously renegotiated.

Camouflaging 'Politics' in the Movement

To understand how the domains of virtue and immorality figure in the political performances of the GJM, we must ask: How does the GJM

[21] Basu (2001). This is not to obscure the fact that the GJM uses violent means to oppress rivals to reaffirm its authority (see M. Chettri, this volume). Here, I am concerned with how the GJM legitimizes (not enforces) its rule.

establish itself as a virtuous promoter of a 'moral' politics in Darjeeling? Critiques of the party mainly concern themselves with allegations of corruption and violence. These critiques intensified after the GJM undersigned an agreement for a new autonomous council, the GTA, in July 2011. For many, this not only signalled an end to the struggle for Gorkhaland, but also indicated that the government had bought the leaders with an arrangement of limited autonomous rights and little territorial expansion. How did GJM president Gurung deal with the challenges to his reputation as a genuine fighter for Gorkhaland? What role did the reference to moral values play in camouflaging alleged deviations from the course of statehood?

The examples are drawn from the following public speeches and statements of Gurung between 2007 and 2013:

i. The GJM foundation meeting at Darjeeling Chowk Bazaar on 7 October 2007, attended by 20,000 persons, and the public meeting at Siliguri on 7 May 2008, attended by over 100,000 persons
ii. A public meeting at North Point College (near Darjeeling town) on 30 May 2010, attended by several hundred persons
iii. A public celebration of the GTA agreement at Darjeeling Chowrasta on 21 July 2011, attended by several hundred followers
iv. A protest meeting against the areal recommendation for the GTA at Darjeeling Gymkhana on 14 June 2012, attended by several hundred party activists
v. The short-term revival of the movement in August 2013.

While I personally observed and audio-recorded the GTA celebration in 2011, and the Gymkhana meeting in 2012, I draw on audio and video material for the examples in 2007, 2008, and 2010, and on newspaper articles and video footage for August 2013. I combine these descriptions with accounts from party followers, tea plantation workers, and rival party members generated during various field-stays between January 2011 and July 2013.[22]

[22] I am grateful to Townsend Middleton for sharing his audio–record of the October 2007 speech, and for helping with my description of the meeting.

October 2007 and May 2008—The Purification of Gorkhaland

Uncommonly, on 7 October 2007, the motor stand at Darjeeling's main bazaar was not crowded with jeeps and buses manoeuvring the parking spaces, while trying to avoid the mass of people crossing between them. Instead, more than 20,000 persons were loudly cheering on Gurung, the man who dared to challenge the so-called 'king of the hills' (Ghisingh), and to announce a new agitation for the long-standing demand of Gorkhaland.

Bimal Gurung, dressed in green, with a traditional Nepali *topi* on his head and adorned in *khatas*, was by that time well-known as Ghisingh's former 'muscle man', inciting fear amongst the town's population. To convince the audience of his dissociation from Ghisingh, Gurung proclaimed a 'new dawn' in Darjeeling and presented himself as a trustworthy, honest, and generous leader—in contradistinction to the 'selfish' and 'corrupt' leaders of the GNLF. His presentation of masculine power was supported by his claim of having received divine inspiration from Mahakal Baba (Darjeeling's local reincarnation of the god Shiva), as he communicated through occasional loud and aggressive shouting. He received a frenetic response from the audience whenever he hit the board with this fist. Gurung defamed Ghisingh's practices as *kutniti* (a term used in Darjeeling for describing dirty politics based on corruption, deception, and self-aggrandizement of leaders) and announced that the voice of Gorkhaland was rising again. Responding to the popular perception that 'leaders are selling the demand', he alleged that the GNLF leaders had pawned their 'mother' (read: Darjeeling hills) with the West Bengal government in exchange for privileges: 'They [GNLF leaders] quickly forget about the land and about the *jati* [community/people], and turn to the money ... But our brothers and sisters are conscious ... This is why you cannot buy them with money anymore. Because they love their mother and they love their land.'[23]

In contradistinction to the GNLF's violent practices, the new movement led by Gurung's newly launched GJM would be 'democratic' and 'non-violent'. His request to other local parties to abstain from political struggles over power for the sake of the movement added to his attempt to dissociate the Gorkhaland demand from the realm of party-political

[23] Gurung (2007).

struggles, while calling for unity: 'So I am declaring that this is not a party flag but a flag of the *jati*. So all you people leave your [party] flags behind and come ... under this flag, and we will get Gorkhaland ... And tomorrow, when we get Gorkhaland and you can hold those flags.'[24]

At a subsequent mass meeting in Siliguri in May 2008, Gurung reassured his claim to leadership of the movement. Swearing an oath on the Gita and the Bible, Gurung promised not to 'betray' the people and installed the GJM as the (sole) genuine representative of the statehood claim. 'Political parties have betrayed the Gorkhas to gain electoral support, but GJM is the voice of Gorkhaland'.[25] In the new movement, 'conscious' people, the logic went, should stand at the apex in order to assure that leaders did not betray. The emotional atmosphere was enhanced by melancholic Gorkhaland songs played before and after Gurung's speech, during which he waved a massive GJM flag on stage matching the rhythm of the songs.

This 'purification' of Gorkhaland from kutniti was accompanied by the sometimes-violent ousting of the leaders of the old GNLF regime by their former followers (who now switched sides to the GJM), and a replacement of the GNLF's territorial markers, such as flags.[26] In resemblance of a people's movement directed against the state, the GJM confronted the West Bengal government (then headed by the CPI[M]) that had been backing Ghisingh for the past 20 years. Intense street agitations, indefinite general strikes, gheraos of public offices and GNLF leaders' houses, and pad yatras (marches) complemented other forms of public disobedience, like the non-payment of taxes.

Thus, rhetorically and practically speaking, Gurung emerged as the leader who had rescued Gorkhaland from the clutches of dirty party politics, and rescued 'mother' Darjeeling from the GNLF. Gurung appeared a strong, generous, honest, and uncompromising leader of a new movement, which was transparent and owned by the people. The mass support and emotional enthusiasm suggested that the movement indeed provided the long-awaited platform to carry the silenced hopes for Gorkhaland.

The GJM spread like a wave over the Darjeeling hills. Hundreds made pilgrimages to Gurung to pledge him their loyalty. Equipped

[24] Gurung (2007).

[25] Gurung (2008).

[26] The transplanting of old GNLF flags with new GJM ones caused violent clashes.

with the flag of the new party they returned to their villages to establish units like Nirman had done. Eventually, in February 2008, the West Bengal government gave in to the immense protests and decided to ask Ghisingh to resign from his post as DGHC caretaker. After protests turned violent in July, Ghisingh fled to the plains, thereby completing the GJM's takeover.[27] By then, the GJM had attained the status of the only government-recognized negotiation partner, a fact that ultimately caused the marginalization of other local parties within the broader movement.[28]

2008 to 2010—Failures, Denial, and Deception

The frenetic beginning of the GJM in Darjeeling, the ousting of Ghisingh, and the seeming liberation of the demand for Gorkhaland from the clutches of party politics and private pursuit, had raised expectations amongst those who believed that Gorkhaland would solve all their identity and development-related problems. Liberated from politics, Gorkhaland was again worth actively supporting. Not surprisingly, in 2009, the GJM-supported candidate of the BJP won the national elections from Darjeeling with a high margin. But to sustain the forceful agitation and to make themselves heard in Kolkata and Delhi, Gurung had to deliver.

Several rounds of tripartite negotiations, however, failed to show any significant progress towards statehood. Gurung's promise to achieve Gorkhaland by 10 March 2010 (otherwise he would 'commit suicide') was not met. Instead, the party began negotiations for a so-called 'interim set-up', another autonomous council to replace the DGHC. The lack of success in achieving Gorkhaland, along with an intense agitation that

[27] On 25 July 2008, during a *gherao* of the house of a prominent GNLF leader, a bullet allegedly fired from within the house killed one female GJM activist, sparking violent protests.

[28] Initially, the agitation was supported by the Communist Party of Revolutionary Marxists (CPRM), which together with the GJM sent a delegation to Delhi to assert resistance to the Sixth Schedule plans. The CPRM later withdrew its support from the GJM, claiming that it had not only left its course on statehood in favour of regional autonomy, but that it also employed violent methods to silence rivals. The CPRM was founded in 1996 as a splinter party of the CPI-M that held a notable following especially amongst tea plantation workers before the rise of the GNLF in the 1980s.

increasingly disturbed public life and business, threatened to weaken the GJM-led movement.

One of the most vocal critics of the GJM was Madan Tamang, president of the All India Gorkha League (AIGL). Tamang did not support the GJM, whom he accused of corruption and deception. He insisted that only 'collective leadership' could assure that leaders did not again exploit Gorkhaland as a 'begging bowl' to gain personal benefits from the government. Defying threats from the GJM, in the morning of 21 May 2010, when he was about to prepare for a public speech at a central place in Darjeeling town, he was attacked by a mob of GJM activists. One of them killed Tamang with a long sword in the presence of the public and the police. This gruesome murder of one of Darjeeling's most respected and outspoken politicians sparked an unprecedented outrage amongst the otherwise silent population.[29] GJM posters and flags were torn; thousands came to attend Tamang's funeral procession. Senior party members resigned. Gurung, who had been in Kalimpong, could only re-enter Darjeeling under police protection.

To reaffirm its claim to leadership, its commitment to 'non-violence', and to present itself as the sole genuine contender for Gorkhaland, 10 days after Tamang's murder the GJM organized a massive public meeting in the northern fringes of Darjeeling town, where Gurung held his stronghold. The venue's set-up was reminiscent of the May 2008 meeting in Siliguri. It was plastered with GJM's flags, and a huge banner over the dais proclaimed 'We want Gorkhaland'. Hundreds of attendants waved GJM flags to the rhythm of a sentimental song, 'Our shared aim is Gorkhaland'. Gurung, meanwhile, dressed in an extravagant red *daura suruwal* and a topi, formed a fist to the beat of the songs to enthuse the crowds. Darjeeling's Member of Parliament Jaswanth Singh (Bharatiya Janata Party, BJP)[30] also attended the event, complementing this powerful performance of unity.[31]

[29] On the assassination, see Middleton (2018).

[30] Singh won the Darjeeling seat in the 2009 national elections, after the BJP declared its intention to 'sympathetically examine and appropriately consider the long pending demands of the Gorkhas' (cited in: Ramachandran, Smriti Kak (2014). 'With hindsight, BJP includes Gorkhaland in its manifesto.' *The Hindu*, April 9).

[31] One major element of the speech concerned the ongoing negotiations on an interim set-up and the contentious question of the territorial reach of the would-be council.

Gurung, flanked by two serious-looking female cadres of the Gorkhaland Personnel (GLP, a paramilitary pseudo-police force established in 2008), began his speech by pointing at the masses that came to attend the meeting because they 'believed in Gorkhaland'. Addressing those who protested against the GJM, he stressed: 'Those who tore the [GJM] flag—they should see the crowd today ... You should remember that it is harmful to touch the fire ... The GJM is the fire of Gorkhaland! It does not cool down easily. It becomes hotter until the aim is achieved. Therefore, don't touch it; your hands will be burnt.'[32]

Reiterating the GJM's monopoly over Gorkhaland, he continued: 'GJM is carrying the issue of Gorkhaland. Bimal Gurung himself is nothing, an aim is fixed on him.'[33] Gurung flanked this equation of himself with the GJM and Gorkhaland with a promise to stay honest and straight. Referring to the ongoing tripartite talks on an interim set-up, he stressed: 'We never betrayed our aim so far. Like milk is white, the GJM has the same whiteness ... They tried to buy us often, but we were not sold ... If I try to turn this issue [Gorkhaland] around ... I will die vomiting blood, I have promised!'[34] He even announced a 'final fight' (*antim ladhai*) for statehood.

An important element in his speech was his strict denial of the GJM's involvement in Tamang's murder. Gurung instead pointed at his commitment to 'democracy' and 'non-violence', and called for an enquiry by the Central Bureau of Investigation (CBI). He alleged the other parties (especially the AIGL) of playing 'politics' upon Tamang's dead body. All this can be read as another attempt to exclude the Gorkhaland Movement and the GJM from any association with 'politics', violence, and repression.

Overwhelmed by this show of strength, the volatile mood in Darjeeling receded, and the GJM continued to lead the movement and negotiations in New Delhi and Kolkata. Yet, despite its denial and deception, it never completely recovered from the public outrage over Tamang's murder, making it even more necessary for the party to sustain its leadership by other, more practical means.

[32] Gurung, Bimal (2010). 'We Want Gorkhaland.' Speech. Public meeting, Darjeeling, May 30.

[33] Gurung, Bimal (2010). 'We Want Gorkhaland.' Speech. Public meeting, Darjeeling, May 30.

[34] Gurung, Bimal (2010). 'We Want Gorkhaland.' Speech. Public meeting, Darjeeling, May 30.

Drawing on ethno-nationalist ideology alone was not sufficient to sustain the agitation. Various accounts of party supporters suggested that they expected their leaders to share their presumed wealth. Indeed, many praised their *dajyu* (elder brother) Gurung for distributing money, and expected to be given jobs through the party.[35] Money was also needed to pay the salaries of the GLP—the aforementioned quasi–police force with about 13,000 members[36]—as well as the cost of transportation and food during demonstrations. Further, since 2008, central developmental institutions like the DGHC and the gram panchayats lacked any elected bodies, which left them somewhat dysfunctional.[37] After 20 years of mismanagement of public funds through the DGHC, people were longing for development. This became especially pronounced in May 2009 when the cyclone Aila caused large-scale devastation in the hills, and the government provided an emergency fund of Rs. 200 million to the DGHC.

To maintain their image as generous 'social workers' caring for the welfare of their constituents, the GJM needed to respond to such demands. The easiest way to do so was to jump into the governmental gap left after Ghisingh's ousting, utilize the money still available with the DGHC, and to engage in other developmental schemes (such as the Pradhan Mantri Gram Sadak Yojana [PMGSY] and the Mahatma Gandhi National Rural Employment Guarantee Act [MGNREGA]).[38] Doing so, however, the GJM risked being perceived as dependent on the government. Not surprisingly, according to an insider, Gurung had initially

35 Wenner (2015).

36 *The Telegraph* estimated an expense of Rs. 22.1 million for the GLP's monthly salaries. Chhetri, V. 'Morcha Peace Pledge with Hint of Threat', *The Telegraph*. 13 May 2011.

37 Elections to the DGHC scheduled for 2005 were withheld by the West Bengal government, which instead appointed Ghisingh as a 'caretaker'. The previously elected members of the gram panchayats resigned in 2008 after their term expired. Neither the DGHC nor the panchayats had elected members afterwards and were instead officially run by government-appointed bureaucrats and administrators.

38 The PMGSY is a centrally funded scheme for road construction to remote areas, and implemented via the State; the MGNREGA aims to guarantee 100 days of employment per year for the unemployed at minimum wages. It is implemented at the gram panchayat level.

refused the secret offer from the West Bengal government to informally run the DGHC. Yet, in April 2012 one zonal president explained to me that the provision for roads, water, and the improvement of the economic conditions were indeed necessary to sustain the party.

As the party-workers' recurrent saying goes, 'all development goes through the party.' This expresses the fact that the GJM gained the authority to channel the DGHC projects. But while those without close connections to the high-ranking leaders complained about exclusion from such benefits, some members of rival parties (especially from the CPRM) proclaimed that they did not *want* such patronage. In their opinion, (government–financed) 'development' and Gorkhaland could not be attained at the same time. They alleged that the GJM was merely a 'broker' (*dalal*) of the West Bengal government, exploiting the demand for Gorkhaland as a 'begging bowl' to access the state's resources. Such dependency on the government resulted in the decline of the statehood agenda. Thus, for them, the GJM's provision of development proved that Gorkhaland had become implicated in dirty politics.

Also Bimal Gurung was aware that this double-dealing risked being interpreted as standing at odds with the GJM's agitation against the West Bengal government. Accordingly, Gurung denied his authority over the DGHC: 'I don't have the 'authority' [Engl.] to issue cheques, to issue work orders, to distribute work. My work is to tell others. Where there is suffering—'build a house there'. Where someone is sick—'give medicine'.[39]

Simultaneously, Gurung continued to invest in his reputation as a 'social worker' with the capability to help the poor in an impartial way, guided by humanitarian principles (and not by instrumental electoral politics).[40]

Such ascription of moral principles expressed in a caring attitude towards the Gorkhas also came to the fore in the GJM's justification of the GTA agreement. On 18 July 2011, barely two months after the TMC had replaced the CPI(M) in the state government after the 2011 West Bengal Assembly elections, the GJM signed a tripartite agreement on the establishment of a new autonomous council—the GTA—to replace the DGHC. Three days later, the GJM set up a huge public celebration

[39] Gurung (2012), interview, 7 July.

[40] Gurung, Bimal (2012). Speech. Indoor party meeting, Gymkhana. 14 June.

at Chowrasta. Hundreds of followers dressed in Nepali attire (Gurung himself this time refrained from the ethnic dress) clapped and danced to the rhythm of Nepali folk songs, and a traditional *panche baja*.[41] After performing the obligatory puja in front of Mahatma Gandhi's picture, Gurung and general secretary Roshan Giri distributed sweets to the people. When Gurung began to dance on stage, some women cheered joyfully. Gurung was celebrated like a rock star.

In their speeches, the leaders promoted the GTA as a way to 'develop' the region, while maintaining their commitment to Gorkhaland. Reciting the Memorandum of Agreement, GJM general secretary Giri stressed that it acknowledged the GJM's objective of Gorkhaland, and then read out the long list of projects to be completed by the GTA.

Gurung then drew a direct connection between the people's movement and the GTA, which he presented as his 'gift' in return for their support. At the same time, he underlined that the GJM held the power to run the council in their position as 'medium' between people and the state:

> And this big gift is not only for Bimal Gurung und Roshan Giri to eat, it should be for all people to eat ... We are only there to provide, to speak and to feed. But you are here to use it ... We are working for the people. Whatever problems there are, please share it; there is the party office.[42]

Such implicit references to the welfare function of the GJM were underlined by Gurung's self-presentation as the 'father of all Gorkhas'.

To counter doubts that the GTA agreement signalled the end of the Gorkhaland agitation, Gurung described the GTA as 'semi-final', and justified the council as a 'trial' for running a state, providing development, and generating employment. Further, to clear any doubts over his commitment to Gorkhaland, Gurung stressed that not he himself but the party's general secretary Giri had undersigned the deal. Accordingly, he promised not to take any post in the GTA and instead to 'watch how it works from the outside',[43] avoiding any conflation with his role as a dedicated movement leader.

[41] *Panche baja* designates the traditional Nepali music band consisting of five players equipped with drums, cybals, folk trumpets, and folk oboes. It is usually performed at ceremonies such as weddings or at festivals.

[42] Gurung, Bimal (2011). Speech. Public celebration, Chowrasta, 21 July.

[43] Gurung, Bimal (2011). Speech. Public celebration, Chowrasta, 21 July.

The news on the GTA agreement received a mixed response in Darjeeling. Gurung attempted to justify the GTA as only a 'step' towards Gorkhaland, thereby preventing it from being used as fodder for allegations that Gorkhaland was being used as a 'begging bowl' in politics. Others welcomed it as an end to disruptions of public life caused by the agitation. Yet, many felt that the council not only signalled an end to the GJM's statehood claim but also proved their fears that the GJM had 'sold' the demand to the government in return for benefits. The work of camouflage had begun to fail.

One year later, in June 2012, the so-called Sen Commission that had been established to look into the GJM's territorial demand to include areas of the Dooars region under the GTA, recommended that only 5 *mouzas*[44] (of the 398 mouzas claimed) be added to the new council. In a last attempt to press for an areal increase of the GTA, Gurung called an indoor party meeting at Gymkhana, gathering hundreds of party workers from all over Darjeeling. Gurung was under immense pressure: he had not only not delivered Gorkhaland, but he also appeared to have lost the territory he promised would be added to the new council.

Gurung's subsequent threat to withdraw the GTA agreement, his call for a 'final fight' for Gorkhaland, his harsh tone towards the chief minister, and his stressing of his social worker image to defy rivals' allegations of clientelism appeared less convincing to followers. After the meeting, some seemed angry, claiming that they had been waiting for the new council and expecting benefits long enough. Meanwhile, the TMC, the ruling party in West Bengal, had begun establishing units in Darjeeling district. This was another indicator that trust in the GJM to achieve Gorkhaland was dwindling.

Confronted with the threat that TMC might contest and win the GTA elections if the GJM refused to participate, in July 2012 the GJM won in all 45 of the new GTA constituencies, 28 of them uncontested. Contrary to Gurung's promise to 'watch the GTA from the outside',[45] he became the new chief executive of the council. Over the coming months, the GTA began its work for 'development'—which for many was a confirmation that Gorkhaland had again become a pawn in the game

[44] *Mouza* is an administrative unit. One mouza comprises several gram panchayats.

[45] Gurung, Bimal (2011). Speech. Public celebration, Chowrasta, 21 July.

between the ruling party and the government, a sinking ship in the sea of kutniti.

2013—Back to Confrontation?

By spring 2013 (roughly one year later), when I revisited Darjeeling, the green, white, and yellow colours of the GJM were complemented by the orange, white, and green of the TMC, and even the GNLF's green came out in the open. Graffiti demanding Gorkhaland had lost most of its colour, and in many places GJM flags had lost their previous shine. The movement for Gorkhaland appeared to be passing.

Growing defections to other parties such as the TMC and GNLF suggested that many of those who had initially supported the GJM had lost their hope of achieving Gorkhaland. As one new TMC leader cynically explained to me: 'We still want Gorkhaland. But for now, there will not be Gorkhaland. So I decided to take some benefits from politics.' The lost hopes for statehood legitimized seeking personal wealth by joining an anti-Gorkhaland party. Others were simply tired of the GJM's corruption, perceived self-aggrandizement, and violent repression.

When I met Nirman, the GJM leader cited at the beginning of this chapter, he seemed even more disappointed: 'The party is like a pot of mud. It is not clean, it is dirty ... *rajniti* [politics] is not a garden, it is a mud island. For people like us there is no place in politics.'[46] His hopes of getting a position in the GTA had not been fulfilled. He left the party prior to the 2014 national elections to support the intellectual and independent candidate M.P. Lama. Another account from a friend from June 2013 summarized the mood of the time. Like many others, he couched his critique in terms of 'selling' and 'bargaining'. Reflecting what had happened to the movement since its inception, he explained: 'Slowly, the movement became an income source.' He continued to criticize the nexus between contractors and leaders: 'There was a need for development and funds from the government. Contractors began to bribe the leaders ... So the leaders were sold. The movement was destroyed by money.' Like many others, he believed that the 'bargaining' also concerned the Madan Tamang murder case, which the government used to exercise pressure on the GJM leaders, many of whom figured in the murder charge sheet (including Gurung). Mirroring the need to keep Gorkhaland free from

[46] Nirman (2013), interview, June.

politics he concluded: 'They did the movement in a wrong way. It became a game in Indian politics,' and estimated that 'Gorkhaland is only 20 per cent really for Gorkhaland. Rather, it is a begging bowl.'

Yet, a development at the central level put an abrupt halt to the GJM's downslide—at least for a short time. In July 2013, the Congress-led national government announced that it would give in to the demand for a Telangana state, to be carved out of Andhra Pradesh. Earlier, the Morcha had regularly claimed that if Telangana were to become a reality, the central government would also have to grant the demand for Gorkhaland. It was a question of saving face and the last bit of credibility. Like other statehood demanding groups in India, the GJM reacted by re-initiating a forceful mass agitation, including a month-long general strike in August 2013 that brought Darjeeling to a stand-still.

To prove his commitment, Gurung resigned from his post as GTA's chief executive. Was this another attempt to step out of the realm of party politics? Afterwards, the other hill parties (CPRM, AIGL) and the Bharatiya Gorkha Parisang (BGP)[47]—which had made Gurung's resignation a condition to join the agitation—mobilized their supporters. Together with the GJM they formed the Gorkhaland Joint Action Committee (GJAC). For many in Darjeeling this legitimized the GJM's renewed call for agitation, and appeared to be the long-sought 'unity' required for statehood. Many of those who had begun doubting the GJM's commitment to Gorkhaland actively re-joined the agitation, sparked this time by drastic means. One GJM youth activist died after immolating himself for the statehood cause. This, and the immense and sustained public attendance at protest meetings, underlined the continued emotional potential of the Gorkhaland claim.

Gurung, who appeared much more confident in his regained role as a movement leader, underlined his commitment to the cause in various interviews. Responding to a High Court verdict that justified the West Bengal government's reaction by force against the agitators by terming the ongoing strike 'illegal', he stressed that: '[T]he current movement ... is no longer a GJM movement, it has turned into a people (sic) movement. The people are coming onto the streets spontaneously and holding agitation to realize their demand for Gorkhaland. No such people

[47] The BGP describes itself as a non-political organization fighting for the rights of all Indian Gorkhas at the national level. It does not have a strong base in Darjeeling.

movement can be stopped by the police and the military.'[48] Ruling out any negotiations with the state government, Gurung promised that: 'this time, we will not leave our movement halfway. We will not stop until the demand is accepted by the Centre ... We are not at all bothered about the GTA. Our aim is Gorkhaland.'[49]

The West Bengal government reacted with force. After deploying several companies of the hated Central Reserve Police Force (CRPF) in Darjeeling, several hundred supporters and GJM leaders (including elected GTA councillors) were arrested. Many male villagers spent their nights in the dense jungles to avoid the nightly raids and arrests. While punishing the agitators, the government rewarded those who refrained from joining the agitation by offering special developmental concessions. During the agitation, the West Bengal government approved the establishment of a tribal development board for the Lepcha, an ethnic group considered aboriginal in Darjeeling, many of whom had over a long time fought for their rights separate from the Gorkhaland agitation.[50]

Yet, the achievements of the agitation remain questionable. Instead of getting Gorkhaland or a central commission to look into the issue, the GJM's internal organizational structure was impacted by the many arrests of its leaders, and the seeming unity amongst the hill parties was called into question based on allegations that Gurung made one-man decisions. Only a month after its establishment, the GJAC broke into pieces and, with it, the possibility of a more inclusive movement was lost. Confronted with state force, the depletion of food and other resources, the agitation slowly declined. In December 2013, at the request of councillors and his supporters, Gurung was officially re-established as the GTA chief. Albeit with mistrust and occasional confrontations, the working relationship between the West Bengal government and the GJM continued. The GJM's struggle now focused on pressing for the transfer of departments promised by the state government to the GTA.

In retrospect, the August 2013 agitation appears to be an exception in the course the GJM took after 2011. Yet, it demonstrated once again, what disruptive power the statehood demand holds as long as people

[48] Sengupta, Tamal (2013). 'Bimal Gurung: Darjeeling Gorkha Leader who is taking on Mamata Banerjee.' *Economic Times*, August 16.

[49] Sengupta, Tamal (2013). 'Bimal Gurung: Darjeeling Gorkha Leader who is taking on Mamata Banerjee', *Economic Times*, August 16.

[50] On the granting of Tribal Development Boards, see also Bentley (2015); Chhetri, this volume; Middleton (2015).

perceive it as a genuine issue led by committed and honest leaders who engage in the movement for the public good and not for private gain.

When Sachin stated that 'Gorkhaland is not a movement for money, but the leaders make it a movement for money,' he expressed where he saw the boundaries between moral and immoral domains. He imagined the demand for Gorkhaland itself as something pure, related to an existential question of the Gorkhas. But because of the 'selfish' practices of leaders, the meaning of Gorkhaland changed—it was made a 'movement for money,' and thereby had entered the immoral domain of instrumentalist politics. This, in the end, weakened the cause, as it opened the door to the West Bengal government to co-opt the movement's leaders.

The fact that people do not generally criticize the pursuit of private gain but rather its conflation with the domain of an idealized movement supports Parry's argument that people object to a breach of boundaries between public (here: the movement) and private domains.[51] In people's imagination a 'true' movement embodied the 'other' of politics. Gorkhaland's existential importance prohibited an intermixing with personal quests for material gain. Such perceived boundaries between moral and immoral conduct are also functional in the GJM's practice and rhetoric. As I showed, leaders responded to followers' multiple demands for sharing their presumed wealth and fighting for Gorkhaland through double-dealing,[52] while camouflaging their involvement in politics as 'virtuous' behaviour. Examples for this camouflaging include the presentation of patronage as social work, the denial of allegations of repression while proclaiming commitment to 'non–violence', and the justification of the GTA agreement as a step towards Gorkhaland. Leaders' legitimacy ultimately rests on their ability to generate trust and responsibility in protecting the group's interest.[53] The aim of such camouflaging was thus to demonstrate that Gorkhaland—after all—was part of the domain of a virtuous movement represented by an honest leader. Resembling the logic of an ideal-type people's movement,[54] the agitation for Gorkhaland should stand outside the realm of party politics in order to avoid exploitation for personal or electoral gain.

[51] Parry (2000).
[52] cf. Jeffrey (2010).
[53] Pardo (2000).
[54] cf. Kothari (1985).

By rhetorically exempting Gorkhaland from politics and portraying it as a social movement, the GJM president responded to popular assumptions of what moral and immoral politics in Darjeeling means, and reestablished these idealist boundaries. At the same time, he attempted to blur such boundaries in order to expand the space for manoeuvre in a context conditioned by followers' multiple demands from below, and by state pressure from above. This simultaneous reinforcement and blurring of boundaries ultimately led to contradictions in his course. In this context, promises of patronage in the disguise of a caring political party engaging in 'social work' can be read as attempts to compensate for transgressions of the line into the immoral, thus helping to expand the 'degrees of toleration of the dirtiness of the game'.[55] It is up to individuals to estimate whether the boundary into the unacceptable has been crossed or not.

In Darjeeling, the GJM has, to date, failed to achieve Gorkhaland and to satisfy its followers' increasing demands for tangible benefits. The growing perception that only the leaders became wealthier over the course of the agitation, and that the party relied on violent means to sustain its dominance, suggests that for many the GJM had crossed the boundary separating the acceptable and the unacceptable. While people had initially equated the GJM with Gorkhaland and the movement, many now equated the GJM with dirty politics (or kutniti), and as such, were willing to criticize how the GJM had directed the movement and even claim that its leaders had sold Gorkhaland.

Yet, the GJM's monopoly in accessing state governmental funds, posed a difficult question for those whose livelihoods depended on the provision of patronage: Was it morally apt to benefit from the GJM's patronage, to voice their private interest in the movement's domain, and thereby to use the system as best as they could?[56] While members of the CPRM decided to stay deprived of patronage as they saw it standing in conflict with their aim of Gorkhaland, others, like Sachin and Nirman, felt compelled to compromise on their moral principles. Possibly, their justifications for remaining with the party indicate that camouflage can be as much of a strategy of followers to cover up their personal moral trespasses, as it is for political leaders.

These distinct and changing motivations of the movement's supporters reflect not only the movement's varying forms of mobilization and

[55] Alm (2006: 103).

[56] cf. Fuller and Harriss (2000), Wenner (2018).

legitimacy;[57] they also reflect how various dimensions of the movement came to be couched between socially held perceptions of 'moral' and 'immoral'. Although people held clear idealist imaginations of how the movement *should* function, in practice it turned out as a space of conflicting values where their emotional-affective desires met with private and particularistic interest. This intermingling of idealist moral desires with an instrumentally driven realpolitik, and the realization that the sphere of public interest has been submerged by private pursuit, led to the realization that a 'true' movement was impossible. Thus, while support for the Morcha dwindled after the GTA establishment in 2012 in a sometimes-cynical fashion, many explored other avenues to make claims on the state. Amongst them stand their membership in other parties, or the participation in movements for recognition as Scheduled Tribes, which promises benefits for select ethnic groups under the state legislature.[58] In December 2015, a new party, the Jana Andolan Party, was established in Kalimpong. Founded by eminent and popular intellectuals (many of them former GJM leaders), it remains to be seen whether it can live up to its promise of practising virtuous politics. Its foundation underlines that the struggle over defining the moral grounds of politics continues, in Darjeeling, and elsewhere.

[57] cf. Wenner (2015).

[58] See, Chhetri in this volume.

6 *The Rowdies of Darjeeling*

Politics and Underdevelopment in the Hills

Mona Chettri*

In September 2015, I was in the middle of a group interview at a settlement near Teesta Bazar with community members who had been affected by the construction of the Teesta Low Dam Powerhouse III, when a large group of men decided that they wanted to be a part of the conversation. As soon as they arrived, our conversation on the prevalence of '*dhamki* politics' in the region (that is the politics of threat during public hearings and meetings) stopped abruptly. My respondents started talking about compensation packages and loss of livelihoods as

* The author would like to thank Townsend Middleton and Frank Conway for their comments on earlier drafts of the paper, as well as Dilip Kumar Chettri, Rinchu Doma Dukpa, Amode Yonzone, and Deoashish Mothey for their insights and assistance in the field.

a result of the dam. I later learnt that some of the men were affiliates of a local party that had been instrumental in stifling public opposition to the dam. The local party had brought *rowdies* to public hearings and their presence had sufficed to keep people away from meetings and ensure that none of the attendees asked awkward questions. Although those men had long changed their political alliances, they still had the reputation of being dangerous rowdies.

In the dialect of Nepali spoken in Darjeeling, *rowdies* or *rowdy*[1] denotes a person who fits somewhere between a gangster and a *goon*, not a professional criminal but an individual prone to crime and violence usually at the behest of political leaders. The term *rowdies* in Darjeeling-Nepali is synonymous with the Hindi term *goonda*. Whether for the GJM, the GNLF or even the TMC, rowdies are the foot soldiers who ensure that the commands of their political leaders are carried out at the local level. Rowdies' tasks include organizing political rallies and attending public hearings, among other things. Often sighted leading political processions, enforcing strikes, and collecting *chanda* (tax) on behalf of their political parties, the rowdies of Darjeeling are a subaltern political phenomenon and part of the distinct political culture of the hills.

The persistence of rowdies in the social and political history of Darjeeling forces an assessment of two important and inter-related aspects of the region's political economy. First, rowdies are crucial to the success of any political party. They are an extension of the political parties they represent and often enforce diktats on behalf of that political party. Whilst acting as mediators between the party and the community, they remain a political underclass with no actual voice in the political decision-making processes of the party. This is telling of the political structure and distribution of power in the hills. Second, their continued existence on the margins of society also requires us to examine the socio-economic stagnation that has enabled the proliferation of this political class for which violence has become a route out of poverty. The phenomenon of rowdies, therefore, helps us analyse the prevailing political structure and rampant poverty in the hills, factors which work in tandem to reinforce and perpetuate a political culture of violence.

[1] The plural *rowdies* was used by respondents in conversations irrespective of the number of people being referred to as *rowdies*. For the purposes of this paper, I adopt the conventional use of the singular/plural. N.B. Pseudonyms have been used to protect the identity of the respondents.

This chapter assesses the political culture of Darjeeling through its rowdies. These subaltern political figures embody a visceral, masculine form of politics that is equally representative of the failure of the development state and of the unrelenting poverty and political inequality in Darjeeling. The first section contextualizes the criminalization of politics in South Asia within which rowdies in Darjeeling might be located. The second section discusses the evolution of the rowdies from solitary, 'community Robin Hood' figures to political musclemen, which reflects the criminalization of hill politics. The third section engages in an analysis of the vicious cycle of poverty and underdevelopment, which makes becoming rowdies a way to surpass economic hurdles. The conclusion uses the rowdies' phenomenon to contextualize the mutually reinforcing issues of underdevelopment and a violent political culture.

Politics and Crime in South Asia

The relationship between politics and criminality is a historic one and remains pervasive across many parts of the world. In the South Asian context, the modern state has created political spaces and opportunities that allow the proliferation of a symbiotic relationship between crime and politics; the number of criminals present is thought to be on the rise even though the exact role or network of the criminals is poorly understood.[2] Scandals and scams have become commonplace, exposed regularly by television stations that relentlessly stream 'breaking news' to the masses. This relationship between crime and politics has also become the subject of caricature, reproduced many times over in Bollywood films and television to the extent that there is now a general perception that no career politician is 'clean'.[3]

Over the years, the nature and extent of the relationship between crime and politics has become more explicit and visible, especially through the participation of recognized criminals as electoral candidates. This phenomenon has been facilitated by political parties, institutions, and powerful individuals who have the power to affect important policy changes.[4] The state (whether it be the central or the regional state) is the key agent in the distribution of public goods and services. Because of

2 Rudd (2014: 324).

3 See Sinha (2013); Suresh (2012). See also Wenner, this volume.

4 Jaffrelot (2002).

this, there is immense incentive to win elections either through money or muscle-power. Intense electoral competition has created new forms of patronage and clientalism, creating extra-legal economic resources and increasing criminality amongst politicians.[5]

Grassroots mobilization and elections are the most important aspects of any functioning democracy, which in turn create space for different political coalitions and machinations. The deepening of Indian democracy, however, has created a gradual shift in models of political authority and allowed the proliferation of muscular politics.[6] Increasing criminalization of politics may be argued to be a manifestation of the failure of the modern state in reaching its poorer citizens on the one hand, and the increasingly fluid boundaries between the state and society on the other. The growing presence and active participation of criminals and gangs in the political sphere has come to symbolize the decay in Indian politics and democracy. It can be understood as a symptom of the fractures in the Indian polity, economy, and society, manifest in broken rules of law, nepotism, corrupt bureaucracy, unemployment, and an election process driven by fear and force.[7]

Politics and criminality are associated through a complex network, which usually leads to the local goonda or muscleman. Changing patterns of authority have generated a '*dada*' (big boss) culture, especially in poorer localities where masculine, assertive, and violent culture is seen as a sign of leadership and a basis for local authority. In the contemporary context, it is deemed impossible to win elections without the support of the muscle-power of goondas.[8] Criminalization of politics is also increasing because politicians need not just money but also goondas, dadas, and rowdies in order to secure/extract money, commit election fraud, and assert their strength through displays of muscle-power. On the other hand, goondas need political figures for protection from the law. Crime and politics are consequently engaged in a symbiotic relationship.[9] This close relationship between corruption, violence, and institutional authority has been a feature of the regional political economy since the early 1970s, especially post-Emergency; a period which saw an ascendency in political manipulation and domination of the economy and society by

5 Michellutti (2014: 284).

6 See Hansen (2001).

7 Berenschot (2011); Piliavsky and Sbriccoli (2016: 1).

8 Berenschot (2011: 10).

9 Jaffrelot (2002).

a single political party.[10] Economic liberalization of the 1990s created new avenues for corruption and crime to infiltrate the social, political, and legal institutions of the country.[11]

In discourses on criminality, goonda, rowdies, and dadas have figured as the citizen's dichotomous other. They have, in turn, become the local face of institutional corruption and crime. The model figure of the citizen upholds rights, duties, and order, whereas the goonda represents disorder and indulges in violations of the same rights and duties.[12] Within this discourse there is a vital difference between a criminal and a goonda, which is related to the public displays of violence or daredevilry of the goonda in contrast to the necessary stealth of any other criminal.[13] The pressure that shapes a goonda's behaviour is very different from that of a criminal whose success depends largely on the capacity to keep his/her activities a secret.[14] Thus in contrast to the secretive nature of crimes committed by mainstream politicians, the violence of the goonda is a performative act; its main target is not just the victim of the assault but also the audience that witnesses the spectacle. Indeed, the reputation of the goonda is built on the amount and intensity of fear that he can provoke in a community that he seeks to control.

Engaging with goondas or rowdies, it is equally important to understand the factors that lure people into the world of criminality in the first place. A primary factor remains the growing divide between the different classes as a result of lopsided economic development. There is a widespread assumption that Indian capitalism benefits the corrupt, the wealthy, and the powerful, which is a result of the rampant criminal entrepreneurship across the region.[15] Straddled between rising aspirations and insufficient means to fulfil those aspirations, a large number of young people drift towards criminality. Growing cities and towns, with their hordes of unemployed denizens, become fertile grounds for gangs and goondas who offer jobs and shortcuts to material success—powerful incentives since they have aspirations for the consumption-oriented lifestyle that has been promoted in the social imagery by economic liberalization.[16]

[10] Sanchez (2012).
[11] Manor (2002).
[12] Nanda (2010: 37).
[13] Nanda (2010: 37).
[14] Berenschot (2011: 19).
[15] Sanchez (2012: 446).
[16] Jaffrelot (2002: 99).

Fragmented systems of authority, especially in postcolonial states, are dominated by local strongmen who occupy strategic positions between state institutions and the population.[17] This is also applicable in the case of Darjeeling, which has been wedged in a political deadlock between the regional West Bengal government and the varying local administrations of the DGHC and, more recently, the GTA. The former DGHC and new GTA are embedded in a loop of complicated separation of powers between regional and local political institutions. For instance, despite a large number of important departments like tea, water, industries, and labour having been transferred to the GTA, decisions around their funding and policies are still made in Kolkata. This disjunction between the state and local governments creates another subset of localized governing processes built on political and ethnic patronage. This system of governance lacks any form of self-regulation, monitoring or accountability for its functioning and is structured around the political authority of a single person whose power is filtered down through the expansive hierarchy, making it a centralized political system controlled by a few.

This phenomenon was evident for over two decades during the rule of Subhash Ghisingh who capitalized on the regionalization of politics by creating a wide network of political patronage crucial for his continuation as the leader of the Darjeeling hills. This trend has continued and flourished under the present regime. The West Bengal government allows and even tolerates criminality amongst the political classes in the hills as long as the demands for Gorkhaland are limited to occasional rallies and muted threats of another political agitation. This translates directly into the administrative set-up of the hills. In comparison to the DGHC, many more departments have been allocated to the GTA. The GTA also manages a significant portion of the projects and funding that come to the hills. Therefore, whether the DGHC or GTA, these administrative set-ups create a system whereby the dominant party and/or politicians are allowed to control the economy and development of the hills, or at least some aspects of it. This arrangement allows for the establishment of a wide network of political patronage dependent on the notion of '*aphno manche*' (our people/people who are associated with the party).

Political patronage is established through a sprawling social network, the smooth functioning of which is dependent on rowdies and their

[17] Hansen and Stepputat (2006: 306).

ability to maintain and sometimes even enforce these networks. Political leaders may not be personally involved in criminality and violence, but, more often than not, most of them would have control of their personal posse of rowdies. The criminalization of politics requires that the leader has a 'tough reputation' and the proven capacity to exercise violence. This brings together the two long valued potencies of a politician–to protect and provide.[18] This trait has historically been epitomized by the leaders of the Darjeeling hills. Their histories as tough men or leaders are institutionalized locally by the rowdies. Rowdies derive power in their community through their physical prowess, potential for violence, and—perhaps most importantly—their political connections, which grant them immunity from any serious repercussions.

For instance, in 2011, two bailable and two non-bailable warrants were issued against Bimal Gurung, the leader of the GJM. He was granted anticipatory bail, which cleared the way for his participation in the 2012 local elections. Applying for anticipatory bail quickly became a legal way out for a large number of GJM activists who were wanted in criminal cases. This allowed them to participate in election processes like canvassing, organizing meetings and so on.[19] The proliferation of rowdies and the impunity they enjoy make a mockery of the rule of law. They are symbolic of the failure of the developmental state, as well as the nature of local politics, which is steeped in hierarchy, patronage, and violence. This is a volatile, self-perpetuating relationship fed by decades of underdevelopment, inequality, and increasingly a system that rewards the strongest who may not necessarily be the bravest.

According to Ganguly–Scrase and Scrase,[20] there are three distinct layers of middle class in Darjeeling; the old middle class (intelligentsia, businessmen, civil servants), the aspirational middle class (post-liberalization educated, successfully employed), and the new middle class (a first-generation subclass that has acquired wealth through political connections or other corrupt means). Political patronage is therefore one of the most important ways through which people hope to access state resources.[21] There is also a general sentiment in the hills that only those with money and muscle-power are able to get ahead, thereby making it

[18] Michelutti (2014: 284).

[19] Express News Service (2011). 'Bimal Gurung Gets Anticipatory Bail'. *The Indian Express*, March 26.

[20] Ganguly-Scrase and Scrase (2015: 248).

[21] Chettri (2014).

imperative to engage in these networks.[22] Political patronage is of vital importance to rowdies, as it is a source that can be tapped to gain political protection and/or to maintain close affiliation with local councillors who distribute developmental contracts. Not all rowdies are successful in extracting favours or contracts from their political connections but, as will be discussed in the following sections, politics is fast becoming a springboard that can propel youngsters who possess the right balance of ambition, brutality, and recklessness into a life of crime.[23]

In the Gorkhaland agitation of 1986, it was rowdies from the nearby *kamans* (tea gardens) and rural areas who primarily carried out the violence in the name of Gorkhaland.[24] In 2007–8, rowdies were again involved, but this time at the forefront of ensuring public compliance with the political diktats of the GJM. The second Gorkhaland agitation was markedly different from that of 1986 with its supposed espousal of non-violent, Gandhian strategies of resistance against the state. However, the political rhetoric of bravery and sacrifice, with undertones of symbolic violence, remained unchanged in the agitation of 2007.[25] There were peaceful demonstrations, road-blockades, *pad yatra* to the Dooars, and cultural events highlighting the culture of the Gorkha, which at the time were blighted by incidents of violence especially in the plains of Siliguri and the Dooars. In the hills, it was generally understood that participation in public meetings and other events was mandatory and participation was monitored by the local *samaj*[26] and/or local rowdies. During the entire period of the agitation (2007–11) violence, or at least the threat of violence, against individuals or members of certain political factions became a permanent feature of the movement. This is a trend that has continued to exist even after the agitation. It remains a hallmark of hill politics.[27]

[22] Scrase, Ganguly–Scrase, and Deuchar (2016: 109); Wenner (2015).

[23] Rudd (2014: 322).

[24] See Subba (1989b).

[25] Chettri (2013).

[26] *Samaj* are mostly localized community–based institutions that play an important role in the social and political activities of an area. Samaj can also be based on ethnicity and caste groups. See also Drew and Rai and Chhetri, this volume.

[27] Criminality and associated political violence is not the preserve of Darjeeling hills only, but it is the explicit, almost flamboyant public display and the impunity with which it is used that distinguishes it from neighbouring Sikkim where such acts of violence are limited in their frequency and intensity.

Sunil sat across from me in a cramped tea shop near Kalimpong motor stand. He was soft-spoken, friendly, and the long yellow tika on his forehead was telling of his religious disposition.[28] We talked about his busy schedule, which comprised almost entirely of community activities. He had to help someone get a school admission, take someone else to the hospital and then later attend a political meeting organized by one of the newer parties of Kalimpong. Sunil was enthusiastic about the upcoming elections. He had been approached by most of the leading parties to canvass for them in his locality, Panchdaara, one of the poorest areas of urban Kalimpong. I asked him which party he would eventually support and he replied, 'whichever party has the money'. He laughed it off as a joke and said that he was organizing a meeting in his locality the next day to gain a consensus on which party they should collectively support. Sunil, the social worker was also known in his circle of friends as 'number one rowdies' of the 1986 agitation; a past he claims is well behind him.

The formation of the DGHC and the GTA did not drastically alter the political and socio-economic status of the Darjeeling hills. Sunil felt that nothing had changed for people like him. Politicians came and went; and he and his people still lived in poverty and squalor, as had generations before him. And yet, ironically, he felt that the elections were a chance to bring about some change in his neighbourhood. While community development might still be a distant goal, political interruptions like the Gorkhaland Movement in 1986, 2007–8, and the 2016 state elections provided small niches in which Sunil and many more like him had finally found some prospect of deriving monetary benefit from parties, or benefiting indirectly through party support in gaining employment, contracts and so on. Not surprisingly then, elections were the busiest time for rowdies, a time for them to prove their mettle and gain favours of their political overlords, who were at their humble, pliant, and community-spirited best.

Political parties and politicians do not necessarily engage with the electorate on broader ideological issues, a characteristic feature of South Asian politics where vote banks are built on narrow claims of caste, religion, region, or on the vague promise of development. Endemic poverty and government dysfunction can play a deterministic role in shaping

[28] Sunil (2016), pers. comm., 14 March.

people's political perspectives. Short-term benefits (like cash/and or entry into the extensive network of political patronage) may influence their electoral choices. This is also true of the Darjeeling hills, which has seen very little expansion of public infrastructure (apart from those under the MGNREGA schemes) and human resource development under the West Bengal government, the DGHC, and now the GTA. Elections therefore, often become an elaborate charade of ethno-nationalistic hyperbole and promises of development. While the TMC promises more development for the hills through the creation of ethnic developmental boards, the GJM and other parties promise it through the formation of Gorkhaland.

Political participation for the candidates as well as the electorate is less about political ideology and more about the best possible means through which to access the very limited resources that flow into the hills. The GJM is still the single largest party, but disillusionment with the GJM is evident through both the successful inroads that the Mamata Banerjee-led TMC has been able to make in the hills, and the proliferation of smaller local parties like the Jan Andolan Party, which was formed by former intellectuals of the GJM, Harka Bahadur Chettri and Amar Lama in 2016.

The success of each of these parties lies in its capacity to influence voters, the most important being those living in the rural and kaman areas. Key to their success is their ability to attract and support as many rowdies as possible. Rowdies along with various other 'party-workers', 'youth', and 'activists' are typically used by political parties as a show of strength in political rallies, to mobilize grassroot support and, if necessary, make threats and engage in violent activities. For example, in 2008, amidst a mix of outrage, enthusiasm, and political pressure, a political diktat known as the 'dress code' was introduced in Darjeeling under the directive of the GJM and enforced under the watchful gaze of the 'party workers'. Pursuant to this new rule, it became mandatory for everybody to wear their ethnic dress during the month-long festival of Dasain and Diwali. While some genuinely welcomed this move by the GJM, moral policing by the GJM Nari Morcha and Gorkhaland Police (GLP, later re-named Gorkha Personnel, a local police force that had been composed of rowdies controlled by the GJM) also highlighted the coercive nature of cultural politics, as non-compliance invited physical humiliation and assault in public.[29] While processions in ethnic clothes and street

[29] Middleton (2015).

performances were received by the public with great fervour, it was all conducted under the purview of the GLP, which was on the lookout for miscreants and detractors of the GJM's version of ethnic nationalism.

The mushrooming of different political parties has made room for the absorption of many more rowdies into the political system. The initiation of many younger people (mostly boys) into the existing rowdies' culture is based on '*asha*' (hope) for future prospects through political affiliation. New rowdies depend on those higher up the rowdies' hierarchy for handouts of money and development work contracts.

The political co-option of rowdies is a phenomenon that can be traced back to the 1986 agitation. Most of the famous pre-1986 rowdies have passed away, but their exploits remain a part of community memory. A senior citizen of Darjeeling, Tika Rai, recounted his experiences of rowdies with a mixture of reverence and fascination.[30] Just like present-day rowdies, the old-timers (as he liked to call them) came from kamans and other economically deprived areas in the periphery of urban Darjeeling. They worked their turf alone and acquired their reputation through solo feats of violence (primarily against the police) and some form of contribution (whether it be material or moral) to the communities in which they lived. Back then, being a rowdy was a display of masculinity, pride, and honour, but it was also borne out of necessity. It was a survival tactic of the poor.

Not everyone succeeded in establishing themselves as rowdies, but those who did gained a license to harass and exploit others as they saw fit; nonetheless, most of these old-timers died penniless and in obscurity. Before 1986, Darjeeling was simply a neo-colonial backwater run on the alms given out by the West Bengal government. At that time, the region was not experiencing the same flow of money it has received in recent years through the DGHC and the GTA. The 1986 agitation proved to be a watershed moment in the history and future trajectory of the rowdies of Darjeeling hills. It was during this time that many rowdies acquired a dangerous reputation, and therefore an economically secure future.

The violent agitation of 1986 has left an indelible scar on the collective memory of the hills. Almost every family has a story of their traumatic experience, not only of the fear and violence perpetrated by the presence of the CRPF, but also of the heartless violence that Nepalis of different

30 Tika Rai (2016), pers. comm., 22 March.

political parties inflicted upon one another. An excerpt from local journalist Saurav Rai's unpublished memoir of the 1986 agitation illustrates the atmosphere of fear and violence that was prevalent in Kalimpong:

> I remember people used to come out of their houses and as soon as the CRPF would start their flag march everyone used to run indoors. I think they had kept people on watch who would shout 'CRP ayo', the CRPF has come ... The sound of the voice would be long, musical and clear. As soon as everybody heard the voice even the cooking used to stop, windows were closed, curtains would be down and people used to huddle in one corner in pin–drop silence ... after a while people would start opening their curtains and windows and everything used to return to normal till the next shout of 'CRP ayo'.

As the 'number one rowdies of 86', Sunil was an active participant in the 1986 agitation and was hardened by the experience. He justified his participation simply by saying that he had truly believed in the fight for Gorkhaland and perhaps, most importantly, that he had nothing to lose as there was not much to live for. As I listened to his nonchalant description of violence and counter-violence, I asked him where the *aat* or courage for such activities came from; he replied, 'the party made us like that'. Political support became an important shield for those engaged in violent activities; it made them immune to the police and the law, a consequential change that has come to define the futures of so many young men.

The socio-political history of the Darjeeling hills is replete with examples of rowdies, intimidating people, and worse, examples of them allegedly assassinating political figures in broad daylight without facing any serious repercussions. For instance, in 2015, the Kolkata Sessions Court issued an Order to the CBI to arrest GJM leaders including Bimal Gurung in relation to the assassination of Madan Tamang, the leader of the AIGL who was killed in 2010. Gurung and other accused members of GJM appealed to the Kolkata High Court seeking anticipatory bail. The court hearing the plea granted a stay on their arrest until their bail plea was disposed of.[31] This news prevented another round of violence

[31] Sengupta, Saugar (2015). 'Tamang Murder Case: CBI questions HC brief over Gurung bail plea.' *The Pioneer*, November 18. http://www.dailypioneer.com/nation/tamang–murder–case–cbi–questions–hc–brief–over–gurung–bail–plea.html. See also, Middleton (2018).

and rioting in the hills that had been in the offing since news of the arrest warrant was released. The case continues in court and the GJM has gone on to win almost all the constituencies of the Darjeeling district in the 2016 General Elections. Such instances have emboldened political criminals and rowdies who know that political pressure on the police and local administration can help to guarantee the continuation of their nefarious activities.

Rowdies have evolved from solitary figures, existing on the borders of criminality, to groups working for various political parties. In exchange, the parties support their rowdies by handing out cash and/or providing developmental contract work. The degree of political support is based on the image that the rowdies have in their local area. This means that rowdies need to display masculinity and unruly behaviour in order to determine their utility to political leaders. The reputation of rowdies is built on violence. Their ability to engage in dangerous and violent activities has a direct impact on the quantum of handouts and benefits accorded to them. According to Sunil, heightened public displays of masculinity and bravado (the pinnacle of which is murder) usually guarantee a greater chance of progress and faster movement up the rowdies' hierarchy.

As stated above, most of the rowdies hail from the kaman and peripheral areas of the Darjeeling and Kalimpong hills. These areas have been continually exploited and deprived both under colonial planters, the West Bengal government, and currently, the regional administration.[32] Although they remain important vote banks, these kamans and villages remain enduring sites of poverty and underdevelopment. In these spaces, people from economically and politically marginalized backgrounds are able to move out of absolute poverty by becoming rowdies, which affords them political and economic opportunities that would have otherwise been inaccessible.

Milan Rai exemplifies the upward mobility afforded by rowdies' culture. Rai gained infamy as a rowdy during the agitation of 1986.[33] Reckless, headstrong, and violent, he quickly became a household name, inspiring fear amongst the local population. He lived, and continues to live in a kaman close to Darjeeling town, but after the formation of the GTA, his life circumstances changed. He is now a wealthy man and

[32] See also Middleton's and Bennike's chapters, this volume.

[33] Milan Rai (2016), pers. comm., 25 March.

moves around with his own small entourage of rowdies. He does not have to engage in actual violence anymore; his reputation precedes him. There is an implicit understanding among local businessmen and contractors about the percentage of their profits that has to be earmarked for him, the non-payment of which can precipitate persistent disruption to the smooth functioning of their business and construction work—not to mention, a risk to their personal safety.

Rowdies can be considered a public manifestation of the anger and frustration of those who are reeling under mounting economic disparities. For the rowdies, this anger at the prevailing economic disparities and sense of social inferiority is channelled through public displays of bravado, masculinity, and violence. Rowdies do not, and cannot, maintain their violent persona forever (especially as they start ageing or have families); nor have all been successful in progressing to any other equally lucrative career path. However, there are a significant number of rowdies who are now respectable contractors and real-estate agents. Their transformations, in essence, provide hope to the young recruits that this is a possible way out of the grime of poverty and desperation.

The Vicious Cycle

The 2012 Annual Status of Education Report states that 0.7 per cent of Darjeeling students aged 6–14 were 'not in school'.[34] By 2014, that figure rose to 2.4 per cent which meant that approximately 45,000 children were not engaged in primary and/or any form of education, a factor which would seriously inhibit their life chances in the future. Of those who were enrolled in schools, the majority attended government schools where the standard and overall quality of education was abysmally low. For most, access to standard private schools is impeded by prohibitive school fees, 'donations', and other costs. Work on tea plantations and growing cash crops like oranges and ginger traditionally constituted a safety-net for those without education, but the recent decline and closure of tea-gardens, coupled with low wages, and the '100 days' scheme

[34] The terminology 'not in school' denoted those students who had either dropped out or not enrolled. According to the Census of 2011, the total population of Darjeeling District stood at 1,846,823. A survey of all the available ASER reports shows a higher male to female dropout ratio (Directorate of Census Operations, West Bengal 2011).

under the MGNREGA reduced the allure of working in the estates or in the fields.

Since the early 1970s there has been a surge of rural-urban mobility as large numbers of tea labourers and agriculturists have moved to urban areas.[35] Further, young men and women from the kamans, especially those closer to the town, are not very keen on working in the estates. The recent boom in the retail and mobile phone sectors has created numerous job openings in Darjeeling and Sikkim and many young people that I have met and spoken to over the years were eager to take up those jobs. Others tried their hands as drivers, handy-boys, guides, and other options. Many have even been willing to migrate further afield in search of better opportunities. Nonetheless, there remain still a larger number of young people in Darjeeling who are unemployed and adrift. Lacking education, employment, and transferable skills, joining a political party is, for many, the only option available.

Political parties and their leadership are acutely aware of the importance of the kamans and rural areas as electoral vote banks. There are hundreds of villages scattered across the districts of Darjeeling and Kalimpong, yet only a handful of towns. Canvassing requires money, time, and manpower. Herein, the floating youth populations especially from the kamans become readily available 'party activists' who are provided with food, money, free transportation, and police protection in the event of clashes with rowdies of other political parties for the duration of the canvassing period. For some, becoming rowdies is also a way of sustaining their drug and alcohol addiction. While I was looking for possible respondents, many of my key informants asked if I wanted to interview drug-addicts. They said that being a rowdy was almost synonymous with being a drug-addict. All drug and alcohol addicts need not necessarily be rowdies, but, according to many local respondents, the majority of the rowdies were drug addicts.

While these benefits of being party activists might be short-lived, there is also another dimension to political participation—asha (hope) for the future—in the form of money or developmental contract work conferred through their connections and acquaintances within the party. Prem epitomized the politics of asha. He lived in a forest village and spent most of his time fishing and swimming in the nearby river.[36] Like

35 Brown (2015: 266); see also Besky (2008); Bhowmik (1996).

36 Prem (2015), pers. comm., 25 July.

most of his friends, Prem was a high-school dropout and he had worked as a daily wage labourer in various local construction projects. However, the completion of these projects had left him, his friends, and many more like them unemployed. With no education or work skills, Prem tried to contribute to his family's income through odd jobs that became available from time to time. Apart from that, he participated in political rallies, meetings, and other events quite regularly. There was not much to show in material benefits for his participation, but he said he did it in the hope of some tangible returns in the future. For Prem and his friends, becoming rowdies did not necessarily translate to constant public displays of violence, just reckless foolhardiness and the willingness to indulge in violence whenever required by political parties. These prerequisites would ensure their success as rowdies and make it easier to mobilize grassroot support, canvass during elections, and enforce blockades on the national highway. Political participation was limited to these exercises and the rowdies, without whom political parties would be rendered inconsequential, had no say in the actual decision-making process.

Prem and his friends were aware that if they were politically active and supported the right party, their chances of getting a contract in a developmental project in the area would be greater than if they chose to remain apolitical. Development projects, whether approved by the GTA or the West Bengal government are distributed between 'youth groups' (comprising mostly of men) based on the recommendation of the local party representative. Depending on the size of the project, they can be further re-distributed amongst smaller group. Those working on these projects are colloquially known as *peti* (petty) contractors. To exist and succeed in this world of 'peti' contracts requires political clout and the ability to prove one's usefulness to the party as rowdies.

This world of peti contractors is tightly controlled by the party hierarchy and what eventually trickles down to people like Prem and his friends represents a miniscule proportion of the total allocated funds. Rowdies and the vicious cycle of poverty and dependency within which they are trapped speak volumes about the state of development in the Darjeeling hills. The rowdies phenomenon is but a violent symptom of the malaise that has shrouded the Darjeeling hills for generations. Decades of economic and political subservience first to the British Raj and then to the West Bengal government has taken its toll on the collective subconscious of the people (see the essays in the first section of this volume). This situation is further aggravated by the stagnant regional and local economy, which offers no new avenues to the thousands of unemployed and under-employed people of the hills.

The tea industry is still the largest employer. It is based on a very high fixed land-labour ratio with 3.5 workers per hectare and the livelihoods of approximately 70 per cent of the total population of Darjeeling is dependent directly or indirectly on the tea industry.[37] However, closure of tea gardens and lower tea production now means that gardens are unable to generate additional employment.[38]

A large portion of the people in Darjeeling are unemployed and live in poverty (19.66 per cent in rural areas and 15.21 per cent in urban areas).[39] While government jobs are difficult to find in general, top administrative positions are occupied by officers from the Indian Civil Services and the West Bengal Civil Services, who are often recruited from different parts of the country. Barring a handful of ST and SC candidates, there are very few non-Bengalis working as civil servants or occupying high positions in the government.[40] Darjeeling is marketed as the 'queen of the hills' but tourism is restricted to only a small area, thereby limiting its impact on local employment. The majority of the employees and almost all of the top ranking officers in West Bengal Tourism Development Corporation are Bengalis; locals generally get employed as photographers, drivers, and guides.[41] Tea has blocked the experimentation and development of many other industries.[42] Meanwhile, exploitation of other natural resources like timber and water (and in particular, the generation of hydro-electric power by the state)

[37] Datta (2010).

[38] See also Besky and Sen, this volume.

[39] This lack of development and infrastructure has to be analysed against the background of the overall performance of West Bengal itself, which is an average performing state owing to excessive unionization and poor labour relations. Within West Bengal, a significant part of the state is relatively more economically backward and also tends to be less advanced in terms of human development. Comparative analyses of various indicators (education, health) places Darjeeling at a better position than other districts like Nadia or even Jalpaiguri. This includes six northern districts (Darjeeling included), three western districts, and the Sunderbans in the south (Development and Planning Department Government of West Bengal 2004).

[40] Bomjan (2008).

[41] Subba (1989b: 312).

[42] Tirkey (2005).

has disturbed the environment in a seismically sensitive zone and caused severe ecological damage.

The absence of the state is most evident in the organized chaos that has become Darjeeling town,[43] where water shortage is now being handled to a large extent by water rowdies, who ensure households of water supply by illegally tapping connections for a price.[44] There are no reliable health services and there is a palpable lack of civic planning. The stories of poverty, squalor, and migration coupled with the political rhetoric of the Gorkhas' bravery in the battlefield and sacrifice for Mother India, have remained the same for decades now. The rowdies represent all of this and more. They represent the lack of opportunities, the absence of change in the governance and the politics, and the increasing gap between those who have and those who have never had. Just like the old-timers, it is necessity that drives the younger generation towards rowdie-ism, as it offers them a possible route through which they can bypass the administrative hurdles that have been imposed by their lack of education, low economic status, and other indicators of social inferiority. Thus, becoming hardened rowdies helps mask not just the social problems they face, but also the economic ones.

Rowdies are the instruments of realpolitik in the Darjeeling hills—small parts of a larger political system that rewards violence and criminality. This culture also draws some reference from the discourse of a Gorkha identity constructed around bravery in the battlefield, thereby making violence an intrinsic part of everyday politics. As enforcers of political campaigns and the face of political activities, the rowdies lack proportional political agency because they are bound by the rules and demands of their political overlords. They have to exist and work within a political structure, which is extremely hierarchical, and the possibility of progress is determined by the degree of violence they are willing to engage in. This also leads to very important questions on how political participation, agency, and popular support are manufactured in the name of representative democracy. One of the primary motives that propels individuals to become rowdies is the region's historic underdevelopment and concomitant poverty. Rising aspirations are quelled

[43] Ganguly-Scrase and Scrase (2015).

[44] See also Drew and Rai, this volume.

by the ever-widening socio-economic gap between different sections of the society. Participating in elaborate networks of patronage through the path of rowdie-ism is seen by many as the only way forward. A lot has changed in the hills over the past two decades and yet much more remains the same. While the character of the pre-1986 and the post-1986 rowdies might have shifted, the imperative has not; it is still poverty. It is indeed a vicious cycle in which, unfortunately, there appears to be no break for the foreseeable future.

7 The Quest to Belong and Become

Ethnic Associations and Changing Trajectories of Ethnopolitics in Darjeeling

Nilamber Chhetri*

Demands based on ethnicity and ethnic identities have been raised in Darjeeling since the colonial period. However, these ethnic demands underwent significant transformations in the postcolonial era, owing to changes in political processes and the responses of the state. Since the turn of the twentieth century, identities such

* I am thankful to the anonymous referees for their observations and comments on the earlier draft of the essay. I especially thank the editors for providing me this opportunity to contribute to the volume. I also express my gratitude to Simashree Bora for reading the earlier draft of the article and providing crucial insights. In addition, I would also like to thank all the informants from different ethnic associations in the Darjeeling hills for their assistance in the field.

as *Hillmen* and *Gorkha* were utilized by ethnic groups in Darjeeling to frame their major demands. Along with these collective identities, individual ethnic groups and their associations have also raised discreet demands. Unfortunately, many of their records have been lost over time. Nevertheless, an understanding of ethnopolitics in Darjeeling requires a diachronic understanding of the growth, perpetuation, and demise of ethnic associations, and a detailed analysis of changes in the repertoire and nature of their demands.

Governing systems in the colonial and postcolonial period—particularly those concerned with minority recognition, affirmative action, and autonomy—provided opportunities for different kinds of ethnic groups.[1] Over time, these shifting administrations of difference have shaped ethnic mobilization and subjectivities in formative ways in Darjeeling. The most recent shifts from 'Gorkha' to 'tribal' politics and back again (sketched in this volume's introduction) reflect the dynamic variability of ethnic politics in the hills. They too shed light on the innovation and growing need with which marginalized minorities are engaging India's postcolonial state. Taking a longitudinal look at the shifting terms of identity politics in Darjeeling from the early twentieth century to the present, this chapter asks what ethnic politics in the hills may teach us about the possibilities of identity, alterity, and subnational politics in South Asia more generally. It argues that recent demands for regional autonomy and ST recognition are closely linked to the quests for both entitlements and belonging as full-fledged citizens of the Indian nation-state.

In order to understand the trajectory of ethnic demands in Darjeeling, we have to analyse the transformations of colonial subjects into citizens

---

I am indeed greatly indebted to them for their kindness and also their keenness throughout the course of this study.

[1] Seen through this lens, the genesis of these ethnic demands in Darjeeling can be traced to the objectification processes and the enumerative modality of colonial governance [Appadurai (1993); Cohn (1987); Dirks (2001); Kaviraj (1992); Sundar (2000)]. In India, categories structured in the colonial period were reproduced in the postcolonial period, thus indicating a perpetual continuity and affinity between anthropological discourse and technologies of governance across these eras [Asad (1973); Cohn (1987, 1996); Dirks (2001, 2004); Dudley–Jenkins (2003); Pels and Salemink (2000); Uberoi, Sundar, and Deshpande (2008)].

of postcolonial India. During the colonial period, subjecthood was characterized by indirect contact with the state. In the postcolonial period, both formal citizenship and substantive citizenship rights have been increasingly shaped by a larger discourse of cultural rights.[2] Whereas liberal ideals of citizenship demand homogeneity, the global indigenous rights movement has articulated cultural rights premised on the notion of difference. The Darjeeling case highlights these dynamics, as the ongoing demands for recognition and autonomy are essentially framed through an idiom of cultural exclusivity and difference, which in varying forms have come to constitute a perpetual quest to establish a clear sense of belonging to the nation.

Discussing the early ethnic associations in hills, this chapter will try to provide an alternative history of identity-based demands in Darjeeling—one that augments, but also challenges, the standard genealogies of the Gorkhaland struggle. I begin by examining the historical processes through which early ethnopolitical identities were forged in the early years of the twentieth century. Drawing on archival materials and oral histories, I then chart the emergence and transformations of ethnic associations in mid-twentieth century. During this period, we see two markedly different trajectories of identity politics take shape. The first concerned the representation and political demands of a collective *Hillmen/Gorkha* community. The second manifested in a range of ethnic associations representing individual ethnic groups like the Mangars, Gurungs, Limbus, Khas—and focused primarily on social welfare and cultural preservation of their respective constituents.

Ethnic associations since the turn of the twentieth century largely reflected the concerns of Darjeeling's civil society; these issues were later taken up by organizations and political parties making overtly political demands. Subsequent years would see the concerns emanating from political and civil domains converge, thus producing a hybrid nature of ethnic demands in the hills. We therefore need to look at the points of convergence between the civil and political domains. This helps us to note the complex trajectory of ethnic demands and analytically trace these struggles as more than mere survival strategies—they are, at once, a way to derive subsistence from the state and redefine a people's place and identity in India.[3]

[2] Jayal (1999).
[3] Gudavarthy (2013: 22).

Traversing complex terrain, the present ethnopolitics in Darjeeling highlights the synthesis of political and civil society. As I will argue, the most recent avatars of ethnopolitics in Darjeeling reflect a powerful admixture of sentiments to become and belong to the region and the nation-state. These subjective and affective ethnic identities produce strong mobilizations and transform the ethnic selves of constituent members. As primary organizers of these movements, ethnic associations—and their transformation through time—articulate a perpetual quest to assert one's position in the national register, and secure rights and entitlements as citizens.

Nomenclatures of Belonging: Early Iterations

As the opening chapters of this volume demonstrate, British colonialism redefined the contours of the Darjeeling region, and largely set the terms of integration into British India for its inhabitants.[4] Darjeeling was included within the colonial matrix as an ambiguous space characterized by its plantation economy, its framing as a site for rejuvenation of health, and its strategic geopolitical position in a frontier region. Amid these exceptional circumstances, a variety of ethnic organizations emerged in the early twentieth century to help forge a collective identity for the Nepali–Indian community of the hills and therein demand an exclusive status for the region. Three aspects were crucial in constituting this collective ethnic identity: (a) the formation of cultural and social organizations to articulate collective demands; (b) the forging of ties amongst ethnic groups to structure a collective ethnic label; (c) the demands for a separate administrative set-up for Darjeeling, citing cultural differences from the rest of Bengal. Issues of belonging and becoming played a significant role in the consolidation of the Nepali-speaking community in Darjeeling. Because issues of nomenclature were essentially linked to questions of nationality, many names were used to refer to the emergent Nepali-speaking community in the hills.

From the start, the Nepali language became a prime symbol of belonging for the peoples of Nepali origin in Darjeeling. The language served

[4] In this regard, what is said of Bastar by Nandini Sundar applies equally to Darjeeling; in both the cases, 'colonialism's distinctive contribution was not in integrating these regions into some wider system, but in changing the terms of this integration' Sundar (1997: 4).

as Darjeeling's lingua franca and furthermore tapped local constituents into a broader Nepali-speech community—a prospect bolstered by the Nepali language course offered at Fort William College in 1820,[5] as well as the role played by missionaries in the development of a Nepali language curriculum. Following recognition from the University of Allahabad in 1911 and Calcutta University in 1918, the Nepali language assumed the status of 'cultural capital'. With the introduction of Nepali instruction in schools, the community's imagination of the world and their position within it expanded considerably.[6]

It was with the growth of the Nepali language that a sense of commonness developed among various ethnic groups inhabiting the hills. Over the course of the twentieth century, the collective Nepali identity gradually gained greater salience over the discreet and exclusive ethnic identities of communities like Mangars, Gurungs, Khas, Limbu, and others.[7] As *jati unnati* (community upliftment) was essentially linked with developments in the Nepali language, early literary figures from Darjeeling emphasized *ekrupta* or uniformity among the various Nepali speaking ethnic groups of Darjeeling.[8] For the purpose of consolidating and standardizing Nepali language, organizations such as *Nepali Sahitya Sammelan* were formed as early as 25 May 1924.

If the question of belonging was bound up in debates over nomenclature, what exactly was this emergent pan-Nepali identity in India to be

[5] The usage of the term *Nepali* for Khas Kura became popular after J.M. Ayton published the first *Grammar of the Nepalese Language* in 1820. A series of Nepali grammar texts were published by Europeans like A. Turnbull's *Nepali Grammar and Vocabulary* published in 1888, and R.L. Turner's *A Comparative and Ethnological Dictionary of the Nepali Language* published in 1931. Dahal (2011: 29).

[6] Onta (1996a: 43).

[7] Historically the communities labelled as 'Nepali' consisted of taxonomically different ethnic, linguistic, and racial groups who were incorporated within the Nepali caste system following the Gorkha conquest of 1769 [see Höfer (1979)]. However, in the case of Darjeeling, caste norms were followed in rudimentary ways and social relations were not. The emergent Nepali community in Darjeeling thus represented diverse ethnic groups such as Mangar, Gurungs, Newars, Jogis, Yakkhas, Khambu Rai, Limbus, Sunuwar, Thami, Khas, Tamangs, Bhujels, and others. Given this history, there was a conflation of *jati* (ethnic) and *jat* (caste) identities.

[8] Chalmers (2003a: 347); Onta (1996a: 51).

called? As terms such as *Gorkhali, Nepali, Bharatiya Nepali, Bharpali, Bhargoli* were debated, the issue of identity proved closely linked to discourses of citizenship and inclusion in British India. Cultural organizations of the time critically experimented with terms to accurately refer to Nepalis in India, while preventing this new-found collective from being identified with Nepal.[9] Early Nepali literary stalwarts like Parasmani Pradhan used both the terms *Nepali* and *Gorkha* interchangeably.[10] Yet, in ensuing years, the ethnonym *Gorkha* gained substantial popularity and consequently became a fulcrum to assert rights and frame major political demands in Darjeeling. The 'martial race' discourse of the British also popularized the Gorkha identity as it inscribed the attributes of bravery and chivalry on the body of 'Gurkha' subjects.[11] Thus early associations of the Nepalis in India like Gorkha Samiti (1906) and Gorkha Dukha Niwarak Sammelan (1932) used the word 'Gorkha' to denote Nepalis of Indian origin. The first Nepali public library was also named Gorkha Library.[12] The name Gorkha was also retained by many of the Nepali journals published in India: for instance, *Gorkha Bharat Jivan* (Benaras, late 1880s), *Gorkhe Khabar Kagat* (Darjeeling, 1901), *Gorkhali* (Banaras, 1915), *Gorkha Sansar* (Dehradun, 1926), *Tarun Gorkah* (Dehradun, 1928), and so on.[13]

The early decades of the twentieth century also saw concerted efforts to institutionalize social welfare organizations in Darjeeling. The most significant being the Gorkha Dukha Niwarak Sammelan (GDNS) established on 3 June 1932.[14] One of the main objectives of the GDNS

[9] Chalmers (2003a, 2009).

[10] Hutt (1997:113).

[11] The name spelled 'Gurkha' as used in Western writings refers to the 'martial race' construct formed during the colonial period, whereas the name 'Gorkha' was a nomenclature adopted by the ethnic groups in Darjeeling to represent their collective identity. See Caplan (1995a: 120).

[12] Gorkha Library was first established in Kurseong on 8 June 1913; it was initially housed at J. Pava's residence and later shifted to a rented building. A permanent building for the library was completed only in 1918 with the generous contribution from Sardar Bahadur Lama.

[13] Pokharel (2009: 332).

[14] The precursors to GDNS were the hosts of theatrical companies formed in the hills mainly by Dhanbir Mukhia. In 1909, he formed the Gorkha National Theatrical Company and staged plays on social and cultural issues of the time. Again in 1909–10, the Children's Amusement Association was formed, and in

in its formative days was to dispose the dead bodies left unattended and perform the death rituals.[15] The GDNS also spearheaded the campaign for social uplift of the poor and the needy and started scholarship schemes for students. The GDNS tried to reach out to the masses through the distinctive medium of Nepali plays. It staged plays at different locales and promoted cultural consciousness among the groups settled in Darjeeling.[16]

While the nomenclature of 'Nepali' or 'Gorkha' identity was gaining ground within the cultural realm, the political voice of the groups settled in Darjeeling was framed and articulated through the 'Hillmen' identity. Along these lines, the demand for the creation of a separate administrative set-up in Darjeeling was initially voiced by some 'leaders from the hills' on the eve of the Indian Council Act of 1907.[17] The demand to create a separate administrative unit for Darjeeling district was articulated in subsequent years by the Hillmen's Association under the leadership of S.W. Laden La, who was an ardent advocate of autonomy for the hills.[18] The memorandums submitted by the Hillmen's Association provide insights into the changing nature of inter-ethnic relations in Darjeeling. The first memorandum submitted by the Hillmen's Association, demanding a separate administrative unit, makes the case for three communities of the hills, namely Lepchas, Bhutias, and Nepalis who are all placed under the label of 'hill people'.[19] It is interesting to note that the

---

1914 the Himalayan Amusement Association was formed. The latter two organizations were clumped together in 1915, and renamed as the Himalayan and Children's Advancement Association. The GDNS was established on 3 June 1932 by Dhanbir Mukhia, Harka Dhwaj Lama, Jitbahadur Khadka, Manbahadur Mukhiya, and Lalu Pradhan. Along with social welfare activities, it was also instrumental in promoting education in the hills. For this purpose, they established public libraries such as Gorkha Jana Pustakalaya and Manovinod Pustakalaya in Darjeeling. Bomjan (2008: 49).

[15] Pradhan (2012: 33–5) Shneiderman (2015: 141).

[16] For more details on the plays staged by the GDNS, see Pradhan (1982) and Rai (1984).

[17] Subba (1992: 76).

[18] Rhodes and Rhodes (2006: 4).

[19] See the Memorandum of the Hillmen's Association, submitted to the Chief Secretary of the Government of West Bengal, dated 8 November 1917 in Moktan (2004: 90–2).

Darjeeling Planters Association and the European Association echoed the demand for the creation of a separate administrative unit for Darjeeling on the eve of Montague–Chelmsford Reforms of 1919. These associations supported this demand, as they wanted to secure their interest in the tea plantations and insulate the hills from the growing influence of the nationalist movement.[20] Such demands were, however, resented by other organizations like the Kalimpong Samiti, which feared that Darjeeling's exclusion from the reforms of 1919 would perpetuate the backwardness of the region.[21]

Nevertheless calls for the exclusion of Darjeeling from Bengal gained ground in subsequent years, as evidenced by the second memorandum submitted by the Hillmen's Association in 1920.[22] On the eve of the Simon Commission, the Hillmen's Association placed similar demands before the government. This memorandum is interesting as it only pleads the case of the Gorkhas settled and domiciled in British India. The memorandum places all hill communities under the generic category of 'Gorkha'.[23]

The division within the Hillmen's Association regarding the question of ethnicity is evident through the memorandums submitted by the association.[24] Tracked diachronically, these demands indicate that

[20] Nag (2007: 210).

[21] Organizations such as the Kalimpong Samiti under Sardar Bahadur Bhindal Dewan and the People's Association led by Sir P.M. Pradhan argued against the separation of Darjeeling from Bengal. See Middleton (2013c: 17); (2015: 38).

[22] See the Memorandum of the Hillmen's Association submitted to His Majesty's Secretary of State for India, Edwin Montague, dated 11 February 1920. Source: Rhodes and Rhodes (2006: 81–3).

[23] See the memorandum submitted by the Hillmen's Association to Sir Samuel Hoare, Secretary of State for India on 25 October 1930. The eight points of the memorandum state that 'The district of Darjeeling, where the Gurkhas population predominate, should be excluded from Bengal and be treated as an independent administrative unit.' Source: Moktan (2004: 93–5).

[24] For instance, the memorandum of the Hillmen's Association no. 9 states, 'the district of Darjeeling should be totally excluded from Bengal by creation of an independent Administrative unit with an administrator at the head of the area assisted by an executive council,' submitted to Sir Samuel Hoare, the Chief Secretary of the Government of West Bengal, dated 6 August 1934 (Moktan 2004: 96–8).

Gorkha identity was transforming from a collective label into an exclusive category representing only the Nepali speaking groups in the hills. Colonial technologies of governance also contributed to the growing rift between the Nepali, Bhutia, and Lepcha communities. For example, the 1931 census classified groups such as Gurungs, Mangars, Khas, Newars, Tamangs, Damais, Limbus, Kamis, Sunuwars, Yakkhas, Sarkis, Ghartis, and others as 'Nepali Tribes', thus leading to the formation of two broad categories: 'hillmen' (Nepalis) and 'other hillmen' (Lepchas, Tibetans, and Bhutias).[25]

These census operations reified ethnic identities in Darjeeling giving them an objective governmental form, which in turn escalated the rift between Lepchas, Bhutias, and Nepalis. The formation of the two categories, 'hillmen' and 'other hillmen' further complicated matters. Added to it was the idea of indigeneity. Nepali groups ('hillmen') were viewed as migrants, while Lepchas, Bhutias, and Tibetans were seen as autochthonous to the hills. In order to resolve these differences, leaders such as Laden La formed the Hill People's Social Union of Darjeeling (HPSU) in 1934, and also published a magazine called *NEBULA* (*Ne* for Nepali, *Bu* for Bhutia, and *La* for Lepcha). However, these efforts at reconciliation failed due to the growth of other political organizations and ethnopolitical associations in Darjeeling.

Early Ethnic Associations and Cultural Preservation

With a broader Gorkha collective in formation, many ethnic groups of Nepali heritage formed their own respective associations.[26] These early ethnic associations were not driven by the logic of securing benefits from the state. Rather, they were concerned with cultural preservation and welfare schemes for their fellow ethnic members. The existence of these associations opens up questions about the nature of the public during the colonial period in Darjeeling. Specifically, their existence suggests that the emergent Gorkha public was crosscut not only by class and gender, but ethnicity and caste. Doing so, these ethnic associations help to chart the prolonged period of gestation in which identities were re-cast and subjectivities remoulded, both by the exigencies of colonial rule, as well as the demands of sociability in the hills. The activities carried out

[25] Porter (1933).

[26] c.f. Pradhan (2004), Shneiderman (2015: Chapter 5).

by these associations suggest a heightened ethnic consciousness among constituent ethnic groups and highlight a discernible effort launched by groups to preserve their exclusive cultural heritage.

During the course of my fieldwork, I gathered histories of these ethnic associations in an effort to understand how they might challenge the conventional narratives of Gorkha ethnogenesis. Photographic and oral records testify to the presence of many ethnic associations in Darjeeling as early as the 1920s and 1930s. Oral records indicate that one of the earliest ethnic associations formed in Darjeeling was that of the Tamangs established in 1922–3.[27] Similarly, the Biswakarma Samaj formed as early as 1924. Shneiderman reports on the informal meeting organized by Thamis in 1936 and the formation of the Bhai Larke Thami Samaj (BLTS) in 1943, which also started Thami Jyoti Primary School in 1945.[28]

Testimonies of ethnic leaders also suggest a vibrant ethnic organization of Limbus existing during this time. The first meeting of the Limbus, Tum Yakthung Hang Chumlung (council of kings), was held at Dungra Busty, Kalimpong on 26 July 1925, with Sardar Maita Singh Thegim presiding over it. A second convention of the Chumlung was held in 1938, and with the generous contributions of Sardar Maita Singh Thegim and Lal Singh Subba (retired police inspector), they had also started a *Nisham Heem* (school) named as Zambuk Memorial Choomlung to impart knowledge about Limbu language and script in 1938 (see Figure 7.1).

A concerted effort to unite the Khambus, Limbus, and Yakkhas under the banner of the Kirati group was attempted in subsequent years.[29] A meeting was called on 25 December 1976 in Kalimpong, which led to the formation of the Sarva Kirat Chumlung (All Kirati Council). According to R.B. Subba, the President of the Pudung Busty Limbu Samiti Kalimpong, the council was composed of both Limbu and Khambu Rais, and the Chumlung was viewed as a site for the rejuvenation of ancient

[27] The existence of this ethnic association is also highlighted by Rhodes and Rhodes [(2006): 84–5] who report the opening of a Tamang Gomba at Lower Beechwood estate on 20 April 1929 constructed by Tamang Buddhist Association of Darjeeling.

[28] Shneiderman (2009: 126–7); (2015: 129).

[29] Groups within the Nepali community such as Limbus, Khambus, and Yakkhas claim an ancient Kirati lineage, thus asserting their endogamous group identity. They claim to be the indigenous groups inhabiting the Himalayan region since time immemorial.

Figure 7.1 Nisham Heem (School) Zambuk School in Kalimpong Established by the Tum Yakthung Hang Chumglung (council of kings) of Dunga Busty, Kalimpong in 1938
Source: Office of the Yakthung Song Choomvo, Kalimpong.

Kirati identity. However, internal differences subsequently emerged within this organization, as Khambu Rais thought the working of the council was being dictated by the Limbus. They also objected to the Limbu name 'Chumlung' for the organization. The main cause of discord was an issue of Sirijunga script and differences in cultures between these two groups.[30] Owing to these disagreements, Limbus formed their own organization named Yakthung Shong Chumpho, which was renamed Yakthung Song Choomvo in 1994.

These forms of exclusive ethnic activity were also carried out by groups such as the Khas who were regarded as *thulo jat* (upper caste) within the Nepali community. Contemporary Khas leaders attest to the fact that their association named Gorkha Hitkari Sammelan was established in 1942–3 (see Figures 7.2 and 7.3). This association organized

[30] According to R.B. Subba, the major source of friction within the organization was the Sirijunga script. Limbus regarded Sirijunga script as a Limbu script whereas Khambu Rais wanted it to be recognized as Kirati script. R.B. Subba (President of the Pudung Busty Limbu Samiti, Kalimpong) (2014), pers. comm., 14 January.

Figure 7.2 Members of the Gorkha Hitkari Sammelan of Darjeeling (Photographs taken during 1942–3)
Source: Collected during fieldwork from the office of Khas Bharatiya Hitkari Sammelan, Darjeeling.

Figure 7.3 The Procession of the Kirati Khambu Rais led by Mangpas (traditional religious specialists of the Khambus) in Kalimpong, Demanding Tribal Status for Their Group
Source: Photograph taken by the researcher during fieldwork on 1 January 2014.

bhajan mandali (prayer meetings), ran schools for adults, and distributed handwritten magazines called *Kamal Patrika* and *Neupane* in 1945. The main concern of the association was to preserve the culture and traditions of the Khas group. The name of this association underwent successive changes in the decades following its inception. Changes in the name also reflected the changes in the approach and the objectives of the organization. The association, when instituted, was named Gorkha Hitkari Sammelan (1942–5). The name later changed to Sri Hitkari Sammelan (1945 onwards), Hitkari Tagadhari Sammelan (1989), Khas Bahun Hitkari Sammelan (1991–2), Gorkha Khas Hitkari Sammelan (1992–3), and eventually Khas Bharatiya Hitkari Sammelan (1995 until present). Unlike the associations of the Tamangs and Limbus, this association was not focused on the Khas-Bahun groups alone. According to a prominent Khas leader of the Khas Bharatiya Hitkari Sammelan, their association was, in the past, guided by a holistic approach, focused mainly on providing education for backward groups in Darjeeling. Given their holistic focus, membership to the organization was open to all groups and the association served civil aims during its formative years. However, all this changed in the early 1990s, owing to the emergence of other ethnic associations in Darjeeling.[31] Similar to Tamangs, Limbus, and Khas, the photographic evidence also shows the existence of the Mangar Samaj in mid-twentieth century Darjeeling. This was more of a caste association which did not engage in any political activity.[32] This early association of Mangars became inactive in later decades; a solid move to revive the association was made only when the Other Backward Class (OBC) status for Mangars was declared in 1994.

From the above discussion we can see that in the past, many ethnic groups had well-functioning ethnic associations. Though many of these associations went into dormancy in subsequent decades, their prior existence serves as symbolic capital for groups currently struggling to be recognized as STs in India. While scant information and documentary evidence exists on these early ethnic associations of Darjeeling, the presence of these associations brings into relief the complex and dynamic history of ethnopolitics in the hills.

[31] R.B. Raya (president of Khas Bharatiya Hitkari Sammelan) (2014), pers. comm. (interview), 3 March.

[32] Bhanu Thapa (General Secretary of the Akhil Bharatiya Mangar Sangh, Kalimpong) (2014), pers. comm. (interview) 8 February; T.B. Thapa (2014), pers. comm. (interview), 26 February.

While the colonial state is notably absent in the oral testimonies I gathered on these early ethnic organizations, there is a curious coincidence of these ethnic associations' emergence with the enumerative practices of the late colonial census. Indeed, with Indian independence on the horizon, concerns over belonging and citizenship gained ascendancy in hills. Politically, the exclusive ethnic identities of groups like the Tamangs, Limbus, Newars, and others offered less traction than the collective identity of a greater Gorkha conglomerate. From the 1940s onwards, Gorkha identity was increasingly articulated and reinvigorated. Thus, the relentless effort of the HPSU to forge a consolidated 'hillmen' identity throughout the 1920s and 1930s faced a serious setback with the revival of AIGL in Darjeeling. With the formation of the AIGL, the 'hillmen' identity was replaced by the claims to 'Gorkha' identity.[33] The formation of AIGL also signalled the demise of the previously mentioned ethnic associations, which had only started to mobilize constituent ethnic members in Darjeeling. Within the changing political discourse, Gorkha identity gained salience as a collective label representing the aspirations of diverse ethnic groups.

As opposed to the culturally and socially oriented projects of individual ethnic groups, the AIGL advanced the collective Gorkha cause as a distinctly *political* project. Calling for the formation of a separate province, the AIGL set the discourse for many of Darjeeling's subsequent subnationalist struggles for autonomy. The postcolonial period would see increasingly strong demands for the creation of a separate state.[34] The efforts of parties such as Pranta Parishad and GNLF ultimately culminated in the Gorkhaland Movement of 1986–8.[35] With the growth

[33] The All India Gorkha League (AIGL) was originally established in Dehra Dun on 15 February 1924 by Thakur Chandan Singh to integrate the Gorkha community into mainstream Indian society. However, following intra-organizational problems, the League became inactive in later decades; it was revived in Darjeeling in 1936, by Dambar Singh Gurung and formally launched as a political party on 15 May 1943.

[34] These subnationalist demands were buoyed by movements for the constitutional recognition of the Nepali language. In many ways these movements were geared towards voicing the concerns of the Nepali community in India and to secure their rights as citizens of the nation. See Pradhan (2012); Samanta (2000); Subba (1992).

[35] See this volume's introduction; also, Chakrabarti (1988); Subba (1992).

of such parties, the concerns raised by civil society organizations and ethnic associations were largely folded into broader pan-Gorkha collective mobilizations.

Tribalism and the Re-emergence of Ethnic Associations

Formation, dissolution, and re-emergence of ethnic associations characterize the history of ethno-politics in Darjeeling. These transformations suggest a dynamic articulation of identity claims, periodically framed to address issues of belonging and becoming in particular political contexts and eras. Tracking the trajectories of ethnic associations through time, we see that the changed political scenario following India's Independence both augmented and altered the interwoven processes of ethnic formation and mobilization. In this regard, the recent demands for ST recognition have to be located within broader logics of postcolonial governmentality.[36]

Insofar as the residual effects of colonial thought permeated postcolonial governance, they, in turn, influenced the mode and character of struggles raised by ethnic groups. As per the various protective discrimination policies enshrined in the Indian constitution, the official recognition of ascriptive social identities through affirmative action instituted a space to claim rights and benefits on the basis of cultural identities.[37] Four communities in Darjeeling (Bhutia, Lepchas, Tibetans, and Yolmos) were originally listed as STs in the 1950s. In the 1990s, the government's decision to implement the recommendations of Mandal Commission significantly affected ethnopolitics in Darjeeling.[38] Regrouping after the turbulence and failure of the Gorkhaland agitation of the 1980s, many ethnic groups revived their old ethnic associations,

[36] Abrams (1988); Coombe (2007); Fuller and Benei (2000); Gupta and Ferguson (1992, 2002); Gupta and Sharma (2006); Hansen and Stepputat (2001); Middleton (2015).

[37] Jayal (1999); Mahajan (1998: 149).

[38] The Mandal Commission was formed in 1978 under the Chairmanship of B.P. Mandal to determine the status of backward classes within Indian society. Though the Commission submitted its report in the early 1980s, the recommendations of the Commission were not implemented until V.P. Singh decided to implement the recommendations, thereby extending reservations to the economically weaker sections of society. With the implementations of the report a new category emerged in India called Other Backward Classes (OBCs).

Table 7.1 Contemporary Ethnic Associations in Darjeeling

Name of the Ethnic Associations	Year of Establishment
Kirati Khambu Rai Sanskritik Sansthan	1994
Akhil Bharatiya Gurung (Tamu) Bodha Sangathan	1992
Tamu Choj Dhi	1992
Tamu (Gurung) Kalyan Sangathan	1999
Akhil Bharatiya Mangar Sangh	2002
Mangar Samaj Darjeeling	1939
Lafa Mangar Sangh	1992
Mangar Sangh Bharat	2006
All India Kirat Yakkha (Dewan) Chhumma	2003
Bharatiya Thami Welfare Association	1990
Akhil Bharatiya Newar Sangathan	1993
Gorkha Yogi (Jogi) Kalyan Sangh	2007–08
Khas Janjati Mahasangh	2014
Khas Bharatiya Hitkari Sammelan	1995
Bharatiya Sunuwar (Mukhia/Koich) Samaj	1992
Bhujel Kalyan (Welfare) Association	1994

Source: Compiled by Author.

while others formed new associations to capitalize on the affirmative action advantages on offer. Throughout the 1990s, ethnic associations increasingly emerged, demanding recognition as OBCs and subsequently as STs, based on their exclusive cultural identity (see Table 7.1).[39]

These movements for ST status marked a significant shift from the Gorkha-dominated politics of the 1980s. The effects of economic liberalization also propelled these quests for affirmative action, as marginalized groups in Darjeeling and beyond sought purchase in India's new economic order.[40] The recognition of the Limbus and Tamangs as STs in 2003 only increased the desire of other unrecognized communities in Darjeeling, as did new demands by GNLF chief Subash Ghisingh to include Darjeeling within the ambit of the Sixth Schedule of the India. According to the provisions laid out in Articles 244 (2) and 275 (1) of the Indian Constitution, certain areas in India's North–East, with their predominantly tribal population, have been declared 'tribal areas' and

[39] Middleton (2011, 2015); Shneiderman (2009, 2015); Shneiderman and Turin (2006).

[40] See Middleton (2015).

administered under autonomous councils. To bolster Darjeeling's bid to become a Sixth Schedule 'tribal area', Ghisingh repeatedly demanded inclusion of all Gorkha groups into the list of STs. These calls for tribal autonomy stirred ethnopolitics in Darjeeling, and further propelled individual communities' mobilizations for ST recognition (see also the introduction to this volume).

These interlinked demands for tribal recognition and autonomy have accordingly been structured by particular technologies of postcolonial governance on the subcontinent—specifically those systems put in place to govern ethnic minorities. As the category ST has assumed new-found social lives, ethnic renewal and ethnic switching, to borrow terms from Nagel, have become a key dynamic of ethnopolitics in Darjeeling.[41] For Darjeeling's aspiring tribes, this renewal includes selective appropriation and active deployment of cultural icons and imagery to present an authentic representation of their tribal culture and lifestyle. In this regard, the present demands for ST status can be read as symptomatic of both a broader pattern within the Indian polity and the emergence of a broader global discourse on indigeneity—a conjuncture that Middleton has called the 'ethno-contemporary'.[42] Given the local and longer histories at hand, these demands also articulate the people of Darjeeling's perennial quest to assert their belonging to the nation, and to claim citizenship rights from the state.

Importantly, these movements for ST recognition have carried a strong cultural bent. Like the ethnic associations of 1920s and 1930s (discussed earlier), today's ethnic associations have focused on cultural preservation and social welfare for their constituents. But unlike their colonial predecessors, these ethnic associations are also explicitly political in their articulations of a discrete ethnic—or 'tribal'—identity. The plethora of demands raised by ethnic associations thus reflect a blend of civil society concerns (raised by earlier ethnic associations) and the more political society-oriented dispensations that have shaped the longstanding demands for subnational autonomy.

These struggles to become tribal are informed by national and global discourses of indigenous rights, social justice, and political empowerment. They can be characterized as what Partha Chatterjee calls the 'politics of the governed', which aims to 'give to the empirical form of a

[41] Nagel (1995: 948); also Karlsson (2013: 34).

[42] Middleton (2015: 19).

population the moral attributes of a community.'[43] On the ground, these movements for belonging, becoming, and rights are mediated through a complex prism of political influence and patronage. Minorities' engagement with the state here entails advancing cultural rights through a locally situated web of political relations, wherein local ethnic leaders must forge a variety of operative relations with local politicians, state officials, and government anthropologists. As Chatterjee's formulations of political society would also predict, these movements for ST status herald a particular form of entanglement between elites and subalterns.[44] Marking a convergence between the civil and political dimensions of the society that cuts across class lines, these tribal movements have produced a complex discourse of becoming and belonging. Importantly, these linkages have extended beyond the confines of individual groups to create a broader network of tribal becoming in the hills.

In these struggles, the existence of ethnic associations in the past is a valuable resource for groups to assert their separate and distinct identities. These historical antecedents enable present-day communities to reconstruct the historical and cultural genealogies required for ST recognition. Knowledge of anthropology and ethnology has also proven vital, as these communities look to showcase their authentic and pristine tribal identity before the state. As Middleton (2011) has illustrated, this has entailed elaborate ethnographic performances, put on by aspiring tribes for government anthropologists sent to Darjeeling to determine the tribalness of the groups in question (see Figure 7.3).

Viewed against the historical images of the earlier ethnic associations discussed in this chapter, these colourful displays—and demands—of tribal identity mark a new era of ethnopolitics. Seen over the *longue duree*, tribalism in Darjeeling marks a prolonged process of subjectification, which has transformed communities into the subjects of particular discourses of power.[45] These projects of ethnic renewal, in which the groups themselves pander to the expectations of anthropological surveys, ethnographic studies, affirmative action policies, and so on, while also internalizing official definitions of tribes as geographically isolated groups practising their own animistic faith, linguistic exclusivity, and cultural autonomy, suggest that we must understand ethnopolitics in

[43] Chatterjee (2004: 57); Middleton (2015: 32).

[44] Chatterjee (2004).

[45] Foucault (1978: 85).

twenty-first century Darjeeling in dialogue with postcolonial forms of governmentality. Subjectification here is not imposed by external powers as much as it is generated through the people's perennial quest to reconstitute their identities and thereby attain the rights and belonging they desire.

Ethnic groups in Darjeeling derive cues from various technologies of postcolonial governance and structure their demands around these systems. 'Subjection is nevertheless,' Judith Butler reminds us, 'a power assumed by the subject, an assumption that constitutes the instrument of that subject's becoming.'[46] Subjection in Darjeeling is inextricably related to both issues of belonging and becoming. It is by transforming themselves into tribal subjects within a legal and political discourse that ethnic groups assert their rights and demand entitlements from the state.

A Politics of Difference

The discourse of tribalism in Darjeeling has generated a space within which identity and alterity are produced simultaneously. This has engendered a complex politics of difference that continues to have unintended social consequences for the individual ethnic groups in question and for the Gorkha community writ large. Although Darjeeling's tribal politics have been shaped by the structures of affirmative action, these ethnopolitical movements also indicate a deeper desire to know about one's past culture and tradition. With an eye towards ethnic rights and renewal, communities seeking ST status have asserted their identities by reviving their historical genealogies and revitalizing traditional practices. Culture has assumed a central place in these symbolic reconstructions of community.[47] The cultural requisites of renewal and recognition pose moral demands upon constituent ethnic members to adopt the 'authentic practices' and thereby perform the 'authenticity' of the ethnic-self in everyday life.[48] Once again, the issue of nomenclature has become a key concern. Ethnic groups have adopted exclusive and 'authentic' labels such as 'Yakkhas' for Dewans, 'Koich' for Sunuwars, 'Tamu' for Gurungs, 'Khas' for (Bahuns, Chhetris, and Sanyasis), and such others. Here, the demands for recognition in Darjeeling have been structured around

46 Butler (1997: 11).

47 Cohen (1985).

48 See Briggs (1996); Middleton (2015), Shneiderman (2015).

the twin axes of authenticity and alterity, with these new labels at once announcing a return to a more authentic ethnic selfhood and clearly distinguishing ethnic groups from one another.

By purging their connection with other groups, ethnic associations have further tried to foster an exclusive tribal identity through various symbolic means like ritual actions. In their quest to affirm their tribal self, ethnic groups have endeavoured to detail and standardize their death rites, naming ceremonies, initiation rituals, practice of ancestor worship, and marriage ceremonies. Details of these rituals are duly communicated through pamphlets and periodicals published by the ethnic associations. In these struggles to redefine the ethnic self, novel elements are added to the cultural repertoire of groups, which are then put forth to substantiate their demands for tribal recognition. If these processes of cultural revitalization have bolstered communities' claims upon the state, the imperatives of alterity and authenticity have also created disagreements within ethnic associations, leading to the formation of splinter organizations.

The first evidence of such splits became evident within the ethnic associations of Tamangs in early 1990s. In the aftermath of the Mandal Commission, internal conflicts started to emerge when organizations like the All India Tamang Buddhist Association (AITBA) gave a call to renounce Hindu customs and stop celebrating festivals like Dasain and Tihar. However, some Tamangs opposed such a proposition. Along with religious practices, other aspects of culture became a source of disagreement among the Tamangs. The issue of OBC versus ST recognition aggravated tensions within the association, ultimately leading to the formation of a splinter group named the Tamang Buddhist Gedung in 1994. One Gedung leader recounted:

> Disagreement on many aspects of Tamang culture and tradition was brewing inside the organization from a long time, but the main cause for the formation of the splinter group within the Tamangs was the disagreement on the question of OBC status. The AITBA had rejected the OBC status while the Gedung had welcomed the proposal.[49]

As the tribal movements spread through the hills in the 1990s and early 2000s, the formation of such splinter groups became a regular feature of ethnic associations. For Gurungs, the divisions hinged upon questions

[49] Tamang Buddhist Gedung (2014), pers. comm. (interview), 13 April.

of religious ascription. As a senior Gurung leader explained to me: because Gurungs in Darjeeling followed different religions, the early organization of the Gurungs did not include religion as the primary marker of their identity; rather the concern was to unite Gurungs under a common banner. However, religion became central in defining Gurung identity especially after the formation of the Akhil Bharatiya Gurung (Tamu) Buddhist Sangathan in 1992. Leaders from this association categorically stated that all Gurungs must write their religion as Buddhists, otherwise they would be boycotted by the association. Highlighting the trajectory of Gurung associations in Darjeeling, in the course of the interview, Saran Gurung stated that an early Gurung association named Tamu Choj Dhi was established in Kurseong. A similar association of Gurungs named Tamu Choj Dhi, Tamu (Gurung) Kalyan Sangathan, was also established in Darjeeling in 1997. This association was started with a secular vision and with a stated objective to bring all Gurungs, irrespective of their religious beliefs, under a collective forum.

However, in ensuing years, the division between the secular and the Buddhist associations of Gurungs grew wider. In the wake of the government's rejection of the Gurung's bid for ST status, a more vocal body, named the Gurung (Tamu) Buddhists' Association, was formed. This organization claimed that the sole cause for the Gurungs' failure to be recognized as a ST was the influence of Hindu religion in their socio-religious practises. They argued that only by making Buddhism the sole religion of the Gurungs would they be able to obtain ST status. According to Saran Gurung, the division among Gurungs further escalated when the West Bengal Minority Development Corporation started providing scholarships for religious minorities. He stated thus:

> When such schemes were launched in the hills, the Gurung (Tamu) Buddhists Association claimed that they have started the scheme in the hills and to avail its benefits all Gurung should write their religion as Buddhists. However, one cannot sleep as a Hindu, Bonist or Christian Gurung at night and wake up as Buddhist in the morning.[50]

The Government of India's rejection of demands for ST status has sown discord within other ethnic associations as well. This is most evident in the case of the Khas, where splinter groups emerged after

[50] Saran Gurung (General Secretary of the Tamu Choj Dhi/Tamu (Gurung) Kalyan Sangathan) 2014, pers. comm. (interview), 28 February.

their proposal was rejected by the Register General of India. In 2014, an emergent faction within the Khas, named Khas Kalyankari Mahasangh (later renamed as Khas Janajati Mahasangh), directly connected their failure to the inclusion of Bahuns (*brahmins* upper caste within the Nepali community) in the category of Khas. The General Secretary of the Khas Janajati Mahasangh, explained:

> Khas are followers of Bon religion and not the Masto followers as defined by the leaders of Hitakri Sammelan as the main religion of the Khas. Similarly, Nepali language is regarded by many as originally a Khas language, but Khas have their own language and script called the '*Kharosta lipi*'. They also have their exclusive dance form known as 'Devra Naach'. Chhetri, Bhujel, Majhi, Jogi, Thakuri, Sanyasi, Malla, Sakya, belong to the Khas community, whereas Bahuns do not belong to the Khas community as they were immigrants from Indian Plains to the hills of Nepal.[51]

Like the cases outlined above, formation of splinter groups from within Mangar associations like Lafa Mangar Sangh, Akhil Bharatiya Mangar Sangh and Mangar Sangh Bharat extends this pattern in Darjeeling. Though attempts were made to ameliorate the difference between these associations, internal differences persisted and proliferated.[52] The formation of these splinter groups highlights the complex nature of ethnopolitics in the hills.

As a short history of ethnopolitics in Darjeeling indicates, the forms and functions of ethnic associations have undergone tremendous transformations since the early decades of the twentieth century. This owes to a range of external factors like the transition from colonial to postcolonial governance, and internal factors such as the formation of a vocal middle class and the changing contours of ethnic identities in

[51] Sachin Khas Chhetri (General Secretary of Khas Janajati Mahasangh Darjeeling) (2014), pers. comm. (interview), 4 March.

[52] A meeting was called to resolve the difference between the Akhil Bharatiya Mangar Sangh, Darjeeling Mangar Samaj and Mangar Lafa Sangh, Kurseong on 20 June 2005 at GDNS Conference Hall. In the meeting it was decided to sort out their differences and work unitedly for a common cause. Source: Minutes of the meeting collected from Bhanu Thapa, General Secretary, ABMS on 16 February 2014, Kalimpong.

the hills. Evolving in dialogue with these conditions, ethnicity and identity prove to be dynamic and fluid categories, which are constantly shaped and reshaped by various sociopolitical imperatives, desires, and opportunities. The spectrum of demands raised by the variously configured communities of Darjeeling raise important questions regarding the historical interchanges between ethnopolitics and specific technologies of governance, which have been reified and re-deployed as resources for popular struggles. In the current scenario, the inheritance and reworking of colonial categories such as 'tribe' has generated multiple possibilities and contestations. Amid varying claims of authentic heritage, culture, and religion, ethnic associations have consequently become a heterogeneous space for the negotiation of identity.

Since the early years of the twentieth century, ethnic identities and their attendant associations have played a crucial part in the social and political transformation of hill society. Ethnic associations raised crucial civil society-oriented concerns like the preservation of cultural heritage and the social welfare of citizens. In the wake of wider political transformations, these civil society concerns were absorbed into large-scale political mobilizations for regional autonomy. During these pan-ethnic mobilizations, exclusive ethnic associations faced serious setbacks and dwindled in time, only to re-emerge later in new forms. The present articulations of ethnic identities and demands for recognition as STs illustrate how older concerns for ethnic preservation and a quest to belong are being restructured and redeployed within the ambit of cultural rights and constitutional provisions.

The politics of identity in Darjeeling thereby emerges at the convergence-point of civil and political society. This interface between civil and political concerns represents the changing contours of ethnopolitics in the hills and brings into relief the perennial quest to become and belong to the nation-state. By subjecting themselves to political influences and structuring their demands around constitutional provisions, ethnic associations try to recast identities and avail the benefits that incur to ethnic minorities in India. The present demands for recognition as STs represents a new discourse of identity politics in which issues of legality and citizenship rights are redefined at times within, and, at other times beyond, broader demands for regional autonomy. We see in these changing forms the ways in which the possibilities and constraints of postcolonial belonging and becoming are interpreted, negotiated, and articulated by a host of actors in Darjeeling.

8 *The Promise of Class Analysis in Understanding Nepali National Identity in Darjeeling*

An Engagement with Kumar Pradhan's Work and Thought

Swatahsiddha Sarkar and Babika Khawas*

The idea of Nepalis outside Nepal has become a subject of burgeoning interest of social science research, pursued by a cross section of scholars from India and

* This chapter owes much to the rigorous review that it underwent. While responding to the critical comments and constructive observations made by the editors at the initial stage, and later by the anonymous reviewers of the Oxford University Press we believe our work improved substantially. We are grateful to them. We would also like to thank Pratyoush Onta and Yogesh Raj of

abroad.[1] Yet the class question related to Nepali national identity has not been discussed adequately. It is primarily in the writings of the late Kumar Pradhan, a historian from Darjeeling, that the class question of Nepali national identity formation has received some attention. Drawing upon Pradhan's oeuvre, the present chapter seeks to illuminate the class question in relation to Indian Nepali national-identity formation. However, the objective of this chapter is not merely to celebrate Pradhan's engagement with class analysis in his four major publications in both Nepali and English, but also to critically engage—and reinvigorate—his thoughts in the context of the Nepali diaspora.[2] Specifically, the chapter will evaluate how Pradhan theoretically conceives of the question of class and attempts to apply class analysis in understanding Nepali national identity formation in the context of the Darjeeling hills. In short, we hope to show why and how Pradhan and his works, which are both inspiring and mystifying, should be considered seriously as a key thinker and texts in Darjeeling Studies.

Pradhan has explored both local and regional social history in the context of the Eastern Himalayas in general, and Darjeeling in particular. Starting his academic journey through his PhD dissertation—that yielded his magnum opus, *The Gorkha Conquests*[3]—his interest in such explorations continued as he worked editing newspapers in Nepali (first with *Sunchari* from 1996 to 2008, and then with *Himalaya Darpan* from

---

Martin Chautari, Nepal, for their insights and helpful comments shared on an earlier version of a larger attempt made on Kumar Pradhan. On a personal note we are obliged to Mrs Purnima Pradhan, Gahendra Pradhan, and Manasa Pradhan (wife, son, and daughter of late Kumar Pradhan) for sharing their time and entertaining our repeated visits to their residence pleasantly. This chapter is a tribute to the scholarship of late Kumar Pradhan, which we offer to a larger readership.

[1] Prominent among those—several are also contributors to this volume—who made substantive contribution in the emerging field of Darjeeling Studies are Subba (1992); Subba and Sinha (2016); Hutt (1997); Chalmers (2004); Booth (2011); Chettri (2013); Shneiderman (2015); Middleton (2015); and Sharma (2016b).

[2] The four major publications of Kumar Pradhan considered in the present chapter are: *Pahilo Pahar* (1982), *Agam Singh Giri ko Kabita Ma Jatiya Bhabna* (2005/1982), *Gorkha Conquests* (1991), and *Darjeeling Ma Nepali Jati Ra Janajatiya Chinari Ka Naya Udaan Haru* (2005). For a detailed list of Pradhan's major publications, see Sarkar (2014).

[3] Pradhan (1991).

2008 until his death in 2013). Doing full justice to Pradhan's contributions demands a full-length study, which is not possible in the present chapter. Rather, we situate Pradhan's contributions as the obligatory starting point for any contemporary discussion of Nepali national identity formation in India. The general transformation and revitalization of community history in Darjeeling over the past century may be read as a dialogue with Pradhan.[4] Pradhan's *Pahilo Pahar*[5] and *Darjeeling Ma Nepali Jati …*[6] effectively set the agenda for the present review. In the following section, we seek to bring out the major analytical threads contained in Pradhan's texts.

Distinctiveness of the Nepalis in Darjeeling

Pradhan's treatment of the history of national-identity formation among the Nepalis of Darjeeling resonates with his earlier intervention surrounding the grave question of conquest vis-à-vis nation building in the history of eastern Nepal. In *Pahilo Pahar* he elaborates three distinctive connotations of the term *Nepali*. First, *Nepali* implies a language. Second, the term implies a political denotation indicating those who speak Nepali language and are citizens of Nepal by origin. Third, he uses *Nepali* as a cultural symbol of a distinctive nation whose members are not confined by the political boundaries of the country called Nepal.[7] The use of the term *Nepali* in all of his texts refers to this latter cultural connotation: an identity formation that might be considered a 'nation', but that transcends the borders of any single state. He further argues that the political subtext of the term *Nepali* refers to identity by citizenship of the subject population of Nepal, while the cultural import of the term *Nepali* refers to a linguistically unified community not constrained by the political boundaries of any nation-state. We argue that Pradhan's contribution can be appreciated properly only when one is ready to accept the term *Nepali* as a culturally articulated, rather than as a politically oriented phenomenon. Ultimately, Pradhan proposes a critique that interrogates the collapsing of nation, state and society or culture into one.

[4] See also N. Chettri, this volume, for a discussion of community history and its relevance for revitalization projects.

[5] Pradhan (1982).

[6] Pradhan (2005 [1982]).

[7] Pradhan (1982: 4).

Pradhan's contributions provide clues towards how to develop such a critical reading regarding Darjeeling's social history on the one hand, and social imagining of community solidarity on the other. Moreover, a cursory look at Pradhan's *Darjeeling Ma Nepali Jati …*[8] reveals that he was reluctant to label the Nepali nationality question in India as an ethnic issue. He considered the concept of an 'ethnic group' to be closer to the Nepali term *janajati*, which refers to different community identities like Kirat, Tamang, Newar, Sunuwar, and so on. The appropriation of these different janajati, or ethnic groups, into a Nepali national identity formation in Darjeeling, was made on a cultural and linguistic plane rather than on a political one. Pradhan begins his analysis by emphasizing that Nepali nationalism in Nepal grew out of a pluralist social fabric, whereas by contrast, syncretic unity served as the basis of forging the Nepali nation in Darjeeling. Nation formation in Nepal has undergone a process that he called *Kamila Prakriya* (a process in which people forage in a group much like ants, or *kamila*) while *Mauri Prakriya* (swarming of bees, or *mauri*) was the actual process that explains Nepali national identity formation in Darjeeling.[9]

By emphasizing the *Mauri Prakriya* model of identity formation in Darjeeling, it may seem that Pradhan has hinted at the diasporic foundation of the Nepali nation in India. Michael Hutt has also labelled Pradhan a historian, who contributed an understanding of Nepali ethnicity in the so-called Nepali diaspora.[10] However, it needs to be qualified as to whether Pradhan himself considered the Nepali nation in India a diasporic nation. This is indeed a significant issue about which others have commented at length.[11] Pradhan's position was not very different from others who denied the diasporic leaning for the Indian–Nepalis, although it was he who perhaps, for the first time, made a critical estimation of what such labelling meant for the Indian–Nepalis in the essay titled *Agam Singh Giriko Kavitama Jatiya Bhavana*.[12] In that essay, Pradhan criticizes not only the efforts of the Indian national leaders to equate the Indian–Nepalis with citizens of Nepal, but also those Nepali leaders who thought that a reference to Nepal would be worthwhile to build up national consciousness among the Indian–Nepalis.

[8] Pradhan (2005 [1982]).

[9] Pradhan (2005 [1982]: 3).

[10] Hutt (1997: 102).

[11] Subba (2008); Subba and Sinha (2016); Gellner (2013).

[12] Pradhan (2005 [1982]).

Hence he thought that the use and popularity of the term *pravasi* (non-resident) would unnecessarily complicate the identity building process of the Indian–Nepalis.[13] This is perhaps why he cautions us about the indiscriminate use of such terms like nation, nationality, and nationalism the way they occur in the Western academia. It is our contention that the thoughts and works of Pradhan elicit a thorough critique of the collapse of the nation (cultural) and state (political)—an understanding that bears resonance with arguments of Prasenjit Duara,[14] Andreas Wimmer, and Nina Glick Schiller.[15] In fact, the issue of a Nepali nation in India itself questions, if not nullifies, the monolingual foundation of the nation-state project. This again, helps us understand why it was obvious for Pradhan to denounce any diasporic leaning associated with the Indian–Nepalis even though the journey to be a recognized nationality within India was mooted through the *Mauri Prakriya* model.

Proletarian Basis of Nepali Nation

After outlining the meaning and connotation of the term *Nepali* in the Darjeeling context, Pradhan shifts his analysis towards locating the sources of the nationality question, with special reference to Darjeeling. While explaining this phenomenon, Pradhan gives us an analytical clue by proposing that the principal causal factor that has augmented the feeling of national unity among the heterogeneous communities of the hills is the notion of class. He considers language the 'second' significant causal factor for explaining the Nepali nationality question in Darjeeling. While locating the production of national consciousness in late nineteenth century Darjeeling, Pradhan held the view that almost all Nepalis settled in the hills were proletariats (*sarvahara varga*) as most of them were from working class backgrounds. Consequently, intra-community class exploitation and coercion had hardly taken shape among the Nepalis. In the late nineteenth century, Nepali society in Darjeeling did not experience in its ranks a significant emergence of capitalists or landed gentries (*jamindar*); nevertheless a lower middle class was germinating. According to Pradhan, the ideas of a ruling versus ruled class did not take shape within Nepali society in the hills, essentially because the alien colonial rulers in Darjeeling reigned over both of them. The British were

13 Pradhan (2005 [1982]: 126–7).

14 Duara (1995).

15 Wimmer and Schiller (2002).

the owners of everything including the tea gardens. They occupied all of the top-ranking positions. Even the subordinate positions in government and non-government offices were filled by non-Nepali plainsmen, with Biharis and Rajasthanis dominating the petty business sector of the hills (for example carpentry, tailoring, shoe making, and so on). The Nepalis of Darjeeling were under the vicissitudes of economic exploitation, as they could only afford to sell their labour power.[16]

Nation Formation without a Middle Class

Pradhan was aware that the middle class had been of utmost significance elsewhere in the world, where processes of nation formation took place in moments of rapid social transformation wherein older (feudal) traditions ceased to fulfil the task for which they were designed.[17] He also points out how the interpretations of Indian nationalism by Marxist historians[18] were informed by such arguments. And indeed, Pradhan held the view that the histories of social change and transformation vis-à-vis nation formation have been most convincingly interpreted by Marxism. But Pradhan maintained that the blind application of Marxist interpretation cannot yield any true-to-life historical analysis. This is precisely why he insisted that the national identity formation of Nepalis in Darjeeling could not be considered the direct product of feudalism or capitalism. The earlier generations of Nepalis were exposed to feudal exploitation in Nepal, and upon their arrival in Darjeeling they had to face colonial capitalist exploitation.[19] Nevertheless it would be naïve to conclude that the situation approximated the state of affairs outlined by Marxist historians. In Darjeeling the nature and degree of exploitation was different from Nepal, and there was hardly any possibility of running away from this exploitation. There were *sipahi* (corps) and *mazdoors* (wage earners) in the barracks and towns, peasants in the villages, and plantation workers in cinchona and tea gardens, but there were no

[16] Pradhan (2005 [1982]: 12).

[17] Pradhan (2005 [1982]: 113).

[18] Variously termed as *bhadralok, literati, or intelligentsia* the role of middle class has often been described by Marxist historians as the foundation of the Indian national movement. Some of the most notable works of this genre were produced by Chandra (2002 [1993]; Desai (1991 [1948]); Panikkar (2001 [1995]); Sarkar (1973).

[19] Also described by Middleton in this volume.

indigenous capitalists, and even the rise of the middle class in the local hill society was minimal. The origins of what Pradhan calls the Nepali national identity in Darjeeling necessarily, then, lay elsewhere. Per his rendering, nineteenth-century Nepali society in Darjeeling became a largely working class or a proletarian society. They did not have land rights or ownership in trade, business, or other enterprises. They only had the opportunity to be sold as cheap labour. Given these economic circumstances, it is absurd to maintain that the nationality questions of the Nepalis in Darjeeling were instigated by the interests of capitalists or by the aspirations of the middle class.[20]

Cultural Appropriation of the Class Question

Pradhan hints at a significant question regarding whether social oppression is as important as class exploitation in understanding Darjeeling's history. Specifically, he questions the ways in which the idea of a Nepali nation evolved through the transposition of class polarization into community aspirations. This becomes evident in his analysis when he points out that:

> Those who had left Nepal encountering the feudal atrocities, soon realized that feudal exploitation of Nepal was usurped by the forces of British colonial exploitation in Darjeeling and became aware of the very fact that *Ramrajya*[21] did not prevail in the then Darjeeling. Nationality question of the Nepalis in Darjeeling was not the brainchild of the rising middle class nor did it even reflect the interests of the capitalist class as the Nepali society of Darjeeling was then entirely composed of *sipahis* (corps), labourers, agriculturalists, and plantation (tea, cinchona) workers.[22]

Unlike in Nepal, he maintains that the origin and evolution of the Nepali national identity formation in Darjeeling was not the result of a state unification process; rather this feeling of national consciousness was encouraged by the common interest of working class Nepalis.

However, Pradhan's notion of class was more cultural than economic. Renouncing the concept of class as a purely economic category, much

[20] Pradhan (2005 [1982]: 118–20).

[21] *Ramrajya*'s literal meaning would be the reign of lord Rama from the epic Ramayana, an expression common in Nepali that alludes to the paternalistic control of the people or subjects by a benevolent ruler.

[22] Pradhan (2004: 11).

like E.P. Thompson,[23] Pradhan viewed class in relational terms and argues that, 'the national consciousness of the Indian–Nepalis emerged on the pretext of a subjective feeling of commonality in the life experiences of the exploited and subjugated classes.'[24] It is also remarkable to note that, in Pradhan's analysis, the white collar workers, small traders, and petty businessmen were not absorbed into the proletariat—as the Marxists would presume—rather they created a distinctive class in and of themselves, separate from the colonial ruling class. This constitutes the crux of Pradhan's analytical synthesis. How a class divided society became culturally polarized along the lines of Nepali versus non-Nepali identity in Darjeeling—even amongst the members sharing similar class positions (when viewed in terms of their structural relationship with the forces of production)—is indeed an issue of theoretical concern. In order to explain how community solidarity rather than class polarization unfolded within the settled Nepalis of Darjeeling, Pradhan extends his thesis beyond a Marxist approach to class and class analysis. This led him to investigate how, in the historical progression of hill society, these relations of exploitation and domination became fertile ground upon which an 'us' versus 'them' division between the Nepalis and the plainsmen grew—even though none of the former owned the means of production. According to Pradhan, the notion of 'us' incorporated not only an economic standing, but also a socio-cultural connotation. Apart from the British, educated clerks and conformist Hindus from the plains considered the *matwali*s—or alcohol drinkers (as the Nepalis were commonly referred to for their drinking habit)—to be *mlechha*s (barbarians), and the vertical difference between Nepalis and plainsmen based on caste, religion, culture, and language differentials continued to increase. Educated *babus* (Bengali gentlemen) and *kaiya*s (moneylenders from the plains) continued to consider the labouring Nepalis derogatorily as 'coolies'. Class experience was expressed more in the ideas, traditions, language, and customs of the people who were exposed to the vicissitudes of colonial modernity (that arrived through the rapid spread of education, communication, science and technology, white-collar professions, urbanization, and the market) and class at the same time. Combining economic and cultural concerns, class analysis for Pradhan thereby emerged as a means of examining and understanding

[23] Thompson (1991 [1963]).
[24] Pradhan (2005 [1982]: 11–12).

the experience of what it meant to be a hill people—or let us say, a Nepali people, in Darjeeling's history.

Social Class, Power, and Mobility Closure: Interlocking of Class and Ethnicity

Surprisingly there is much similarity in the theoretical position Pradhan held and the position maintained by social class analysts.[25] On many counts Pradhan's analysis echoes Marshall's, who holds the view that the objectivity of class consists not of the criteria that distinguish it, but of the social relations that it produces, with its subjectivity being the basic need for mutually conscious recognition.[26] In this sense, Pradhan's emphasis on the class basis of the Nepali nation fundamentally implies the importance of power relations. We argue that much like Parkin, who developed a neo-Weberian interpretation of class,[27] Pradhan seems to reason that class relations arise out of market capacities, and that class relations were in fact maintained by a process that Parkin calls 'mobility closure'. Reading between the lines in Pradhan's work leads us to claim that his arguments could be framed in line with the neo-Weberian formulations of class. Pradhan's insistence that community consciousness—rather than class consciousness—found a stronghold in the social history of Darjeeling implies a theoretical proposition. We explore this theoretical position by arguing that the greater the mobility closure (that is the less individual mobility or fewer chances for the individual to acquire the opportunities available in the local resource niche) between groups with different market capacities, the more readily social class will assume a communitarian cleavage. Hutt has also noted such courses of mobility closure in the economic domain of Darjeeling.[28] Ultimately, mobility restrictions make class-community cohesion more probable. It is worth noting that in Pradhan's analysis, the class-community nexus of the Indian Nepalis that occurred through a societal process of mobility

[25] Social class analysis flourished through the writings of a host of American social scientists like T. H. Marshall (1934), Milton M. Gordon (1949), Llewellyn Gross (1949), J. H. Goldthorpe (1987) who extended Marx's class analysis with a Weberian tint and led it towards the direction of a more inclusive category of what they called 'social class'.

[26] Marshall (1934: 61).

[27] Parkin (1972; 1979).

[28] Hutt (1997: 119).

closure projected inter-class differentiations as a species of power relations, while intra-class differentiations were usurped by community solidarity. This resonates with what Parkin labels 'usurpationary closure', by which he meant 'collective attempts by the excluded to win a greater share of resources'.[29] Much like the social class theorists, the essence of class for Pradhan lies not in the qualities or the possessions that cause the treatment, but in the ways a man is treated by his fellows and how he treats them in return. In this way Pradhan shows how inter-class differentiation provided leeway to the 'us' versus 'them' differential necessary for nation formation, which perhaps prevented intra-class differentiation from assuming greater significance than national unification.

This approach helps us understand the theoretical problem that Pradhan unpacks rather convincingly: the overlap between class and cultural boundaries. Returning to the central question once again, how does this class and cultural overlap help explain the class basis of the Nepali nation in Darjeeling? Let us review. Pared down, how did the class interests of the manual labourers from Nepali janajati[30] backgrounds vis-à-vis the babus and other plainsmen (the majority of whom fell under the petty–bourgeois category) transpire in ethnic 'us' versus 'them' terms and further the sentiments of a nation? In fact, Pradhan's emphasis on the 'us' versus 'them' syndrome implies the existence of a 'cultural division of labour' situation,[31] in which the people from Nepal were placed grossly in the working-class category. They were looked down upon by the plainsmen in general and the Bengali babus in particular, who shared a different (metropolitan) culture and occupied all available high status occupations. This helped create a commonality of interest amongst a culturally diverse mass relegated to the bottom of the stratification system. The roots of national identity mobilization among

[29] Parkin (1979: 45).

[30] It would be interesting to note that his preference for the term *janajati* was more prominent in his later writing (2005) however, in earlier writings [*Gorkha Conquest* (1991), *A History of Nepali Literature* (1984)] he mostly used the term 'Mongoloid' and at places *Kirata* to denote what he later terms *janajati*.

[31] The notion of cultural division of labour as used here follows Michael Hechter (1978). By 'cultural division of labour', Hechter meant a system of stratification where objective cultural distinctions are superimposed upon class lines. High status occupations tend to be reserved for those who share metropolitan cultures, while those who belong to indigenous cultures cluster at the bottom of the stratification system.

the people of varied caste and community backgrounds from Nepal was viewed by Pradhan as an outgrowth of the persistent economic segregation of a community from the 'other', and the associated cultural expressions of such materially rewarding positions enjoyed differentially by the two sets of communities. This was how class and cultural questions overlapped. This overlapping paved the way for the growth of a nation as a higher order form of cultural integration for a host of culturally and linguistically divergent communities, irrespective of the fact that some among them did actually emerge as petty bourgeois elements. One can, of course, disagree with Pradhan's theoretical position, but perhaps not with his convincing argument that helps us appreciate the interlocking of class and ethnicity questions, without which the emergent Nepali identity would have remained fragmentary.

A Critique of Pradhan's Propositions

Taken together, the above propositions form the crux of Pradhan's thesis that mark a significant reworking of the problematic of class formation among Nepalis in India. However, Pradhan's texts provide a less systematic alternative theory of class formation than a set of admonitions whose value is largely determined by their place in a specific polemic. Pradhan urges us to avoid sterile formalisms and to be ever-aware that there could be contradictions between classes but not necessarily amongst members of the same class. In fact, Pradhan implicitly assumes the essential correctness of the theory of class that he seems to be denying. Pradhan's conceptual categories are so formed upon his polemical opponent, that his attempt to transcend classical Marxism is far from satisfactory. He is unhesitant in using the term sarvahara varga (proletariat) rather loosely to imply the plantation (tea and cinchona) workers, agriculturalists, labourers, and even the sipahis (corps). Far from being a concept, 'proletariat' in Pradhan's treatment appears more as a denotative term. That is why a concern for the proletariat as an historic force, or for that matter, the stages in the development of the proletariat into a class—cardinal questions for Marxist class analysis—are difficult to trace in Pradhan's otherwise excellent account. In fact, Pradhan's analysis of the class question of Nepali national identity in Darjeeling is not restricted to the quintessential Marxian notion of class. Treating the proletariat more as a denotative term rather than as the historic role player in the Marxian sense, Pradhan actually hints at the inflections of the term 'proletariat' in the non-industrial settings.

Furthermore, his insistence that Darjeeling's Nepali society was not internally class divided seems to be an overstated assessment. At least since the early twentieth century, if not earlier, traces of well-off Nepalis are available in Darjeeling's history.[32] Some others have even traced aristocratic elements represented by the landholding class and the retired army and police officials.[33] In fact, to accept at face value Pradhan's emphasis on the absence of internal class differentiation among the Nepalis of Darjeeling would be a debilitating move for further analysis—particularly if we wish to understand the emergence of palpable class differences in the twentieth century Darjeeling hills.

The history of Darjeeling suggests that theoretical claims and actual practice can be at great variance, as traced through the contradictions among the Nepalis whom Pradhan called sarvahara varga. The mechanisms of contradictions are not found only at the level of two extremes—the ruling class and the ruled—but also among the several referents of Darjeeling's diverse population, most importantly ethnicity and gender. Not all inner contradictions of the sarvahara varga of Darjeeling manifested in the form of exploitation of one group by another—except in the context of gender relations—but they were definitely divided in shared spaces of the public domain. The socio-economic experiences of sipahis, *kanyas/kaiyas* (traders) and even *sardars* (labour agents) differed more widely than the experiences of wage earners, coolies (plantation labourers) or *bhariyas* (porters). Their interests cannot be reduced to their class positions. Although intra-class economic exploitation was not that prominent in the social relations of Darjeeling in those days, the growing social and cultural hiatus that historically defined much of their intra-community relationships was inescapable. Likewise, women workers in the plantations shared an exploitative relation with the owners of the means of production who used their labour, as well as the labour of their male counterparts. However, for women, the exploitation doubled in the domestic sphere, where they were also exploited by men.[34]

Pradhan viewed class through its primary contradictions that arise in terms of ownership of the means of production, and the relations that they bestow. Primary contradictions of ownership regarding the means of production shed light on relations of exploitation based on wages or earning power. However, exploitation arising out of control relations in

[32] Biswas and Roy (2003: 128–9); Sarkar (2010).

[33] Dasgupta (1999: 56–7).

[34] See also Sen this volume; Sharma this volume and (2014).

the means of production (management and employees) often crosscuts class trajectories in gender terms. Similarly, control over the labour process (closure of professional occupations, salaried positions, and wage earning categories) may manifest in cultural or ethnic terms. Pradhan manages to hint at these possibilities, but fails to address the impact of gender in solidifying the existing divide between men and women. The far-flung preponderance of gendered forms of labour exploitation in the plantations generated a class of labouring women whose exploitation and toil weighed much more than their male counterparts', even though they constituted what Pradhan called sarvahara varga.

It is curious to note that though Pradhan makes frequent use of terms such as sarvahara varga, *vargiya swartha* (class interest), *sramajibi* (working class), *samanti byavastha ko soshan* (feudal exploitation), and *punjibadi vargiya swartha* (capitalist class interest), in none of his texts does he spell out the divisions in the agrarian social structure of the Darjeeling hills. Unlike plantations where the radical separation between capital and labour has been quite marked, the agrarian class structure in the hills has been informed by structures of kinship, locality (in the sense of neighbourhood),[35] and labour exchange, giving rise to a system of inequality and exploitation on the one hand, and mutual respect and cooperation on the other. Studies have shown that it is extremely difficult to break the categories of native agrarians of the Darjeeling hills—*mandal* (village headman), *pattadar* (landlord), *adhiar* (share cropper), and agricultural labourers of various sorts such as *pakhure*, *khetala* or *gothala*—into clear-cut class groups.[36] Within this close-knit network of agrarian relationships, the entanglement of class, culture, and community questions could have unleashed a new analytical frame of reference for understanding Nepali national identity from the vantage point of agrarian social formations. This is unfortunately missing in Pradhan's scholarly efforts.

Another crucial facet, which Pradhan does not adequately account for in his class analysis of Nepali society in Darjeeling, is the structure of caste and its elements of inequality. The old structures of caste prevalent in Nepal encountered a period of transformation in the context of Darjeeling, a view held by Pradhan himself. However, this transformation cannot be regarded as a complete project because caste is still a social reality—if not a pervasive problem—for the Nepalis of

[35] See also Drew and Rai in this volume.

[36] Subba (1985, 1986); Sarkar (2010).

Darjeeling. Pradhan considered dress, weaponry, or even *topi* (the typical Nepali cap) as significant national insignias, yet he negated—or at least significantly downplayed—the significance of caste or religion as important factors influencing the identity formation process in Darjeeling in the same way as language or class. He makes it amply clear that he is not convinced by the argument that the caste system has significantly influenced the Nepali national identity formation process in Darjeeling. Other than the Newars, all communities referred to as *matwalis* lacked an elaborate system of caste. The absence of upper caste hegemony, the predominant numerical presence of the matwalis, the instances of inter-caste and intra-community marriages, and the emergence of religious reform movements (like *Josmani*[37] and the *Arya Samaj*[38] in particular) in Darjeeling during the latter half of the nineteenth century, all contributed to the formation of a social system which was relatively free from the strict observance of caste principles. Pradhan's overemphasis on the fact that religious cults have thwarted the growth of the caste system needs to be attended critically. The reformatory zeal of these perspectives—Christianity on the one hand and the Hindu reformatory sects like Josmani and Arya Samaj on the other—and their subsequent spread in Darjeeling were limited mostly in their strategies of conversion. On the whole, the social system of Darjeeling contained multiple faiths but none at the cost of Hinduism or the caste system. It is our argument that by narrating the significance of multiple religious creeds, Pradhan is actually hinting at the difference at the level of social system

[37] Pradhan traces out the origin of the *Josmani* cult sometime in the mid-eighteenth century as most of the early generation rebel poets (like Dhirjedil Das, Sasidhar) were contemporaries of Prithvinarayan Shah. The basis of *Josmani* thought involves a higher philosophy of devotion to *nirguna*—the attributeless God. Much like Christianity it was an iconoclastic creed that was against casteism, commercialization of spiritual knowledge, and many other vices of Brahmanical Hinduism, see Pradhan (1991: 171). The spread of the *Josmani* creed in Darjeeling started with the coming of Saint Jnandil Das, who took his birth in a Upadhyay Brahman family of Fikkal village located in Ilam district in eastern Nepal in 1878 v.s. (Sharma 2020 v.s.: 60).

[38] Much like the *Josmani* creed, the activities of the Arya Samaj, the well-known Hindu reform movement initiated by Swami Dayanand Saraswati in 1875 in India, also flourished in Darjeeling during the end of nineteenth century. Dilusingh Rai—Darjeeling's first Arya Samajist—joined the Arya Samaj at its inception at Darjeeling in the year 1882 (Pradhan 1984: 49). It would also be significant to note that Pradhan himself belonged to an Arya Samajist family.

between Nepal and Darjeeling. He noted the significance of caste in a way to show how it had a different formulation, and how it did not influence the formation of Nepali national identity in Darjeeling as strongly as other factors like class and language. In fact, attention to these lapses in Pradhan's study may enrich the class analysis of the Nepali identity issue in postcolonial times.

All said and done, the reference to class in Pradhan's interpretation of Nepali national identity formation may be considered as a statement of methodology and a programme of research. This seems to be a justified statement when we weigh up his contribution in terms of concepts, theoretical presumptions, and propositions. We argue that throughout his writings on the issue, Pradhan elaborates class in tandem with its 'nominalist' and 'realist' versions.[39] He begins with the 'nominalist' version of class and attempts to identify different classes in correspondence to a set of facts but not to any specific phenomenon of reality. Class in this sense became useful to him as a methodological tool for classifying different categories of the population according to certain criteria, thereby giving his historical account theoretical precision. Such a nominalist view of class even led him to ignore the historicity of actually existing intra-class differentiations in hill society. While situating the 'realist' conception of class in the history of Nepali national identity formation, he viewed class as a historical phenomenon that arises through social relationships, and not merely as a structure or a statistical aggregate. Enactment of such relationships involved experiences of living, acting, and suffering. Theoretical discussions of national identity formation, in the final analysis, cannot remain purely diachronic and experiential. Nor can national identity formation can be solely attributable to the structural dynamics of early industrial capitalism. Pradhan's significance in this regard lies in his historical journey with the nominalist and realist notions of class, which have both illuminated and mystified his position on Nepali nation formation in Darjeeling.

Situating Pradhan in His Life and Time

A thinker's scholarship needs to be judged in light of the corresponding historical conditions in which s/he grew up, matured, and contributed. Our reading reveals that Pradhan sought to emphasize the gap between

[39] The notions of nominalist and realist class analysis are drawn from Schumpeter. For details vide, Schumpeter (1951: 105).

an essentially knowable past and an imposed, often arbitrarily constructed representation of the present (as evidenced in various contemporaneous writings and public statements that attempted to vilify Indian–Nepalis as people of Nepal).[40] Non-Nepali writing on Darjeeling during his time[41] tends to ignore the character of this gap. In contrast, Pradhan's contributions emerge as commentaries on the facts and empirical traces of Darjeeling Nepalis' distinctiveness as an Indian community. His commentaries counter the pejorative popular projections wherein Nepalis are understood merely as a community of Nepal with little or no anchor in India. It is vital to understand Pradhan in these contexts.

For Pradhan and scores of others across Darjeeling, these matters were intensely personal. During all phases of history, Nepalis came from the Himalayan region now recognized as the modern nation-state of Nepal. Pradhan's father Maniklal's arrival in Darjeeling in the late 1920s seems to have given Pradhan a stronger sense of being Indian, since his family's history in India dates back to before the Indian nation-state was formed. This is reflected in his various scholarly and popular writings (some of which we discussed in the present chapter), as well as in his political activism relating to the language movement and his moderate and democratic stand on the issue of a Gorkha homeland within India. Pradhan was a patron of the local Pranta Parishad party and later politically affiliated himself to the Indian National Congress.[42] Clearly, Pradhan's

[40] See, for example, books like *Gorkhaland Movement: A Clandestine Invasion* (2009) by D.P. Kar, where he, the president of *Janachetana*, a major social activist group, maintains the claim that there has been a huge penetration ('invasion') of Nepali immigrants from Nepal who now are strengthening the demand for an ethnic homeland. Besides other things, this book sets forth a particular agenda to tarnish the image of the Indian–Nepalis as citizens of Nepal and therefore rule out the movement of Gorkha identity as a non-issue, or make it an issue of 'illegal migrants' who clandestinely invaded Indian territory.

[41] Studies on Darjeeling by Misra (1986), Chakrabarty (1988), Dasgupta (1988), and Datta (1991) to name a few, are some such works which were contemporary to Pradhan's own contributions.

[42] As was confirmed in a personal interview with Mrs. Purnima Pradhan (wife of late Kumar Pradhan), Pradhan keenly supported the idea of a Gorkha homeland in India. However, he vehemently opposed the violent path to achieving it. He was invited many times to join the GNLF, but he always denied such offers and instead maintained his image as a fierce critic of Subash Ghishingh, the chief architect of the violent Gorkhaland Movement in the 1980s. In the late 1990s, after he moved to Siliguri to run *Sunchari Samachar* (a Nepali news daily),

scholarship did not emerge in a vacuum, or without influence from his personal experiences, political concerns, and ideological inclinations. This paradox—which we prefer to label as politics in a certain sense—is clear in Pradhan's attempts to write a number of school level history text books during the 1970s—a period when vernacular text books in social sciences for Nepali schoolchildren of Darjeeling were not available.[43] Pradhan's political tilt is made clear by his incessant attempts to trace out Nepali settlements in many quarters of Darjeeling and Sikkim. In these books, he draws the readers' attention to early traces of Nepalis in places like *Magarjung* or *Nagri* at Darjeeling. He also emphasizes the Limbu matrimonial links of the Sikkimese kings and the presence of the Magars in Sikkim's history during the seventeenth and eighteenth centuries.[44] Moreover, he himself claimed that the history he wrote about Darjeeling beginning in the 1970s[45] —a period when he affiliated himself with Pranta Parishad and later to the Indian National Congress—is an attempt to make known the fact that Darjeeling–Nepalis are Indian by birth and by deed. Pradhan was trying to emphasize Darjeeling–Nepalis' role in building up the society, economy, and polity of the emerging hill station—and how they, in the process, acquired their own distinctiveness from their ethnic counterparts in Nepal. Pradhan's emphasis on

---

bombing attempts were made to destroy his newspaper office at Pradhan Nagar. The attacks were allegedly carried out by GNLF miscreants because *Sunchari Samachar* had emerged as the popular mouthpiece against Ghisingh's misrule through the DGHC that time. Purnima Pradhan also added that her husband did participate in the public rallies that took place in Darjeeling in the late 1970s in opposition to the discriminatory statement made against Indian–Nepalis by the then PM Morarji Desai. (Interview conducted by authors on 12 May 2017.)

[43] His first textbook of history for Class IX was published in 1974, and thereafter school level history textbooks in Nepali were published for Classes VI to X. Reprints and new editions of these textbooks were regularly published until 2008. In this way, Pradhan pioneered a movement to address the need for school-level history textbooks in Nepali. At the same time, by writing Indian history in Nepali, he actually accelerated the process of Indianizing Nepali at a time when the Nepali language movement for (Indian) constitutional recognition was emerging.

[44] Pradhan (1982).

[45] He began writing about Darjeeling's history in the form of a paper titled 'Darjeelingko Nepali Jati: Euta Aitihasik Adhyan' (Nepali Nation in Darjeeling: A Historical Reading) in the early 1970s, which was completed in 1973. He later published this piece as the first chapter in his book *Pahilo Pahar* (1982).

the class question of Nepali nation formation in Darjeeling, we argue, is an attempt to make these personal-political preferences amenable to his scholarly work focused on the materialistic and empiricist history of Darjeeling.

In lieu of conclusion, there is a certain politics in Pradhan's work that merits consideration—namely his attempts to foster acceptance of the possibility that different interests, traditions, and even nationalities can co-exist within a territorial unit under common rule. It matters very little why territorial units (such as nation-states) have been constructed—whether for reasons of custom, tradition, conquest, negotiation or geographical circumstances. What matters more are the distinct and complex social structures that arise within these units. It is our contention that most of Pradhan's writings call for a tolerance of differing truths on nation and nationalism—truths that have called into question the linear histories of national time and identities in a way that rescues the history of the nation from that of the nation-state.[46] The tendency to equate nation and nationality with mono-lingual/mono-cultural foundations may have epistemic value in the West, but it is insufficient for understanding the intricacies of nation formation in the East. We believe that this revelation, as articulated by Pradhan, indicates his continued relevance in discussions of Nepali nation formation in Darjeeling and questions of nationality in broader historical and contemporary contexts.

46 c.f. Duara (1995).

Section III
Environments and Labour

9 *Subnational Occupations*

A Year in the Life of the Darjeeling Tea Management Training Centre

Sarah Besky*

On 4 July 2008 a large group of 20-something men sat on a concrete patio outside an office suite in the bustling bazaar in Darjeeling. They had been lured by an advertisement for a new management-training institute. The advertisement had appeared the day before in the local Nepali language newspaper. Retired Indian–Nepali (or 'Gorkha') tea plantation managers, supported by a host of Gorkha dignitaries hailing from the local political party, West Bengal state offices,

* Funding was provided by the Fulbright Hays Doctoral Dissertation Research Abroad Program, the Andrew W. Mellon Foundation, and the American Council of Learned Societies, the Michigan Society of Fellows, and Brown University. All errors are my own.

and nearby universities, were forming the Darjeeling Tea Management Training Centre (DTMTC). In Darjeeling, there are many privately run training institutes, from computer programming to English language accent-reduction courses, and even a local air stewardess-training program. But the DTMTC was different.

Many of the other institutes were aimed at training Nepalis in jobs for which they were seen to have a particular racial proclivity. Since the British colonial period, Nepalis in India have been profiled as suited for low-level service work like masonry, gardening, and nannying.[1] For example, common racial stereotypes include the belief that Nepalis speak English with less pronounced accents. Nepali men, consistently portrayed as both courageous and physically tough, have long been steered into military service and manual labour. Meanwhile, Nepali women, depicted in popular discourse as unusually alluring and sexually available, have been pushed into domestic service and hospitality work. At the time of the DTMTC's opening, most of the job training institutes in Darjeeling focused on these kinds of work, perpetuating racial division and exclusion. The DTMTC's explicit purpose was to correct this long history of racial discrimination and profiling. The institute would prepare Gorkhas (particularly men) to be plantation managers.

Darjeeling tea is world-renowned for its light body and muscatel taste. Expert tasters insist that the distinct sensory experience provided by the tea is connected to the geographical location in which it is grown. Tea bushes (and tea workers) are also well known across India as the landscape backdrops for Bollywood dance scenes. Within India, tea plantations are a space apart, both ideologically and materially. The mode of production on the tea plantations that blanket Darjeeling's foothills has changed little over the last 150 years. Darjeeling tea can sell for hundreds of dollars per pound, but the workers who pluck, process, and package it on plantations make as little as Rs. 132.50 per day.

Since the inception of the Darjeeling tea industry in the 1860s, Nepalis have dominated the field and factory labour force, but their ability to advance beyond manual labour in the plantation labour hierarchy has remained severely limited. During the colonial period, plantations employed British managers (and to a lesser extent, Bengalis, Punjabis, or other non-Nepalis). The exclusion of Nepalis from the management

[1] See Newman & Company (1900: 66–91).

ranks continued after the takeover of plantations by Indian companies. This history of poverty and discrimination undergirds a longstanding movement to separate Darjeeling from the state of West Bengal and form a new state of Gorkhaland within the Indian union.

Tea plantation fields and the workers within them are prominent in the political symbolism and discourse of the Gorkhaland Movement. The movement seeks both to undo the political economic inequities of the plantation system and to vigorously counter racial stereotypes that portray Nepalis in Darjeeling as exotic outsiders, rather than rightful residents. The tension between these two aspirations was palpable in the youth sitting outside the DTMTC on that summer day. Many of the would-be students hailed from tea plantations. Some had worked in call centres elsewhere in India, but had returned home because they were unsatisfied with nocturnal urban work. Most had finished high school, or even college, but had been unable to find employment. When I talked with them outside the inauguration, students did not frame their decisions to attend the DTMTC within the overtly political rhetoric of the Gorkhaland Movement. Rather, they described themselves as unemployed and looking for work. Management training, which offered translatable, compartmentalizable, and commensurable knowledge, would land them a job. A job, in turn, would enable them to become upwardly mobile citizens of India, but not necessarily of Gorkhaland.

The students huddled together; nervously chatting, as official speeches inaugurating the DTMTC proceeded inside. They knew the story that the speakers would tell. They would talk about how, on or off the plantations, few skilled jobs were available to the growing number of young men and women with high school or college educations. The DTMTC would answer a growing call by the GJM, the leading local political party that advocates for an independent federal state of Gorkhaland within the Indian union, to create jobs in Darjeeling for what politicians called the 'educated unemployed'. With Gorkha sovereignty, quality local jobs would go to Gorkhas, to whom they rightfully belonged. According to the DTMTC's founders, Gorkhas, by virtue of building, occupying, and maintaining Darjeeling's plantation landscape for generations, possessed an innate knowledge of the tea industry. This knowledge was valuable, but it needed to be honed. Training Gorkhas to be managers would also contribute to the GJM's larger political project of exerting territorial sovereignty over an area controlled by capital interests that politicians and laypeople alike identified as sitting in Kolkata, not Darjeeling.

The notion of linking subnational recognition to education is not a new one in Darjeeling. Indeed, the idea of locally sourced and locally appropriate education has long been at the core of Darjeeling politics. The idea dates back as far as the 1960s, to the Nepali Language Movement's efforts to make Nepali a recognized state language in government and educational contexts. More recently, however, Gorkha politicians have tended to describe the region's educated youth as wayward and in need of discipline. In this, the situation in Darjeeling is distinct from the situation in other parts of India, where subnational subjectivity and education have been closely linked,[2] or in Nepal, where student political activism is strong.[3]

Across India, subnational struggles have consistently been articulated on the basis of underdevelopment. The newly formed states of Uttarakhand and Telangana are good examples. In the Gorkhaland Movement, however, issues of unemployment, precarity, and distribution of resources have consistently taken a back seat to rights based on the recognition of identity, whether ethnic, tribal, or Gorkha. As I describe below, the DTMTC was thus an attempt to reconcile the tension within the movement between an aspiration of economic development and an aspiration of ethnic recognition.

For the DTMTC to be successful, teachers and students alike had to find a way to see themselves as both potential managers and as proud Gorkhas. Over the course of the single year in which the DTMTC operated, these two subject positions proved to be difficult, if not impossible, to occupy at the same time. In what follows, I situate the story of the institute within a broader history of tea management in India. An analysis of colonial era texts aimed at would-be plantation managers reveals deep-rooted tensions over how tea management should fit into politics and over who should occupy managerial positions. I trace these tensions into the present through my own ethnographic observations of the DTMTC's inauguration, its classes, and—most importantly—a series of charged exchanges between DTMTC instructors and students.

These in-class debates underscore an abiding concern among the educated unemployed about those same questions—how management should fit into politics and who should occupy managerial positions. The students at the DTMTC were born and grew up during the years

[2] Singh (2015).

[3] Snellinger (2006). See also Jeffrey, Jeffery, and Jeffery (2008).

between the first major Gorkhaland agitation in the mid-1980s, and the second, which began in late 2007. It was these young people who were often portrayed in GJM rhetoric as the main beneficiaries of territorial sovereignty, but as the case of the DTMTC highlights, they were also the group perhaps most cynical about the movement's potential to effect change. Students had to reconcile a spatial disjuncture between Gorkhaland and management training as an educational genre. They had to figure out how to be subjects of both a place-based movement for ethnic recognition that valued territorial fixity, and a national trend in vocational and managerial training that valued mobility over identity.

The students' vision of training required a suppression of politics, while the teachers' vision saw training as always already political. The assertion that education has non-political value, as Matei Candea has argued, is not simply a sign of the anti-politics of the market or of development discourse.[4] In Candea's account of Corsican education, teachers who identified elsewhere as Corsican nationalists insisted that the classroom was a non-political space. In Darjeeling, by contrast, it was students who resisted the politicization of education. The educated unemployed I met at the DTMTC believed in the idea of Gorkhaland, but they were less convinced of its potential to effect meaningful change in their lives. GJM rhetoric couched the struggle for Gorkhaland as a long-term goal that might take generations to achieve and as a revolution to which youth might need to sacrifice years of their lives. Managerial training, on the other hand, oriented students to what Jane Guyer calls the near future.[5] Across India, students seeking management training thought not in terms of distant political horizons but in terms of the monthly, weekly, and yearly economic planning and personal discipline required to advance through the ranks of corporate and social hierarchies.[6] Management training was one step in planning for the near future. At the DTMTC, it was ultimately students—not teachers—who had to reconcile these temporalities. Maintaining a distinction between education and politics, between the near future and the abstract future, mattered greatly to students. The DTMTC, however, was based on a collapse of these very ideas.

4 Cadea (2011); Ferguson (1990).

5 Guyer (2007).

6 See Jeffrey (2010).

The Right Kind of Man? Or the Right Kind of Training?

A central justification for the founding of the DTMTC was the continued dominance of non-Gorkhas in the ranks of management in Darjeeling. That dominance was facilitated—indeed underwritten—by tea management training centres located outside Darjeeling. By the time the DTMTC opened, such centres were in operation at Assam Agricultural University, North Bengal University, and the National Institute of Tea Management. The founding of these centres is a relatively recent development in the history of the Indian tea industry. Before the mid-1990s, getting a job as a plantation manager was as much a matter of honing social connections and demonstrating a dexterity with middle class manners and speech as it was about mastering technical skills.

Tea management was cloistered in a closed, guild-like circle of experts. It was what Julia Elyachar, drawing on the work of Michael Polanyi, calls tacit knowledge.[7] Training institutes promised to make tacit knowledge explicit—to package and distribute it to anyone who desired it regardless of background, language, or ethnicity. This tension between tacit knowledge and technical training dates back to the days of British colonialism. Beginning in the early 1800s, tea plantations were established in Assam, the North-West Provinces, and later Darjeeling, the Dooars, and south India.[8] By the 1830s, books were circulating around Britain and colonial India that not only demystified the tea production process, from propagation to factory finishing, but also attempted to lure European men to tea management, popularly called tea planting. These texts reveal a history of the linked projects of capitalist accumulation, management, and colonial territorial sovereignty.

In these texts, tea management is described as a means of social and economic mobility. An early account instructs:

> To those (and the class is numerous in England) who, possessing but a moderate sum of money, wish, nevertheless, to maintain the position in life to which they have been educated, to whom trade or the professions are obnoxious, who, having no military tastes or nautical tendencies, are still anxious to use that energy and enterprise which are said to belong to the British—to such, tea planting offers peculiar inducements.[9]

[7] Elyachar (2012).

[8] See Sharma (2011). See also Middleton, this volume, for historical detail and contrasts between Assam and Darjeeling.

[9] McGowan (1860: 33).

In addition to details about the technical challenges of tea planting (from climate and altitude, to soils, to labour costs), these texts describe the qualities of work with a view to reassuring potential European planters, of the viability of planting as a career path.[10] Indeed, the authors of these manuals frame the aspiration to tea planting almost exclusively in terms of self-cultivation and individual mobility. Authors address a range of concerns that might be preventing the would-be tea managers from embarking on a life in tea. They touch on issues ranging from how to save money for a trip home, to how to read under a mosquito net,[11] to how to burn down a forest to plant tea,[12] to which ethnic group's women might make the best nannies.[13]

Alexander McGowan, an army surgeon serving in the North-West during the mid-1800s, describes the attractively low amount of upfront capital expense that was required for an individual to purchase, clear cut, and seed a tea plantation.[14] He portrays tea planting as:

> An employment in itself agreeable, entailing no hard physical labour, but merely sufficient exercise for both body and mind as is essential to their healthy preservation, and eventually so lucrative as to amply repay the anxieties incidental on the earlier years; with a property safe against the many ills that other crops are liable to, [planting can allow] ample time for recreation, or even ... permit a prolonged absence.[15]

Many of the early manuals describe European social life, including the social clubs and domestic accommodations in the tea districts, that would allow managers to maintain and hone their English manners, perhaps even to a higher degree than they would in England.[16]

To succeed, one needed not wealth, but character. Tea planting was best suited for men who would appreciate the opportunity to better themselves not only economically but in terms of what scholars today might call cultural capital.[17] Former tea planter Samuel Baildon's widely

[10] See *Tea Cultivation* (1865); *Papers on Tea Factories* (1854); *Notes on Tea* (1888); *Tea Cyclopaedia* (1881).

[11] Baildon (1882).

[12] *Tea Cultivation* (1865: 23).

[13] Newman & Co. (1900: 29–30).

[14] McGowan (1860: 37).

[15] McGowan (1860: 33–4).

[16] Baildon (1882: 60).

[17] Baildon (1882: 35); Bourdieu (1984).

circulated *The Tea Industry in India: A Review of Finance and Labour, and a Guide for Capitalists and Assistants* explains: 'Now, it is, of course, a very essential thing that only the right kind of men should become tea planters, both for their own sakes, and also for that of the industry.'[18] Baildon outlines a typology of men and dispositions, and the degree to which each type was suited to the lifestyle. He describes the lifestyle in painstaking detail, so that the reader will be able to determine whether he is the right kind of man for such a life.[19] He fills one entire chapter with descriptions of his own ability to occupy his mind, 'without all mediums of resource for occupying leisure that I might possess—musical instruments, paint-boxes, drawing materials, etc.'[20]

Baildon's purpose here is to hedge against the romanticism that can accompany colonial adventure narratives. Certainly, a manager could have a social life beyond the plantation on which he was posted, but given the demands of the job and the distance that would need to be travelled, such a life would be sporadic. Even more sporadic would be trips back home to Europe. Considering this, he explains: 'One fact should receive the earnest consideration, *primarily*, of all persons thinking of leaving home for India. It is that the only possible recompense for so leaving home is money. For this they will have to give up almost everything which, to the studious, makes life enjoyable.'[21] Almost everything. For his leisure would be to participate in the cloistered social institutions and practices that came to define British social life under the Raj. Tea management in colonial India was about economic mobility. A pre-existing appreciation for the virtues of music, manners, and art was a prerequisite to the social clubs and houses that provided a facsimile of English life in the tea districts. It was in settings like the Darjeeling Planters' Club, that upwardly mobile young managers could demonstrate their manners and share knowledge about the technical and economic process of growing tea. It was in clubs and house parties that tacit knowledge changed hands.

As the industry grew in the years leading up to Indian Independence in 1947, a new wave of tea planting books came to the market. This later group of books aimed to unveil and codify the managerial secrets that

[18] Baildon (1882: 39).

[19] Baildon (1882: 39).

[20] Baildon (1882: 41).

[21] Baildon (1882: 42).

had been cloistered in spaces like the Planters' Club.[22] By the early twentieth century, when the Indian tea industry was at its peak, the number of managers and assistant managers across India (nearly all of them white and male) had swelled considerably. With this expansion came a need to make tacit knowledge about the industry more explicit. Tea planters frequently moved from region to region. A person might start in Assam before finding a more lucrative post in Kerala or Sri Lanka.

Such mobile managers were the target audience for this second wave of tea planting texts. While earlier texts by the likes of McGowan and Baildon were dominated by vivid narrative descriptions of burning down forests and reading under mosquito nets, this second wave of tea planting manuals took on a more scientific tone, working to make tea cultivation techniques—including pruning, planting, fertilizer application, and pest management—not only explicit but also commensurable across space.[23] They are filled with lists and charts of an array of procedural concerns regarding numbers (from temperature figures to wages), timings (for pruning, planting, and plucking), and inputs (of urea fertilizers, irrigation, and labour time).[24]

Many of these texts were written by experts who had done agronomic research, most notably at the quasi-governmental Tea Research Association (TRA), the main arm of which is located in Jorhat, Assam. Still in existence today, the TRA has been conducting field experiments on tea cultivation for over 100 years.[25] The TRA's research and publications aim to support managers as they move from post to post

22 By the late 1880s, the entrepreneurial land acquisition that McGowan and early writers describe gave way to a corporate plantation landscape (complete with social clubs, golf courses, and sprawling manager's bungalows). With this shift, the entrepreneurial planter became integrated into a hierarchical management structure in which there was a manager (often referred to as a planter) and one or many (depending on a plantation size) assistant managers. This model of organization persists. Today, there are 87 plantations in Darjeeling, and each plantation has a head manager and a number of assistant managers, who oversee the field, office, or factory (or subsections of these on a larger plantation).

23 These later books can actually be divided into two categories. In addition to technical how-to manuals, a series of memoirs written by retired planters were published. The purpose of these books was less to inspire new planters than to capitalize on British readers' desires for nostalgic tales of life under the Raj. See: Fraser (1935); Longley (1969); Hetherington (1994); Ramsden (1945).

24 See Bald (1903); Johnson (1953); Ukers (1935).

25 Banerjee (1993); Hajra (2001); Singh (2005).

between plantations across India and to other British tea producing post/colonies. In the manuals based on TRA research, the manager is not the right kind of man, but any man willing to be trained. Indeed, as British planters were replaced by Indian managers in the 1950s and 1960s, the codification of management in such manuals could be seen as a democratizing trend.

The conversion of management knowhow from a genre of tacit knowledge to one of technical training was not limited to the tea industry. Indeed, the tea management training institutes of Assam Agricultural University, North Bengal University, and elsewhere were founded well after other similar institutions. Despite the proliferation of tea management training centres since the 1990s, the tea industry has not been so easily divorced from a past in which race, manners, language, and cultural capital mattered. Indeed, if training manuals developed through organizations like the TRA made management thinkable as a scientific or technical skill, they also created space for management to become a focal point for the operations of ethno-nationalism. The DTMTC, whose curriculum was modelled on those of other technical training institutes, was also designed as a space for the cultivation and celebration of ethnic identity. A key tenet of the DTMTC's charter was that the right kind of man for Darjeeling plantations must also be a Gorkha man. Turning now to ethnographic material, I will show how colonial ideas about cultural capital, modern notions of technical proficiency, and an emerging ethnic consciousness intersected in Darjeeling.

Inaugurating the DTMTC

It was a rare sunny morning in the midst of the monsoon. Attendees of the DTMTC's inaugural ceremony milled around a rooftop patio, enjoying the unusually dry conditions. Among those assembled were several prominent GJM leaders, whom I had come to recognize from party rallies and meetings, as well as a slew of suited men I had never seen before. The dignitaries were seated in a circle of plastic chairs, while the potential students stood together on the far side of the patio, looking over the bustle of Darjeeling's main bazaar. At the appointed hour, one of the suited men called for the attendees to come inside. 'But not you,' he said to the future students, 'we will call for you in a minute.'

A minute turned into over two hours. With everyone seated around a small conference table, the DTMTC's principal welcomed and introduced the honoured guests. These included Gorkhas who had become high-level civil servants, professors, politicians, and business owners in Darjeeling. They also included the DTMTC's staff of teachers. One was a retired factory manager who would teach classes on bookkeeping. Another was still employed as a factory manager at a remote plantation on the eastern side of the Teesta and would teach classes about manufacturing while he was on extended sick leave. A third was a retired field manager who would lecture on plant biology and pests, including how to deal with blights and properly manage pesticide application. The principal was a retired assistant manager who had run a small, remote garden on the Nepal border. In addition to leading the DTMTC, he offered a class on pruning and planting tea bushes.

In his opening speech, the principal described the origins and objectives of the DTMTC. He gave a scathing critique of the current state of Darjeeling's tea plantations before explaining how he and his colleagues intended to fix it:

> The reason why we are starting such a tea management institute in Darjeeling is out of necessity, because since 1820 ... the planting and cultivating has been done by our ancestors only. But our people are still labourers, and they [non–Nepalis] are still occupying the executive posts. Today most of our [Nepali] young brothers and sisters are educated. They are all competent ... If we open such an institute here, then these kinds of youths will get an opportunity.

The audience was sympathetic. The DTMTC's principal and the other teachers had all succeeded in becoming assistant managers (*chota sahibs* [little sahibs]), but none of them had managed to reach the rank of head manager (*burra sahib* [big sahib]).

Still the DTMTC's staff were all inordinately successful. When I interviewed them later, I asked how they had been trained. They each insisted that they had made it into the management ranks through discipline and hard work. There was a posting. They applied for it. They got it. In a way, then, the teachers were implying that they were the right kind of men for management jobs. They had honed skills in speaking, deportment, and manners that allowed them to overcome the systematic racial discrimination that kept most other Nepalis out of the management ranks. When these men were seeking employment in the 1970s and 1980s, tea management institutes did not exist. They had learned how to manage plantations by exploiting personal connections and economic capital to work themselves into the spaces where tacit knowledge was exchanged—spaces like the Planters' Club and the local private colleges.[26] Despite this success, outsiders still took most management jobs. Today, they told me, outsiders were succeeding not because of cultural capital but because of formal training. What they sought to do with the DTMTC was provide Gorkha youth with such training. By doing this in Darjeeling, rather than in Siliguri, Assam, or Kolkata, they could prove that the right kind of man could also be a Gorkha man.

The speech by the principal was followed by a series of lectures by other distinguished guests, some from the tea industry, some from elsewhere—but all Gorkhas. A rhetorical pattern emerged. Just as colonial tea manuals shifted between the 1800s and the 1900s from anecdotal stories of personal triumph to technical outlines of best practices, each inaugural speech at the DTMTC morphed from the personal to the technical. Each person began by recounting their own individual experiences, telling stories about how perseverance allowed them to be successful. Their resolve was rooted in their Gorkha identity. Gorkhas were brave, cunning, and resourceful, but that was not enough. For the good of the Gorkhaland Movement—and for Darjeeling's tea industry—discipline and resolve rooted in ethnic identity had to be combined with technical training.

The lone woman speaker at the inauguration, a former high-level regional bureaucrat and active member of the women's wing of the GJM, was particularly vehement in her insistence that Gorkhas pursuing jobs on tea plantations were being systematically sidelined by outsiders. 'The basic knowledge that we have had from our parents,' she said, 'they [outsiders] do not even have that. They just have the degrees.' The degrees to which she was referring were not bachelors or master's degrees in language or science. These degrees were from tea management training institutes.

Tea gardens were at the heart of Darjeeling, she went on, and the DTMTC would keep them alive. This new crop of Gorkha managers, by virtue of having grown up in Darjeeling, would understand the particular demands of growing tea in the hills. She and many of the speakers repeated this point. A premise of the DTMTC was that Gorkhas possessed not only courage and dedication but also their own kind of tacit knowledge about how to cultivate tea. She broadened this argument further, explaining that Gorkhas didn't just have an innate

[26] Elyachar (2012).

sense of when to prune, when to pluck, and when to apply fertilizer; they also had an intimate understanding of the plight of plantation workers. This understanding would be a trait that only Gorkha managers would have. The DTMTC, she maintained, was a vehicle for blending politics with ethical values.

While this bureaucrat saw the DTMTC as a means of keeping Gorkha youth on Darjeeling plantations, not all of the dignitaries who spoke at the inaugural event shared this vision of the spatial boundedness of management training. For example, a former professor at Darjeeling Government College drew on plantation history to argue that the DTMTC's success might lie in its ability to provide the educated unemployed of Gorkhaland not just with economic mobility in the form of higher-paying, higher-ranking jobs, but also with geographic mobility. Certainly, the graduates would make excellent tea managers for the 87 tea plantations in Darjeeling, but the possibilities that might come from managerial training were expansive. He compared the new cohort of trainees at the DTMTC to their British predecessors: 'Just as the sahibs sacrificed their lives by leaving their homes in England, our young men must also make sacrifices ... Not just here, but in Assam. They could run the Tata company too.' For the professor, part of linking economic development to ethno-national recognition was carving out a presence for Gorkhas on the national economic stage. For him, training must put Gorkhas into the upper tea management structure across India, including (but not limited to) Darjeeling.

After almost two hours and several speeches, the students were invited inside to introduce themselves. Each prospective student was asked to state his name, where he came from, and what his qualifications were (that is the highest educational degree he had received). Having read the DTMTC's recruitment materials and listened to the series of speeches, the students astutely tailored their introductions to the centre's mission. Most students began by naming the plantation on which they grew up. Those who did not grow up on plantations were quick to name not only the villages or peri-urban settlements in which they were born but also the nearest plantation. Identification with plantations was not enough. The students also trumpeted their technical backgrounds. Nearly all students had at least a B.A. pass from a local college, and some had master's degrees, in subjects ranging from biology to Nepali literature. Like the speech givers who preceded them, each person told his/her individual story while at the same time trying to bind himself/herself to an institutional and political mission.

They faced the challenge of positioning themselves as both Gorkha subjects and as (potential) managerial subjects. As I show in the next section, this dual positioning proved more and more difficult to maintain as the year of DTMTC training progressed.

Between Affiliation and Recognition

The DTMTC' s classes took place at Roy Villa, a stately turn-of-the-century building perched on a hillside overlooking a tea–covered valley. The most famous occupant of the building was Sister Nivedita, a disciple of Swami Vivekananda, who died in 1911. After Sister Nivedita's death, the building was converted into a youth hostel. Classrooms were added to the original structure, complete with chalkboards and writing desks. Inside were several dormitory rooms in which students unable to commute back and forth from college in Darjeeling could stay for a modest fee. By 2008, however, Roy Villa had long sat unoccupied, and it was rumoured to be haunted by Sister Nivedita's ghost. In the summer leading up to the DTMTC's inauguration, the GJM commandeered the house from the state of West Bengal.

In early October 2008, I sat in the back of a room, squeezed into a tiny wooden school desk and scribbling notes as a DTMTC teacher droned on about the different techniques of tea bush pruning. He read in English from photocopies, stating the intervals between LP (light prune), MP (medium prune), LS (light skiff), and DS (deep skiff) prunes. Each of these different cuts was differentiated by a particular—the number of centimetres from the top of the bush or mark left by the last prune. Like many DTMTC teachers, he read his lesson from the tattered texts and photocopies of circulars he had received from the TRA when he was an active assistant manager. The technical information in these documents was heavily geared to environmental conditions in the plains of the Dooars and the gentler foothills of Assam.

When students interrupted the lectures to ask about how the techniques described in the TRA materials would apply to Darjeeling, the teachers did their best to provide an extemporaneous response. While the lectures I observed proceeded in English—the standard for both tea planting and the science of agronomy—the teachers' attempts to tailor information to local conditions tended to be in Nepali. As students pressed (in Nepali) for more instruction, teachers would (switching to English) remind them that even though planting conditions varied, it was important to know the standards and the theory.

By the time of that class in October, students had begun to complain regularly of a lack of practical education at the DTMTC. It was all well and good, they told their instructors, to discuss the ways in which planting tea on a steep mountainside might present challenges that went unaddressed in manuals written for the plains or Assam, but in order to understand these differences, students needed to be allowed into the field. In response, teachers told students that they did not need practical training. After all, they had grown up playing around the tea bushes. As one teacher suggested, if they wanted to know how to pluck or prune, they could go ask their mothers.

In these debates about the relationship between theory and practice, and between agronomy and embodied knowledge, a discord between the cultivation of a Gorkha subjectivity and the cultivation of a managerial subjectivity became evident. Was tea management something best learned on the job, or was it a set of discrete skills that could be corralled in books and taught in standard modules?[27] In some moments, the DTMTC's curriculum seemed overly rigid and excessively deferential to the techniques laid out in TRA circulars. In others, it seemed excessively dependent on vague ideas about the deep connections between Gorkhas and Darjeeling plantations. How would a student's completion of a year at the DTMTC be recognized by would-be employers? Would their work be recognized outside of Darjeeling at all? And if students did secure jobs on Darjeeling plantations, would they be regarded as managers, or as *Gorkha* managers?

For students, these mounting concerns became crystallized in an unfulfilled promise the GJM leadership made early in the school year. When they matriculated, students were assured that the party would help the DTMTC secure an affiliation. The students reasonably took affiliation to mean accreditation by a university or other technological training institute. For students, affiliation would increase the chances that training would yield job placement. To be recognized as a trained manager, they reasoned, a person needed a certificate from an accredited institution.

Despite the party's promises, the question of the DTMTC's purpose had never been fully resolved by the school's leaders. For some,

[27] Two women students were accepted to the DTMTC, but they quickly realized that the teachers did not see them having a future in tea management. They (and I) were fed a steady line about how they could be tea tasters in the plantation factories. They stopped showing up when the second tuition payment was due in November 2008.

like the bureaucrat who spoke at the inauguration about ethical values, the DTMTC's mission was one of territorial development. The very founding of a tea management training centre in the heart of Darjeeling was already a powerful form of placement. It would keep the educated unemployed from seeking work elsewhere. Moreover, Gorkha managers would care more deeply about improving the lives of lower-level tea workers who comprised the party's rank and file membership. For others, like the professor who spoke at the inauguration about the need for Gorkhas to leave home and make sacrifices for the movement, the DTMTC's mission was one of national and subnational recognition. The centre's purpose was to propel Gorkhas into the managerial ranks in plantations outside Darjeeling.

As the school year proceeded, this unresolved debate about the DTMTC's ultimate purpose—and about the relationship between development and recognition—coalesced around the question of affiliation. In and out of class, many teachers began to talk of affiliation not as alignment with another institute of higher education, but as alignment with the GJM itself. If the DTMTC were affiliated with an outside university, it would need to admit students from outside Darjeeling. The territorial and developmentalist mission of the DTMTC prohibited this kind of inclusion. Even those who favoured seeking affiliation saw a risk. On the one hand, a denial of affiliation by the likes of the National Institute of Tea Management (NITM), North Bengal University (NBU), or Assam Agricultural University would call the centre's legitimacy into question. On the other hand, if affiliation were to be granted, teachers would find themselves subsumed to another institution's bureaucracy. They would risk being recognized not as teachers in the management training system, but as *Gorkha* teachers.

As in Candea's Corsican case, the question of the limits of the political in education was played out performatively in classroom debates.[28] By November, DTMTC lectures were punctuated not only with questions about how theory written by TRA experts conflicted with the practice of Darjeeling plantation workers but also with breakout discussions in which affiliation, placement, and recognition alternately took on political and technical meanings.[29] In one typical such debate, the principal

[28] Candea (2011).

[29] See Bagchi (2012); Middleton (2015); Sarkar (2013, 2016); Shneiderman (2015); Wenner (2013, 2015) for discussions of recognition in the context of Darjeeling politics.

responded to a student's questions about the DTMTC's affiliation with a reminder that, affiliation or no affiliation, students had to pass the course before they could ever get a certificate. Unfazed by discussions of grades, students pressed for assurance that the certificate that was said to await anyone who passed the training would mean something in the tea industry, and that this certificate would continue to mean something over the course of their careers.

Another DTMTC teacher responded to questions about certificates by telling the students to go and ask the managers on their home tea plantations where *their* certificates were: 'Please ask them to show you their certificates. From which institution did *they* get it? What is *their* educational background?' The students were well aware that DTMTC teachers did not have certificates. They also knew that most managers across India and beyond did not have them either. But times had changed. The students were headed out into a world in which certificates from training institutions were now critical to securing jobs. As the previous generation of plantation managers aged and retired, they would be replaced by managers who held training certificates. Since new jobs might crop up not just in Darjeeling but across India, these certificates and the training to which they attested had to be commensurable.

In one class I observed, a student posed a hypothetical situation to the principal. What if, after completing the DTMTC training course, he secured a job on a plantation? 'Suppose,' he suggested, 'I leave that company because I may not want to work in the same company for a long time. To go to another company, I have to have a certificate.'

The principal responded: 'It is completely up to you. Once you have joined any tea garden, then it is up to you whether you progress or not. Another other company will pull you from your company. They will say that you are doing great, please come and join here.'

The principal then tried to change the subject and scope of the discussion. The student's hypothetical example concerned the fate of a single individual in a relatively depoliticized marketplace. The principal wanted to talk about the fate of the student body as a whole.

> I have been saying from the beginning that even if you do the training, there can be no guarantee of a job. Nobody can guarantee a job. But there is one thing. And that is that we are putting forth a sincere effort. And our boys *here*—and not boys from *somewhere else*—have to get placement. Maybe it will be quick or slow; this is what we have to do.

What was significant for the teacher was the physical location of the DTMTC. He was adamant that the act of training Gorkha men to be managers here at Roy Villa, in the heart of Darjeeling's colonial centre, was of paramount importance. While the student's hypothetical scenario concerned one man's career, measurable in the weeks, months, and years of salaried service to a company, the principal's counter-hypothetical approach reached for a more distant time horizon.[30] No one knew exactly when Gorkhas would be granted their separate state. From one temporal perspective, the students were affiliated with a system of management training in which certificates were passports for economic and geographical mobility. From the other, they were affiliated with a social movement in which grounding oneself in place was both an ethical and a political stance.

'But sir, there has to be an affiliation', one student pleaded.

'What is this thing called affiliation?' The principal asked.

'It's like this. Say you are affiliated with Assam [Agricultural University]. If we are affiliated with Assam, [then] *we* have to comply with *their* terms and conditions. We would have to run *our* class according to *their* syllabus. *We* have to work according to *their* holidays. But our main problem is here, in Darjeeling. In the tea gardens of Darjeeling.'

As long as the GJM stayed in power, an affiliation to the party might be beneficial, but the students had seen one politician and party, Subash Ghisingh and the GNLF, ousted. They were far from confident about the longevity of the GJM. As the GJM intensified its campaign for a separate state throughout 2008 and 2009, DTMTC teachers doubled down on their desire to be linked to the party. Over the same period, the GJM backtracked on concrete development schemes like the DTMTC in favour of more symbolic projects, such as month-long cultural programmes: performances of Gorkha-ness in dance and song as a means of proving to the rest of India that Darjeeling and its people were different and thus deserved their own state.[31]

A couple of weeks later, during the height of the month-long puja celebrations in Chowrasta, when townspeople were required to wear traditional dress, (*daura suruwal* and *chaubandi choli*), a student asked

30 Guyer (2007).

31 See Besky (2013); Golay (2006). See also Chettri (2016); Middleton (2015); Shneiderman (2015), for a discussion as it relates to ST/SC political action.

pointedly: 'What if the political party changes—'. The principal cut him off: 'No matter what political party comes in, the garden will still be there. The garden is always there. And what can be said about political parties?' Another student interjected: 'Sir, it *can be said* that the political party cannot influence anything.' To which the principal replied:

> We have to convince everyone.... A person from a place is supposed to be employed in the same place. We can tell owners to put our people in the tea garden. We can say that they have to put 80 per cent of our people in the tea garden. If we cannot fight against them, then we will be the suppresser *and* we will be the suppressed.... We have to face this, because it is our mother and father working and we are not doing anything for them. We do not do anything, even when we have the ability to do something.

In this exchange, a generational divide between students and teachers became a divide about the role of politics in education. The student saw political affiliation as ineffective at best, while the teacher saw a suppression of politics in the classroom as tantamount to a betrayal of mothers and fathers.

The principal confided: 'A student just came to me and said: "Sir, I got a job in the call centre, so I am going."' He paused. 'Do you understand? It is because he has no confidence in his future.' He continued:

> When boys like you have been trained, you have to revolt. You have to bring revolution.... You can't just wait and think about whether you are going to get a job. I am fully dependent upon you. If you all become slackers and think that you will not get a job and lose hope, then you will be nowhere. You all should have guts. You all are being trained. The tea estates are *here* and we have to get the outsiders out. With this determination of mind, if you study hard, then it can happen.

This shut down the discussion momentarily. The principal portrayed employment in a call centre—underwritten by training in English pronunciation and perhaps a degree from an affiliated university—as surrender. A young man's concern for a near future of steady pay cheques and marginal economic gains was at the same time a lack of faith in the promises of a more distant future of territorial sovereignty.[32] The principal continued:

> Whether there is a certificate, or not ... Take training from here as your certificate. *That* is affiliation, because you are the son of the soil, and you

[32] Guyer (2007).

> have got every right to get a job in a tea garden. In ... the tea gardens in this district, because you have *the training of the tea garden*.... Are we so weak? If you are asking me to give you a guarantee, I cannot do that. You have to give it to yourself.

In this exchange, as in the others, two different subjects are in conflict. The 'I's, 'we's, and 'one's of the students' discourse are individual managers. The 'you's of the principal's discourse comprise the collective class of Gorkha educated unemployed.

The principal paused as the students murmured and shifted in their chairs. Then continued: 'So you should all give me a decision, should this institution be an independent one or should it be supported by the local university?'

In this way, the principal left the decision about the DTMTC's fate and its ultimate purpose in the hands of the students. Soon, he had his answer. After the long winter break, a fraction of the students came back to class. Some of those who left had taken insecure clerical positions—neither managerial nor on plantations—around town. Others told me that they did not feel that making the final tuition payments would yield any benefits. In the summer of 2009, Roy Villa was taken back by the GJM and allocated to the Gorkhaland Personnel, an informal organization of men and women that patrolled Darjeeling wielding *lathis* and clad in green and yellow jumpsuits, enforcing the dress and behavioural codes that were part of the GJM's cultural programmes. In 2013, the state government, having re-exerted control over the building, facilitated the turnover of Roy Villa to the Ramakrishna Mission. At the time of writing, the Ramakrishna Mission runs skills development projects and language classes out of the building, much as it does on its main campus in Kolkata.

As I have argued here, the story of the DTMTC's rise and fall illustrates fundamental contradictions embedded in two concepts that are central to the Gorkhaland Movement: development and recognition. In the discussions about the purpose and operations of the DTMTC, development sometimes referred to the aspiration among the educated unemployed of Darjeeling for economic and social mobility. As it was elsewhere in India, management training was seen as a means of individual improvement. Among older GJM activists, including the DTMTC's teachers and founders, development indexed something different.

Training meant not mobility but stability—what the bureaucrat at the inauguration referred to as an ethical investment in Darjeeling's plantations. Training was a form of collective solidarity and territorial control.

Among some students and teachers involved with the DTMTC, recognition came in the form of accredited certificates. As economic and geographical passports, certificates would permit the advancement of the Gorkhaland cause by permitting more trained Gorkhas to work, in more places, with higher degrees of responsibility. Among others involved with the DTMTC, it was the institution, not its certificates, which must be recognized. From this point of view, the DTMTC would only succeed if those outside Darjeeling recognized the capacity and right of Gorkha people to devise their own homegrown forms of training.

Ultimately, the story of the DTMTC provides a more general lesson about the problem of occupation in Darjeeling. Management is an occupation in several senses. Management is about filling and controlling physical and institutional space. The post of manager is one that individuals can fill interchangeably, but it is also a location in political economy, between labour and capital. It is a location on a plantation. The promise of a comfortable bungalow and membership in a social club once lured men from Europe, just as it now lures young Nepali men raised in plantation villages. Finally, management is the institution that enables the occupation of space by corporations and states. Tea plantation management positions in Darjeeling continue to be filled by those whom Gorkha activists consider to be outsiders. Although management is occupational in all these senses, it has tended to be somewhat immune from politics. It is hard to imagine management as a position from which to take political action or as an institution through which to assert political beliefs. Management remains largely a function of politics rather than a set of political actions in itself.

Over its short lifespan, the DTMTC thrust management and subnational politics into an awkward relationship. In India, the idea of management is both bigger and smaller than the Gorkhaland Movement, or any movement for territorial sovereignty. Management is bigger in that it pulls young people away from their homelands, luring them to other states and other countries with promises of individual mobility, underwritten by certificates and affiliations. Management is smaller in the sense that its economic appeal—the offices, the houses, the salary, and the petit bourgeois social clubs—is individual rather than collective. The recent rise of management training centres in India, predicated on unmasking the tacit knowledge once housed in guilds and social clubs, changes little about this individual appeal. Like management based on the right kind of gender, race, or character, management based on training produces individual economic mobility through geographical flexibility, rather than place-based commitment.[33] In this way, management could easily be seen as undermining subnational movements. In the end, the DTMTC put students in a double-bind, between training and tacit knowledge, between development and recognition, and between economy and identity. Though the DTMTC was ultimately a failure, the story of how its students faced this bind can provide insights into the articulation of Darjeeling politics with both India's colonially rooted plantation economy and its liberalizing national economy.

[33] Elyachar (2012).

10 *Connection amidst Disconnection*

Water Struggles, Social Structures, and Geographies of Exclusion in Darjeeling

Georgina Drew and Roshan P. Rai*

It must be a relief for tourists visiting Darjeeling in the heat of the Indian summer to ease into the cooler temperatures of the former hill station. The lush green mountain landscape, fed by monsoon

* Georgina Drew and Roshan P. Rai extend their gratitude to the *samaj* members of Jawahar Busty, Mul Dara, and Mangalpuri. We thank them for their generosity and inspirational stewardship, as well as for welcoming us into their homes. We are also grateful to the Darjeeling Municipality, especially the Water Works Department, whose staff enabled us to get insights into the complex dynamics of water management in Darjeeling. Lakpa Tamang, of the University of Calcutta, deepened our work with his demarcation and mapping of springs in Darjeeling. Georgina also acknowledges the support of the Australian Research Council (DE160101178).

rains, is likely soothing to visitors' senses as they leave the parched earth of the plains behind. And it must be odd for new arrivals when, after checking into their hotel, they read a sign posted in the lobby or the bathroom announcing 'acute water scarcity'. This notice is invariably met by a plea that guests use water sparingly. To such a visitor, the question must arise: How bad can it really be? The confusion is likely made worse by the visibility of water moving through pipes and natural springs as one roams about Darjeeling. This chapter is an effort to partially explain this very basic question. It stresses attention on the pockets of the township where a resource lack is felt along with the social responses emerging to address Darjeeling's water access challenges.

If you have read anything about water stress in India or South Asia, you may be thinking that you know what is to come in this discussion. Many readers will likely be aware that access to water is patchy across this region of the world and that those with better access are often from higher socio-economic sectors of the population.[1] True enough. Should you choose to continue beyond an overview of how this plays out in Darjeeling, however, we will share an unexpected twist to the issue of inequitable water access as it plays out in the hill station. We will explain why, even within the overall context of water stress in Darjeeling, select people do not push for better access to municipal supplies. We will also share the specificity of the hydrological features and the ingenuity of the social structures, known as *samaj*, that enable these residents to take this curious position. Samaj are community organizations that are often made up of multi-ethnic residents living in close proximity to one another. These neighbourhood groups provide support networks that help mitigate a variety of resource vulnerabilities and economic struggles, as well as the shocks associated with life cycle events such as births, weddings, and funerals.

To explain the nuances of water access in Darjeeling, we need to examine several issues relating to the themes of connection and disconnection. In what follows, we discuss who is connected to municipal waters, who is not connected to them, and how a physical disconnection to municipal water supplies fosters social affinities that lead to productive adaptations. We also clarify the limits of those social connections and the difficulty of generalizing the examples we highlight, due to the particularities of the Darjeeling experience. Towards the end of this

[1] Lahiri–Dutt (2006); O'Leary (2016); Sultana (2009, 2010, 2011); Truelove (2011).

discussion, we additionally offer insights into the relevance of geographies of exclusion to our case study. Our contention is that geographies of exclusion do persist in contemporary Darjeeling, but that social structures such as the samaj counterbalance this tendency in ways that create geographies of inclusion. The effort is to show how Darjeeling is emblematic of the wider challenge of water inequity facing Indians across the country, while also affording a relatively unique glimpse into the power and promise of social collectives.

The arguments to follow are based on a mixed set of methods. As co-authors we have engaged in collaborative studies of water management in Darjeeling since 2011, with joint periods of investigation in 2013, 2014, and 2016 ranging from 10 to 20 days each time. In this work, we have met with officials of Darjeeling Municipality as well as community activists and a selection of leaders from Darjeeling's multiple samaj.[2] This involved focus group discussions with several samaj representatives from 2013 to 2016. We have also walked several of the water transmission and distribution lines that stretch across the length of Darjeeling Township to examine the ways that people are connected to, and/or disconnected from, the municipal supplies. Our efforts benefited from previous studies that pinpoint the location of Darjeeling's numerous springs.[3] Archival materials, historical documents, academic literature, and Roshan Rai's decades spent living in Darjeeling add to the data set from which our text draws.

Municipal Connections and Colonial Legacies

Let us return momentarily to the signs posted in Darjeeling's hotels. They do not exaggerate: the lack of availability of water in Darjeeling can be acute.[4] As interlocutors pointed out when we started our discussions back in 2011, those signs also obscure the fact that tourists often have far more water at their disposal than residents. It is not uncommon in the dry season, for instance, for people in Darjeeling to get by with little more than a litre of water to wash their bodies with per day. Many such

2 As of April 2016, we have met with three municipal representatives, two technical water experts, two senior NGO representatives, and 28 samaj leaders. This amounts to a total of 35 key interlocutors.

3 Boer (2011).

4 The water deficit is estimated at 1.33 million gallons per day (Darjeeling Waterworks Department n.d.).

people go to great lengths to reuse grey water, reduce the frequency of toilet flushing, and to refrain from washing clothes unnecessarily. One of the reasons that the situation is so dire is that the water infrastructure in Darjeeling is still heavily reliant on the system instituted by the British. To explain more, we share a brief history of Darjeeling's colonial era water management.

The water management system upon which Darjeeling relies was designed around the turn of the twentieth century. When finalized in the 1930s, it was originally meant to service 10,000 to 20,000 residents. It may well have been an appropriate model at the time that it was implemented, but the system has struggled to accommodate the growth in Darjeeling's population. From 1981 to 2011 alone, the population of Darjeeling doubled. By 2011, Census figures put the number of people living permanently in Darjeeling town at 120,000. Given the persistent appeal of the picturesque hill station, there is every indication that this number will continue to increase. In addition to the permanent residents are the 200,000 people who constitute a transitory population.[5] The visitors inhabiting Darjeeling on a part-time basis include students, tourists, and migrant workers. The system servicing the Darjeeling's water needs relies on a reservoir built by the British, which is located below the Senchel Wildlife Sanctuary some 15 kilometres upstream of Darjeeling. The system is now stretched to its limits. The two lakes that make up this reservoir were manufactured for the storage of 33 million gallons of water that is perennially recharged by 26 springs[6] and an average rainfall of roughly 3,000 millimetres.[7] Overseen by the Darjeeling Municipality, the system relies on a gravity-based design to move the water through a series of pipes, a filter house, and two distribution tanks before arriving in town.

According to the municipality, the water supply system for Darjeeling includes about 35 kilometres of pipes for the transmission of water from Senchel lakes, and 83 kilometres of pipes to distribute water within the

[5] Census of India (2011).

[6] The lakes are demarcated as North and South. The North Lake, constructed in 1910, can hold up to 20 million gallons. The South Lake, constructed in 1932, can hold up to 13 million gallons (Darjeeling Waterworks Department n.d.).

[7] The rainfall is concentrated in the monsoon months of May to September when the deluge flows quickly down the steep slopes of the Darjeeling hills. While most of this is lost, some precipitation infiltrates the system to emerge as springs.

municipality. A public report notes that 95 per cent of the existing pipeline and valves were laid by 1930. This system is in great need of repair, revitalization, and improvement. A 2012 report of the Waterworks Department of the Darjeeling Municipality makes this point clear. They note: 'Not a single work was done in the past to replace the old pipeline or leaking valves.'[8] The lack of maintenance is part of the reason that water leaks are prominent through the entire supply and distribution chain. According to a water engineer at the Waterworks Department, interviewed in early 2014, the loss of water in transmission from Senchel lakes to the township is about 30–5 per cent of the total water supplied. The employee commented that about as much could again be lost within the distribution main. This means that another 30–5 per cent of the water supply could be lost after 65–70 per cent of the town's water capacity reaches the distribution point.

Once the water from Senchel arrives in town, it follows a distribution network that prioritizes the settlement patterns of colonial era Darjeeling. This settlement zone, located at the top of the hill, is now Darjeeling's most coveted—and expensive—land. As one moves away from this central hub, the downhill areas are marked by settlements of increasingly lower income residents. These poorer residents often have significantly less access to municipal waters. This fact recalls the work of others who have persuasively argued that water is a conduit and symbol of power differentials.[9] The observation is historically accurate, as water works have been a vital engineering tool used for perpetuating hegemonic cultural and socio-political models since, at least, the period of India's colonial experience.[10]

The inefficiency and inequity of the municipal water network is a visible feature of everyday life in Darjeeling. As one walks through the township, one often sees massive bundles containing dozens of pipes meant to distribute water to those fortunate enough to have their own supply. This water can come from the main distribution line or from tapping into any one of Darjeeling's numerous springs. Not all pipes in the bundles that are scattered around Darjeeling are for single households, however, as some of those pipes go to neighbourhoods where the water

[8] Darjeeling Waterworks Department (2012).

[9] Donahue and Johnston (1998); Swyngedouw (2004).

[10] Chapman and Thompson (1995); Drew (2015); Gilmartin (1994); Stone (1984); Whitcombe (1972).

is shared. The visual result is impressively rhizomatic,[11] especially when the myriad water pipes on the ground are seen in conjunction with the numerous electrical wires hanging overhead.

With these observations in mind, we suggest that there are ecological factors that play into Darjeeling's water stress but that, to a large extent, the issue of inadequate water supply is in part a manufactured crisis.[12] In saying this, we assert that the resource management system in place has exacerbated a schism between those who have access to water and those who do not (Figure 10.1). Such schisms reflect the overall

Figure 10.1 A Darjeeling Resident Manually Carrying Water while Walking Past Water Pipes
Source: Photograph by Georgina Drew (January 2014).

[11] In labelling it rhizomatic, we flag the seen and unseen networks discussed in philosophical detail by Deleuze and Guattari (1988).

[12] This observation draws on the work of Barbara Rose Johnston (2005). Her work encourages us to think about the ways that water stress is a feature of management and governance failures rather than merely a quantitative issue of overall water availability.

trajectory of development in Darjeeling.[13] It is within this manufactured crisis of water stress that Darjeeling's 'village societies' or *gau samaj* play an important intervening role. For ease of reference, we will henceforth refer to them simply as samaj.

Municipal Disconnections and Samaj Affects

Darjeeling's samaj are geographically clustered collectives. These collectives are often multi-ethnic and based on residential patterns, rather than shared cultural or religious practices.[14] Given the diasporic population and the heterogeneous nature of Darjeeling's settlement patterns[15] the samaj are often a stand-in for kin and ethnic-based networks.[16] That said, residence alone is not enough to ensure samaj affiliation. A neighbourhood might have a samaj, but not all neighbours may belong to it in an official sense. Rather, people join samaj after a selection process is complete and a membership fee is paid. Once a person belongs to a samaj, he/she is entitled to emergency financial assistance as well as a considerable amount of social support. In a sense, they are akin to an informal insurance system that also serves as a social safety net. Members argue that the system simultaneously provides members 'self-reliance' as opposed to dependence on municipal or state governing bodies.

A driving concept of the samaj is the idea that they provide *kalyan*, a Nepali term that can be translated as 'welfare'. As a samaj member adamantly stated when asked, people join the samaj because they offer an 'invisible structure' that buffers the risks and insecurities associated with everyday life. By taking monthly fees, often of about Rs. 100 per member,

[13] Development, propelled by tourism and the need to accommodate increasing rates of rural to urban migration, has changed Darjeeling's landscape. The rise of quickly made and visually uninspiring cement buildings is a source of contention. When these buildings are constructed alongside historic and aesthetically pleasing colonial era structures, residents are apt to lament the loss of the city's former 'charm' and character (Scrase and Ganguly–Scrase [2015]).

[14] Shneiderman (2015: 210).

[15] Shneiderman (2015: xv–xvi); see also Middleton, this volume.

[16] As a result of this clustering, it is common to see ethnically diverse samaj members participating in the cultural or religious activities of their neighbours. By way of example, when the ethnic Thangmi host life-cycle rituals in Darjeeling, it is common for a large portion of attendees to come from non-Thangmi households (Shneiderman 2015: 210).

the samaj have a pool of resources to distribute in times of need, such as medical emergencies, weddings, funerals, and disasters. When needed, these funds are disbursed as a one-time grant, or as a loan. Additional funds can also be collected depending on the circumstances. In some samaj, for instance, each member is likely to give an additional ₹20–₹50 to a family that has experienced a trauma such as a medical emergency or a death. When pooled, these funds help cover hospital fees and the high costs that can be associated with funerals.

Important for our discussion, the samaj also fight for basic resource provisions for their members. In the formerly unplanned settlements, the samaj have been particularly active in the effort to access and manage water not provided by the municipality. Spring water features prominently in their provision strategies. In this chapter, we highlight three samaj that have been highly involved in securing water for their members. These are Muldara, Jawahar Busti, and Mangalpuri (Figure 10.2).

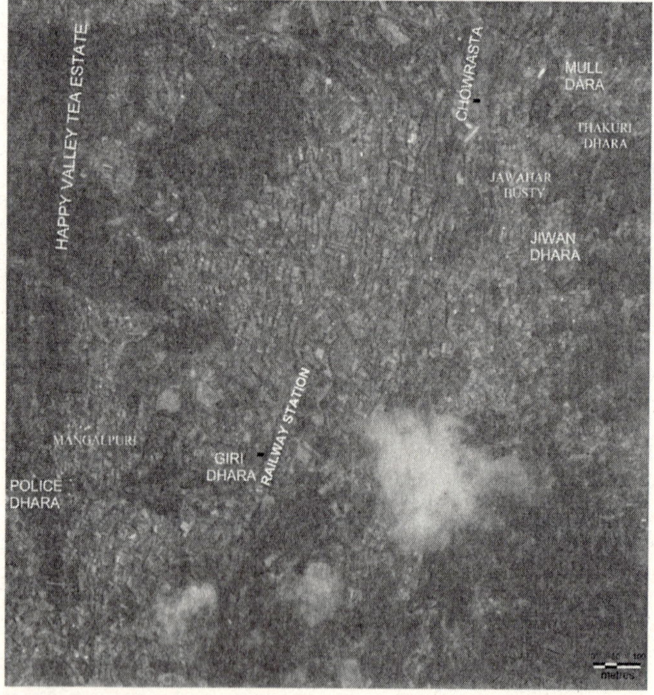

Figure 10.2 Map of Muldara, Jawahar Busti, and Mangalpuri Samaj in Darjeeling

Source: Photograph by Georgina Drew.

The first two are located on the south–east, just downhill from Darjeeling's iconic gathering point known as Chowrasta. The third is located on the south–west side of town, a section that is witnessing rapid residential expansion due to its proximity to a series of established and under-construction roads.

The three samaj that we emphasize are connected in varying degrees to municipal water supplies.[17] Yet in all cases, the samaj members and leaders we encountered were highly critical of the quality of these municipal waters. While the samaj members did not always know the details of how the water was managed, many had the impression that water supplied by the municipality was inferior to the spring water upon which many of them depend to a much greater extent. In a focus group with four Jawahar Busti samaj members in 2016, for instance, interlocutors used a barrage of adjectives including 'rusty', 'muddy', and 'smelly' to describe the municipal supplies. These descriptions were met with laughter as several members pinched their faces in disgust when speaking of the rancid materiality of that resource.[18] The spring water to which they have access was, in contrast, most often described as 'sweet' and enjoyable to drink.

Jawahar Busti has a continually evolving relationship to the municipality and its waters. Inhabited since at least the early 1960s, the enclave was called the Manpari Busti, which translates to the 'do what you like colony'. This name was used primarily when it constituted unplanned residences built on Public Works Department land. Nowadays, the top 75 per cent of Jawahar Busti is zoned as municipal while the lower 25 per cent remains in a rural zone. With their municipal incorporation in 1997 came the expectation that Jawahar Busti residents pay a *dhuri* tax.[19] This is a temporary landholding tax that is paid up until the finalization of

[17] Jawahar Busti and Mangalpuri receive varying increments of municipal supplies whereas Muldara receives almost none.

[18] This was punctuated by a story, told with gusto, of a suicide at Senchel lake back in 2008. For three days after the event took place, the municipality let flow an uninterrupted supply of water to all municipal taps without telling the public the reason for their flushing activities. When it came to light that they were cleaning the lake after recovering a body, people were incensed to discover that they consumed contaminated resources.

[19] *Dhuri* is a Nepali word for that which is above you (such as the roof over one's head). It also refers to the household unit, especially when written as *ghardhuri*.

ownership. The Jawahar Busti residents negotiated with the government for a municipal water line and seven hydrants after the incorporation. Even with these provisions, the samaj leaders of Jawahar Busti with whom we spoke did not see much benefit in being connected to the municipality. The incorporation had only resulted in a few more hydrants than they would have had otherwise; the municipal water quality was poor; and they did not necessarily enjoy paying the dhuri tax. At the time of our last meeting with samaj members, in April of 2016, their temporary solution was to try and lobby municipal officials for improved services.

The experience of Mangalpuri samaj further softens the expectation that being a part of the municipality brings with it improved water quality and water security. Located a short walk downhill from the Darjeeling train station, Mangalpuri samaj has been considered a part of the municipality since at least the 1970s. Samaj residents contend that they have long constituted an important vote bank for regional politicians. With 1,400 voters, their numbers are certainly sizeable and significant enough for close–call elections, especially that of the Municipal Commissioner. To court the votes of their samaj, politicians regularly make promises that hardly ever materialize. One woman wryly commented on this with the observation that, 'Up is up and down will always remain down.' Her point was that, despite performative efforts at inclusion within the municipality, the Mangalpuri samaj members seem to be unassociated with what happens uphill towards the administrative and political centre of town. As a part of this disconnected 'down', the Mangalpuri samaj members are often forgotten.

Other Mangalpuri residents echoed the claim that they receive few benefits from being a part of the municipality. Aside from the right to vote, the only provision was a single pipe leading to their enclave. Each member contributed their own money (roughly Rs. 300 each) in order to create five water points for distribution within the samaj. From each water point, a family can get between 10 and 20 litres of municipal water per week. This water, they complain, is yellow, foul-smelling, and not fit for even washing clothes. In recent years, in fact, they have threatened to secede from the municipality as a protest for their poor treatment. If they were no longer a part of the municipality, some quipped, they would not have to pay dhuri tax and they would no longer serve as pawns in Darjeeling's municipal politics. What's more, if they were part of the panchayat system, then they would be able to access government-sponsored rural livelihood schemes as well as provisions for water storage and pipe connectivity.

Several of these concerns were shared with us, while we were sitting in a small indigo-painted room in the middle of Mangalpuri with four gentlemen (and later, with three women). An old photo of Nepal's royal family, apparently taken months or years before the 2001 massacre, hung from an electrical wire, along with a portrait of a man in army uniform and several bouquets of plastic flowers, all of which were set in frames. The person speaking the most was the owner of the house in which we were convened. As we looked at the pile of letters for other Mangalpuri residents sitting on his desk and awaiting collection, he joked that he also serves as a de facto postman. His home's roadside location and the lack of accurate addresses for the other samaj members meant that his house was an ideal receiving point. This man, whom we shall call Naveen, spoke at length about the benefits of being in the samaj, stressing many of the points we made earlier. He also commented on how the quality of one's contributions to the samaj 'affects how people respond to your death'. As he explained in jest, a person's efforts to help others via the samaj impacts whether people feel sad when you die, or whether they nod and say with satisfaction, 'that is good' upon hearing the news.

Like the others, Naveen emphasized that despite their incorporation within the municipality's boundaries, Mangalpuri residents receive no 'benefits' from the municipal organizations that are supposed to provide services. In an attempt to get better provisions, they were briefly in touch with those campaigning for an independent federal state of Gorkhaland. In particular, they met with Subash Ghisingh, the chairperson of the DGHC to request help in acquiring more facilities and permanent land rights. In response, they got a terse reply, stating that all the samaj's problems would be solved 'as soon as Gorkhaland comes'. Because of such refusals of help from authorities in specific municipal organizations and in the DGHC, Naveen lamented, 'we feel like refugees in our own land.' As time went on, feelings of being a marginal population caught in a wider political game were elaborated by transitions and internal disputes within the local administration and the inception of the second Gorkhaland Movement. In 2007, the DGHC lost momentum after Ghisingh's position was usurped by his second-in-command, Bimal Gurung, who established the GJM (discussed elsewhere in this volume).[20] The DGHC was finally dissolved in 2012 and replaced by

[20] See also Besky (2013); Chettri (2013: 299); Shneiderman (2015: 25–6).

another semi-autonomous organizational body, the GTA.[21] For the samaj leaders with whom we spoke, these political twists and turns meant that their everyday concerns—including their worries for water provision—were overlooked amidst wider struggles for power.

When asked if the promise of Gorkhaland still held their hopes, a reply was initially given in the form of knowing chuckles from all the men gathered in the room. The verbal response that followed was that there are too many parties and no real unity to foster such a development. Rather, the demand for Gorkhaland has become like a 'begging bowl' for the political parties. Implied in these statements is an assertion that threats of further agitation for Gorkhaland are now used primarily to force payouts for specific programmes (and potentially to specific people). They use Gorkhaland, in other words, as a leveraging device to get funds instead of the actualization of an independent state. Regardless of the accuracy of this assessment, such impressions are a reflection of the widespread skepticism of political parties, and of Darjeeling politics.

Social Connections and Samaj Affects

As self-described 'ordinary people', the Mangalpuri samaj members try to stay out of politics as much as possible. They focus instead on maintaining the spring pumping systems they set up to distribute water to each of the samaj households on a rotating, alternate day basis. Two employees maintain this system with precision and are paid ₹2,500 a month to look after the pumps and the distribution network. The programme is successful, and the samaj receives regular petitions from others to join so that they can benefit from this system. New applications for membership that the samaj feels are primarily aimed at acquiring more water (rather than more social connections) are put on indefinite hold. Still, they often help out neighbours in times of need, even when they are not samaj members. This willingness to help extends to other samaj. When a nearby samaj faces a crisis, the members of Mangalpuri samaj often share goods or offer donations.

Unlike the Jawahar Busti and Mangalpuri samaj, the Muldara samaj receives no municipal water supplies. In our conversations with

[21] The word semi-autonomous is used to describe the GTA because it has administrative, executive, and financial powers but it does not have legislative authority.

members, this was not often seen as a problem. In an impromptu focus group meeting by the main spring, located directly downhill from Chowrasta, three women and three men explained that the experiences of neighbouring samaj served as cautionary tales for being on the water grid. Two adjacent samaj, for instance, had recently received municipal connections, but these connections had taken nearly a year to materialize and brought with them new fees for the samaj and its members. Anyone wanting more than just access to a municipal tap—for instance, a piped connection to one's home—also has to pay a fixed price of Rs. 35,000. When contrasted with the low maintenance and low fee requirements of spring water collection, the municipal supply seems unnecessary. Some of the women with whom we spoke even declared that their trip to collect water offers a means of daily exercise and a chance to see neighbours. The main drawback is the limited amount of water that one can collect. Due to the physical limitations of what a person can carry and the rules for water collection, a samaj member can only take 30 litres of water at a time.

Set in contrast to the problems of quality resource provision associated with the municipality, our interlocutors expressed pride in what they have accomplished together. For many of these people, the samaj efforts did more than just help people access resources; they also created strong social cohesion. This is manifested in feelings of connectivity to one another, as well as feelings of belonging to their samaj.

Whether in Jawahar Busti, Mangalpuri, or Muldara, it was the regularity of interactions related to water that people most often cited as a source of robust connection to their samaj. There are pragmatic reasons for this. Whereas weddings, funerals, and emergencies are occasional events, water management is an everyday activity. Members see each other day-in and day-out when accessing water supplies at one of their communally managed spring sources and at communal hydrants.[22] Samaj members might help each other collect water on days when neighbours get sick or busy. They may even assist each other in carrying their heavy 20 to 30 litre loads of water up the mountainside. It is these banal acts of camaraderie to which people point when trying to explain their strong sense of samaj affiliation.

[22] Members in locations like Muldara also regulate one another to make sure they are only taking their due share. When they see others breaking the rules, they might opt to publicly chastise them. If that does not work, they might bring the matter to the samaj leaders and call for punishment.

It is possible, of course, that samaj members emphasized the everyday acts of water collection because that was our topic of study and the point of enquiry that we repeatedly stressed. Upon reflection, it is likely a range of affiliations and social interactions that contribute to feelings of belonging. So along with the salient component of resource sharing and resource management, some additional aspects of samaj belonging are important to note. These include statements about how samaj members see themselves, as well as how they are seen by others, especially when situated in lower socio-economic neighbourhoods. A more in-depth look at these factors helps to further explain the complexity of the samaj and the role they play in Darjeeling.

Added Layers of Samaj Belonging and Identity

When asked about their sense of identity at focus group meetings, interlocutors declared that they most closely identified as samaj members rather than as residents of Darjeeling. In evidence of this, several interlocutors maintained that their feelings of belonging to the samaj were as strong as their feelings of affinity for their particular caste, ethnic group, or religion. For instance, a Muslim man in the Mangalpuri samaj stated that he feels just as connected to his fellow samaj members as to other Darjeeling residents who share his faith. And as another man in Jawahar Busti stated, he might tell others he is from Darjeeling when he is out of the region, but, when he is in the district, he uses geographic indictors and his samaj affiliation to situate himself in relation to others. To some, these sentiments may additionally reflect a strong sense of class solidarity since the samaj are geographic clusters of residents who often have similar socio-economic standing. The idea that class is more important than other caste, kin, or ethnic indicators is something that scholars like Liechty argue is occurring in places such as Kathmandu.[23] Brown et al. have noted a potentially similar trend in Darjeeling. They assert that class affiliations are now so prominent that during their period of research, 'no one was bothered about being a Nepali or a Bengali or a Marwari.'[24]

[23] Liechty (2002).

[24] Brown, Ganguly–Scrase, and Scrase (2016: 12). They also assert that class-based divisions are to blame for an increasing level of tension between middle class and lower class residents. Their study shows that the better off urban residents actively worked to maintain their own 'cosmopolitan' cultural

Three observations are worth noting in relation to the aforementioned statements and analyses about the importance of the samaj. First, many comments about samaj affinity were given when in the presence of other samaj members and there is likely a performative element to such assertions. Second, many samaj have been around since the 1970s, so several decades have allowed for the solidification of shared practices, and of a shared samaj identity. Scholars such as Holland and Lave argue that identities are shaped by the intersection between historical institutions (including social and governmental structures) and the lived experiences that help people understand who they are and where they belong.[25] The resulting identity formation is rarely singular; people can articulate multiple components of their identity and these may vary in place and time. After all, certain aspects of a person's identity become more prominent according to the circumstances, location, and company in which they find themselves (such as when they are home, at school, at work, or in a faith-based organization). The third point is related to the second. It includes the assertion that notions of belonging to a certain class, ethnic group, or religious following can still be important and influential to how residents see themselves and their neighbours. Co-author Rai of Darjeeling, for instance, connects to his samaj affiliation, his ethnic Rai heritage, and his Catholic faith. The aspect of his identity that is most prominent at any given time depends on the context in which he finds himself. To bring the point back to the samaj, therefore, we do not find it surprising that the primary identity that a person often asserts when situated within the geographical boundaries of the samaj is their samaj affiliation.

Notably, the feelings of samaj affinity were not without a touch of the 'anxious belongings' outlined by Middleton in his study of the embodied and affective dimensions of political life in Darjeeling.[26] In other words, the feelings of belonging within the samaj were not necessarily stable, and the prevailing sentiment of how samaj members relate to one another, as

---

capital and habitus in ways that were derogatory towards lower class Darjeeling residents, and especially the ones that have recently migrated from the rural areas. Their arguments draw from the practice–theory work of Pierre Bourdieu (1977, 1984). His articulation of habitus emphasized the durable dispositions that are passed down across generations in ways that are susceptible to change yet are not frequently challenged due to assumptions of their naturalization.

25 Holland and Lave (2001).

26 Middleton (2013a).

well as to Darjeeling at large, could vary. The Jawahar Busti samaj members gave an indication of this. In a focus group meeting, four interlocutors were initially vocal in their expressions of pride for the ways that they have organized themselves as a cohesive collective. The men repeatedly called their samaj 'strong', using the English word, and said that they are able to effectively lobby administrators and politicians. They also elaborated on the nuanced rules and regulations that govern the use of spring and municipal waters in their samaj. Their system includes rotational family use of the springs at allocated hours publicly listed near several source points. They also oversee the upkeep of the springs, of which there are three public ones (and two that are privately owned). It was in light of their extensive efforts, and the high degree of social organization they have achieved, that they commented with dismay that the municipality ended up labelling them as a 'slum' when they were included in the municipality. This English term was used rather than a Nepali or Bengali translation. They found this nomenclature upsetting. When asked to describe how it felt to be classified as a slum, one interlocutor announced, 'it stinks'. In this example, we see the carefully constructed articulations of self-worth upset by an externally imposed label that tests the strength of the samaj's pride, and which potentially impacts notions of belonging to the municipality.

Resource Precarity and Social Vulnerabilities

Despite the impressive ways that the samaj have worked to get water for their members, there are problems that persist, which may continue to grow. To start with, the energy, physical fortitude, and time required for spring water collection is considerable for some samaj members. Women in Jawahar Busti pointed to the long line of plastic containers surrounding one source point to indicate that, even when the spring is no less than five minutes from their home, they often have to spend one to two hours each day collecting water (Figure 10.3). This is particularly true on days in the dry season of March to May when the flow of water is reduced. In Jawahar Busti and Muldara, interlocutors similarly stated that the walk to the spring was nothing in comparison to how long it took to fill containers and carry them back up the hill. For those living close to the top, nearly within arm's reach of Chowrasta, yet still without access to tap water, the time needed to collect water was too great. One interlocutor, with two children and jobs as a lawyer and part–time shop owner, confessed to paying Rs. 600 a month to have others deliver spring

Figure 10.3 Waiting for Water at Jawahar Busti
Source: Photograph by Georgina Drew (April 2016).

water to his doorstep. When these issues are taken into consideration, the two main upsides to the reliance on springs are the perceptions of the high quality of the water and the fact that they can be distributed efficiently within the samaj.

While the reliance on springs is presently adaptive, the nature of development in Darjeeling means that they may not be a source upon which residents can depend entirely in the long term. There are numerous reasons for this. The first is an indication that the springs are susceptible to cross-contamination with the waste and sewage that flows in drains alongside many of Darjeeling's springs. There may also be contamination that takes place along the spring lines at susceptible points. Mystery illnesses are now rising. In Mangalpuri, residents worried about the safety of their spring water after five cases of cancer and 10 cases of tuberculosis (TB) were diagnosed in 2015. The cases of TB were cured—and the samaj helped to make sure that those suffering from TB had access to medications, and that they took them regularly—but worries persist about environmental conditions impacting overall public health.

Development is another key issue that raises concerns about the long-term viability of springs. A lot of the past development took place above the springs. But as the township continues to grow, buildings are emerging nearer to the downhill springs. On our last visit to Muldara, a house was being constructed just a 100 feet above the main source point for samaj members. Mud from the construction site was flowing down the sewage drains and there was concern that the digging for the foundations could put the spring in jeopardy by shifting the underground channels. Alongside these development practices is the threat of human-induced and natural disasters. Development activities uphill put pressure on the land and increase the chances of landslides when necessary guidelines are not followed. Aware of this connection, residents talked at length about their fears of landslides. Muldara samaj members pointed to an exposed and deforested patch of earth above their spring explaining their fear of being crushed under a landslide when the next monsoon arrives.

Our interlocutors were particularly adamant that the pace of development was too swift, and that not enough precautions were being taken. One samaj member declared the township to be overcrowded and he worried that the scarcity of development-eligible land near the market meant that people were building higher than they should. The development fears overlapped with concerns about what will happen when an earthquake strikes. A woman living at the bottom of Jawahar Busti wondered aloud why the residents above her couldn't see that they were putting the lives of those downhill in danger with all of the risky construction that could topple in a sizeable earthquake. In a heart-wrenching commentary, she declared that she and her family would not have time to say 'Aay–ya!' as the buildings fall on them, taking their homes and lives in a single blow. She and others recalled recent earthquakes that underscored their vulnerability. The 2015 earthquakes in Nepal were felt in Darjeeling, as was the 2011 quake in nearby Sikkim. The media images that followed these events showed in shocking detail the devastation that an earthquake can bring to poorly planned mountain habitats.

In addition to these concerns, there is also the worry that springs' plentitude will suffer as the landscape transforms, via a loss of green cover and forestry, and as the climate continues to change. Within the last 20 years in Muldara, the spring flow has slowed significantly. While the spring used to fill a 4-inch pipe, it now barely fills a 1-inch pipe. Before, residents could fill up a water container of 10–15 litres almost instantly. Now, it takes five minutes to fill up their containers. As the rate of water flow declines, the lines back up. This puts pressure on time schedules, making the act of water collection even more difficult and painstaking. To emphasize the significance of this point, it is important to realize that time spent collecting water is time that is not spent doing other tasks that are also important. Men and women, for instance, may experience a decrease in their ability to earn household income while students lose time to study.[27]

Discussion and Comments on Geographies of Exclusion

The chapter highlights the resource challenges, as well as the social subjectivities, found within Darjeeling's diverse hydrological landscape. The subjectivities touched upon are influenced by varying degrees of connection to municipal waters, as well as the affinities that are produced through belonging to a samaj. In Darjeeling, the subjectivities associated with water arise in parallel to what some call 'geographies of exclusion'. Sibley's approach to geographies of exclusion contains the idea that space is always contested and that 'relatively trivial conflicts can provide clues about power relations and the role of space in social control'.[28] Put in other words, attention to geographies of exclusion helps illuminate how inequalities and identity-based conflicts are spread across spaces and places. While postcolonial water management schemas make clear how such geographies of exclusion operate in Darjeeling, we suggest that the samaj simultaneously create what we might call 'geographies of inclusion', especially within their locational clusters. Neither of these domains is pure, of course, so in saying this we do not mean to institute a binary that demonizes the municipality or overly sanctifies the work of the samaj. Rather, the two are on a relational continuum. The

27 See also Joshi (2014).
28 Sibley (1995: xiii).

extent of the exclusion or inclusion operating in either domain can vary over time.

Geographies of exclusion are known to produce feelings of abjection.[29] Anand's work demonstrates how abjection, or sentiments of unwantedness and otherness, arise in the slums of Mumbai when residents do not have access to adequate water supplies.[30] While we would not go so far as to discount the prevalence of abjection, the data on Darjeeling's samaj softens our ability to end this discussion with a focus on that sentiment alone. The reason for this is both biophysical as well as social.

On the biophysical side, the spring water that the samaj enjoy is perceived as clean, good, and sweet. It is far preferable to the dubious colonial legacy municipal water supply that appears less pure to the naked eye, is harder on the palate, and is likely carrying unwanted bacteria and heavy metals. While lower income Darjeeling residents who do not receive municipal waters might not have the same type of 'hydraulic citizenship'[31] as those on the water grid, the high quality and adequate quantity of the spring waters they receive help to offset the sentiments of abjection that this might inspire. On the social side, the samaj create means through which people are able to connect to one another in ways that are in direct response to municipal inadequacies and erstwhile exclusions. This has created social bonds that our interlocutors described as strong. The feelings of affinity and solidarity are forged through the structures that the samaj create, and they are reconstituted daily in practices of water collection and management. While there is animosity and anger over how the municipality treats the samaj, including labelling them as slums, the sentiments of abjection that might occur are therefore tempered, to restate the point, with feelings of social inclusion. These affinities are layered into varying degrees of association with the Gorkhaland Movement, which studies credit to communal efforts to fashion a common regional identity among people from diverse backgrounds sharing longstanding connections to one another and to the Darjeeling hills.[32]

To close the discussion, we stress again that our findings on the simultaneity of sentiments of connection and disconnection are possible because of the resilience of Darjeeling's samaj, along with their ability

29 Sibley (1995: 8).

30 Anand (2012).

31 Anand (2011: 545).

32 Chettri (2013).

to provide for themselves basic necessities such as water. The emplaced and location-specific attributes of the samaj are uniquely positioned to address the water struggles that emerge in and around the township. They do this in ways that capacitate the multi-lingual and multi-ethnic populations that have come to inhabit Darjeeling through decades of migration to an otherwise sparsely inhabited region. Put in other words, the story of connection amidst disconnection in Darjeeling shows how the experience of resource struggle in this postcolonial settlement is intricately tied to past and contemporary settlement patterns of an ethnically, culturally, and religiously heterogeneous population. Having said that, we celebrate this distinctiveness with a sentiment of caution. Should the viability of environmentally sensitive springs diminish, or should the cohesion of the samaj deteriorate, then future investigations may uphold arguments leaning more strongly towards the abject relations created through geographies of exclusion. Such studies might echo insights into the exclusionary urban water ecologies of Delhi,[33] Mumbai,[34] and Kathmandu.[35] Until the resource base or the level of social resilience deteriorates, Darjeeling's experience remains distinct and difficult to generalize due to the prevalence of vital support networks such as the samaj.

[33] Baviskar (2011); O'Leary (2016).

[34] Anand (2011, 2012).

[35] Rademacher (2011).

11 *Women, Fair Trade Tea, and Everyday Entrepreneurialism in Rural Darjeeling*

Debarati Sen*

The iconic image of a nimble-fingered Nepali plantation worker dominates the gendered tropes which sustain popular imaginations of economic life in Darjeeling. Such gendered tropes about women's labour and economic life conceal more than they

* I would like to thank *Feminist Studies* for granting permission to use material from a version of this chapter that appeared in the journal in 2014. I am grateful to Kennesaw State University's College of Humanities and Social Sciences for their seed grant that enabled follow-up research in Darjeeling in recent years. A major part of my research in Darjeeling has benefited from a Wenner Gren Foundation Individual Research Grant (no. 7495), and an NSF DDIG Grant (no. 0612860). The respective feedback from editors of this volume, as well as the anonymous reviewers of this collection is much appreciated.

reveal about everyday life in Darjeeling's out-of-the-way places. The aesthetics of plantation life produce a 'lie of the land' that obscures our understanding of women's economic and political lives in Darjeeling. My objective in this chapter is to broaden our understanding of the contemporary economic and social lives of Darjeeling's rural women. It is important to understand the critical work that women in rural Darjeeling do—their everyday entrepreneurialisms—that sustain households and much more in the hills (Figure 11.1).

Such entrepreneurial work is also deeply political at the community and household level. This work has been affected and shaped by successive interventions of the local state, as well as NGO initiatives.[1] Women's entrepreneurial work remains in deep dialogue with patriarchal systems, both local and transnational, that affect the reputation and resource access potential of women in rural Darjeeling. Most recently transnational Fair Trade initiatives have endeavoured to claim women entrepreneurs as their beneficiaries. This chapter explores how women

Figure 11.1 The Multicropping Arrangement of Tea Farms as Opposed to the Monoculture of Plantations
Source: Photograph by Author.

[1] Darjeeling Laden La Road Prerana (2003a).

engage with Fair Trade, make sense of its potential benefits, and act upon its governance practices.

During my ethnographic work among women organic tea producers in rural Darjeeling, I frequently faced difficult questions about the meaning and materiality of Fair Trade. Women smallholder tea farmers were gradually becoming conscious about the global popularity of the organic tea they produced. I would often engage in conversations with women like Prema who farmed organic tea and attended organic and Fair Trade training organized by her cooperative Sanu Krishak Sanstha (SKS) or Small Farmers' Organization. Prema, and other women like her, remained deeply skeptical about the potential of these transnational sustainability and justice-promoting ventures. Whenever I showed Prema Fair Trade publicity materials with smiling faces of women tea producers like her, she always commented with statements such as:

> Another one! You know that smiling woman on that tea package is not us. It's nice to know people around the world care about us so much, but why now? Where were these people when we had no roads, when no one gave us loans, when we ate only stale rice? What can they do for us if they do not care about what we women want?

Prema's sarcastic response provides a powerful critique of the moral basis of the Fair Trade movement's empowerment directives that govern tea cooperatives in producer communities and have specific consequences for smallholder women tea farmers' political lives within that context. It was also a rebuke of the virtualities through which Fair Trade maintains its legitimacy.[2]

Such pointed reflection and the accompanying juxtaposition of 'Fair Trade' and *swaccha vyapar* (a Nepali iteration of Fair Trade which means 'clear business') gradually revealed to me how certain intended beneficiaries of the global Fair Trade movement understood the value of Fair Trade in the context of their situated identity struggles and their efforts to gain social and economic justice. Local NGOs and visiting Fair Trade officials used the term *swaccha vyapar* in their information sessions and residents of rural Darjeeling had adopted the phrase as a way to express their understanding of Fair Trade. As will become evident in the rest of this chapter, the use of *swaccha vyapar* constituted more than simply using a Nepali translation of an English term. This terminology was posed as a critique of the intentions of global Fair Trade.

[2] Sen (2016); West (2012).

As a trade-based, transnational social justice movement, Fair Trade's key tenets are to empower marginalized producers, to ensure their participation in key decision-making institutions in their communities, and to promote social justice in general,[3] with a core focus on women's empowerment.[4] It is an alternative economic system, but what distinguishes it from 'free trade' is its imperative to measure and manage the working of social justice through this trading system.[5] Fair Trade promoters and activist consumers believe that ethical buying and selling of Fair Trade tea across national borders can fulfil these goals by channelling new resources and governance mechanisms to producer communities. The Fair Trade product label stands as a proof and promise of trade-based justice work.

What remains unexplored within this abstract global discourse on Fair Trade is how subjects of transnational justice regimes, in this case smallholder women tea farmers in rural Darjeeling, understand and mobilize around the governance practices of ostensibly ethical transnational justice regimes like Fair Trade. More specifically, how do they understand and engage with Fair Trade in the context of their specific identities (as housewives and savvy entrepreneurs) and histories of contention over gendered access to resources in their own communities? It is critical that we understand these sites of critical negotiation with Fair Trade as an example of gendered navigation, and as a critique of globalization and its imbrication with local patriarchies.[6] Through long-term ethnography of Fair Trade operations and their effects on a small-holder tea farmers' cooperative in rural Darjeeling, I contend that Fair Trade interventions can inadvertently strengthen patriarchal/gendered power relations in producer communities, but that smallholder women tea farmers also make creative use of specific Fair Trade interventions to defend their own priorities and rupture Fair Trade's complicity with male domination in their communities. The gendered contestation around Fair Trade is also a critique of these so-called 'sustainability' campaigns to address women's everyday abilities to lead an economically satisfying and respectful life.[7]

[3] Dolan (2010); Moberg and Lyon (2010).
[4] Lyon (2008).
[5] Sen and Majumder (2011).
[6] Sharma (2008).
[7] Sen (2017).

As I will demonstrate ethnographically, the repeated juxtaposition of Fair Trade and *swaccha vyapar* in regular conversation was a rhetorical strategy by which smallholder women tea farmers articulated the shortcomings of Fair Trade in promoting their specific economic pursuits, which they had nurtured during previous participation in other transnational justice regimes like micro-lending. More importantly, women's situated reading of 'fairness' in Fair Trade was filtered through a localized, gendered political economy in which they had to struggle to gain respect and recognition for their daily labour and entrepreneurial ventures, which were critical for their families' and communities' survival in a context of shrinking economic opportunities for men. As I detail later, women's entrepreneurial ventures involved illegal sale of tea and sale of alcohol, milk, and other produce from their farms, ventures they financed through micro-loans. For them 'Fair Trade' could become swaccha vyapar only if it helped them to meet the needs of their families with dignity through their women-only business ventures, and allowed them to mitigate the domination of local middlemen who became virtual brokers of transnational market-based justice regimes in their communities.

In recent years, feminist scholars have nurtured healthy skepticism about empowerment strategies.[8] More worthy of critical feminist examination is how rural women, who contest gendered resource inequities in their own communities, strategically mobilize around transnational justice regimes like Fair Trade. I see women's critique of Fair Trade as centred on its use of their images to sell tea in Western markets, while leaving their labour and struggles unrecognized.[9] Therefore, the images on tea packaging and posters that show women happily plucking tea obscure the male domination of the actual process of justice delivery. To challenge this opaqueness, women use the phrase swaccha vyapar, which at least rhetorically foregrounds their work and challenges the male domination that devalues their labour and entrepreneurship. To contest how they are represented, they seek to represent themselves. The rhetoric of swaccha vyapar connects the discursive contestation with the actual ones by linking women's struggles over recognition and respect for their labour with competition over resources. My findings are based on ethnographic research I conducted in Darjeeling between 2004 and 2015.

[8] For more on feminist critiques of liberal empowerment strategies, see Grewal and Kaplan (1994); Kabeer (1999); Karim (2011); Rankin (2004), Spivak (1993).

[9] Chatterjee (2001).

I conducted close participant observation of the economic and social lives of a core group of smallholder women tea farmers, and interviewed many people associated with them, both male and female. To further situate these critical gendered contestations around Fair Trade, I first elucidate Fair Trade's gradual imbrication with local patriarchies, then demonstrate the ways women contested this imbrication helping develop a 'vernacular calculus of the economic'[10]—a gendered evaluation of Fair Trade from the vantage point of everyday struggles for resources and recognition.

The Emergence of Smallholder Tea Production and Fair Trade in Darjeeling

Smallholder tea cultivation is quite frequent outside plantations. But the fact that some of this cultivation has become organic is a recent development, and was discovered quite by accident in the mid-1990s. SKS members were part of a plantation, which was abandoned soon after India's Independence. Plantation workers became like refugees squatting on state land without any proper economic prospect. The years of tea mono-cropping had made their land unsuitable for subsistence agriculture, leading some farmers to uproot the bushes. Desperate plantation workers engaged in illegal timber trade, looked for jobs in Darjeeling town, or migrated to other places in India. Women in these households, however, harvested teas, hand rolled and dried them and sold them to local tea vendors. Sometime they also made treacherous trips (of 20 kilometres) to Darjeeling town to sell such dry contraband tea to local tea shops in order to get a better price than what was offered by local middlemen. The picture below (Figure 11.2) shows how tea is processed at home. This tea is still designated 'illegal' by the Darjeeling Tea Association.[11]

However, key transformations in the global tea market since the 1990s—especially the growing demand for organic and Fair Trade certified teas—brought non-plantation tea production in Darjeeling into the limelight. Darjeeling tea plantations were forced to adopt organic tea production in the 1990s and to give up the chemical-intensive agriculture that was popularized by the postcolonial Indian state in the 1960s.

[10] Ramamurthy (2011).

[11] Darjeeling Laden La Road Prerana (2003b).

Figure 11.2 Woman Tea Farmer Handrolls Tea in Her Kitchen
Source: Photograph by Author.

The switch to organic methods and abandonment of chemical fertilizers resulted in an average 30 per cent decline in total tea production per plantation.[12]

Before the advent of Fair Trade and the organic tea boom, local NGOs engaged in relief and development work, intervened to help these marginalized tea producers in many ways, encouraging them to form a cooperative and explore animal husbandry and other economic ventures. The cooperative that the women in this study belonged to was formed in the mid-1990s, but was not registered with the state until about 2007. Sensing the economic potential of Fair Trade alliances for small tea producers, an NGO helped them formally register their cooperative so that they could better bargain with plantations. Since

[12] Bisen and Singh (2012).

small-farmers' cooperatives could not afford expensive tea processing equipment, they had to sell raw tea leaves to plantations. NGOs intervened to ensure that the cooperative received a competitive price for the raw tea sold to plantations. They also instated safeguards to prevent plantations from selling small-farmer-grown tea under their own label, obliging them instead to help with processing the tea and marketing of it as cooperative-produced. Additional Fair Trade certification of the cooperative ensured good contracts with plantations monitored by Fair Trade Labeling Organization International (FLO), a transnational governing body overseeing the trade and governance aspects of Fair Trade's operations across the world. At present in Darjeeling, two formal tea cooperatives represent smallholder tea producers living outside plantations, one of which is studied here.[13]

Due to acute lack of economic opportunity in rural areas, local male middlemen and male members of tea farming households sensed an important economic opportunity with the advent of Fair Trade. They gained prominence in the process of formalizing the cooperatives, even though women overwhelmingly did the actual work of tea production. The local NGOs had to rely on these patriarchs since they were literate and had the skills to run an organization. SKS's women farmers realized their worth in the organic tea production and Fair Trade certification process, but simultaneously felt a sense of loss as male community members and local middlemen came to dominate the newly formed SKS and ultimately control tea profits. This realization of self-worth led women to battle the male-dominated tea farmers' cooperative over its failure to acknowledge their efforts in sustaining organic tea production in the region.

As Fair Trade's economic premium money started pouring into the cooperative, smallholder women tea farmers realized the resources they were amassing were inaccessible because they were being invested in community development projects not involving women. Women's contention that Fair Trade was not swaccha vyapar was a way to signal their disenfranchisement within their own cooperative. Swaccha vyapar was also a critique of middlemen within their own communities who now dominated cooperative affairs. Therefore, swaccha vyapar was a creative and powerful iteration of the Fair Trade philosophy that indexed a gendered awareness that male cooperative heads, male traders from their villages, and male Fair Trade officials controlled the Fair Trade network.

[13] Thapa (2012).

Women continually debated what Fair Trade meant in everyday talk, since the current operations of the tea cooperative were inimical to their aspirations of running their own businesses (that is, *thulo yojana*). Thulo yojana was a pet plan of smallholder women tea farmers who also belonged to self-help groups and accessed microcredit based loans. Thulo yojana was a component of swaccha vyapar because it questioned the business-as-usual approach of SKS and its gendered ramifications. After the formation of the cooperative in 1997 to trade in milk, a women's wing was established so that collectively, they could access resources from government programmes for maternal and reproductive health. Later, with the arrival of micro-loans, the Women's Wing provided the structure for the formation of self-help groups through which loans could be obtained. When I began my research in 2004, Women's Wing members were mostly involved in micro-credit and assisting the cooperative in ways that I detail later.

The Women's Wing devised thulo yojana in order to begin an organized business of their own that sold everything they produced besides tea, the trade of which, was now monopolized by men. Women lamented that the success of the Fair Trade cooperative did not directly help them. The juxtaposition of Fair Trade and swaccha vyapar was a rhetorical strategy smallholder women tea farmers used to make visible the precarious forms of labour that maintained their households and sustained organic tea production (albeit by default). Furthermore, the uncompensated labour of women was critical for running Fair Trade programmes, including managing internal control of organic standards and helping run organic farming trainings that sustained the cooperative's Fair Trade certification, which, in turn, was the cooperative's ticket to the financial resources of the global Fair Trade movement.

Despite the marginality of Darjeeling's smallholder farmers within the tea industry, their land ownership and practice of agriculture—in contrast to lower-grade manual work like coolie *kam* (menial or plantation labour)—shaped the identity of smallholder tea farmers' families. They believed themselves to have more freedom than plantation workers. Smallholder women tea farmers in this study also highlighted this distinction, since as Piya Chatterjee has noted, plantation work was seen as demeaning and plantation women were viewed as wanton.[14] Smallholder women tea farmers' self-identification as housewives

[14] Chatterjee (2001).

working on their own farms and their receipt of micro-loans shaped their subjectivities as housewife-entrepreneurs. As I will demonstrate in the next section, this is the lens through which they assessed the significance of Fair Trade. The articulation of swaccha vyapar and thulo yojana was a way to question the separation of business from housework and the housewife identity. Women may take pride in being non-coolie housewives, but they questioned the economic and social limitations of being housewives in SKS.

Middlemen, Gendered Spatial Politics, and the Government of Women's Work

> Why is it that we get these stares when we walk down the village road? Are we different, now that we are trying to do big business?
>
> –Minu

Minu's comment alludes to the crisis of respectability that Women's Wing members experienced after they formally asked the cooperative for money to start a women-only business. Male middlemen called them names like *bathi* (overly clever, cunning)—a derogatory term when applied to women. What precipitated this slander was women's questioning of how middlemen used their clout and monopoly to control the women's entrepreneurial practices.

Before this cooperative was founded in 1997, and before the advent of Fair Trade, local people depended on middlemen for credit and to sell some of their produce and dry, 'illegal' tea on the local market. These middlemen were not sardars[15] or liaisons between the plantations and adjoining communities who recruited tea plantation labour. They were middle to upper caste, relatively wealthy Nepali men who negotiated between farming communities in rural Darjeeling and urban markets. Smallholder women tea farmers identified four important reasons for middlemen's role: (a) middlemen had good contacts in town to sell products from the village; (b) they had money to hire people to transport merchandise from the villages to town; (c) they were necessary because women's family members resented them making frequent trips to town; and (d) the middlemen brought back supplies of food and other essential commodities to these remote villages. Smallholder women tea farmers

[15] For more on sardars in this region, see Middleton's chapter in this volume.

often took loans from the middlemen and were obligated to sell their produce to the middlemen in return. Some had become wealthy over time, and many also held important positions in the cooperative after it was formed.

With the formation of the Women's Wing, members started taking out lower-interest loans from a government bank through a micro-credit scheme. The middlemen subsequently saw their income from moneylending to women decline. This history formed the backdrop of the hostility between Women's Wing members and middlemen, who spared no effort to impugn women's respectability, as Minu's comments in the epigraph attest. Smallholder women tea farmers welcomed the comparatively low-interest loans available from NGO-run government micro-credit schemes, and they reported their family members did so as well. The advent of micro-credit enabled women to free themselves from high-interest loans offered by middlemen. However, they still had to depend on the middlemen to sell their produce so that they could repay the loans.

The middlemen were not pleased with the NGO involvement and the micro-credit schemes. Those who served on the cooperative board had tried to monopolize the sale of other local produce, such as turmeric, ginger, cardamom, milk, and vegetables. Most smallholder women tea farmers complained that the middlemen offered the villagers very low prices for their produce, but because of the lack of adequate transportation and contacts, the villagers had few alternatives for selling their goods. The formation of the cooperative had further entrenched middlemen's power, as they could control who did or did not become members of the cooperative and who got to learn how to get organic certification for their land. Most respondents also reported that they expected the cooperative to sell more goods besides tea in the future. Thus, the local middlemen would become the virtual brokers of transnational market-based justice regimes in the villages.

After Fair Trade funds for development started pouring into the cooperative, Women's Wing members devised their plan of thulo yojana (big plan, big business), to ensure that cooperative households would also get fair prices for their agricultural products other than tea. The Women's Wing had asked the cooperative board for a share of Fair Trade funds in 2005–6 just before the annual visit from the Fair Trade certifying officer. Binu, one of the active members of the Women's Wing, filled me in on this background. The cooperative received Rs. 222,000 (close to $6,000 USD) in Fair Trade premium money. The Women's

Wing members were happy because the governing board told the villagers that the money would be used for development. Leaders of the Women's Wing requested ₹10,500 (less than five per cent of the funds) as startup capital for a produce business, as an alternative to approaching a bank and burdening themselves with a loan. Many smallholder women tea farmers described this money as a reasonable reward for all their work on behalf of the cooperative. The cooperative immediately refused the request, which angered the women. As Binu explained:

> You know, it was all fine until we asked for our share of the FLO money; somehow we became everyone's enemy. We could not even imagine that the men would show their true colours, and there would be so much hostility. We have been taking individual loans from the bank for the last couple of years and always repay the money. After all, we get periodic suggestions and encouragement from the NGO and government officers running the SHGs (self-help groups) on how we should stand on our own feet and learn new skills. When we are selling *raksi* (rice wine) and *bidi* (cigarettes) it is fine, but when we want to found a big business, that is just not accepted. When we put pressure on the cooperative men to give us some money from FLO funds, they immediately asked us, 'Who are you, what is your identity? Your group is nothing without the cooperative, why are you asking for a separate share of the money? If we invest the money into the community as a whole, you all will benefit, what makes you all special? Women also benefit from our rising tea sales, don't they?' I replied saying that women are the ones who provide the labour in the plucking season from which you get this money, and we are going to use this money to learn new skills. To tell you the truth, we absolutely have to make this business a success and show these men that we can do the things they can; otherwise, they are going to make fun of us again.

Binu further explained that if the Women's Wing dissolved and joined the main cooperative, then women would never get any money for this separate business. The middlemen in the cooperative would never allow the women a separate share of the money to start a business, arguing that funds spent on the entire community would benefit everyone. Women's Wing members like Binu were proud that they preserved their group and that the male governing board had to deal with 'probationary action' because of their resolve. This was a key moment when the women felt they had received some redress for the cooperative's unwillingness to share any monetary resources with them.

From running Fair Trade trainings, they knew that Fair Trade supported women's income earning. When the Women's Wing floated their business plan involving this other produce, open animosity erupted between the middlemen and Women's Wing members. The middlemen defamed Women's Wing members, making use of existing gender ideologies to undermine the women's respectability. They spread rumours that the smallholder women tea farmers were becoming like market vendors or women plantation workers, who were considered *bathi*.

One needs to understand the competing gender ideologies in Darjeeling to understand the power of these shaming practices for women's self-identification. Smallholder women tea farmers had a particular investment in distinguishing themselves from women plantation workers, who were considered inferior in social status due to their wage work and lack of control over their leisure activities. Women and their families took pride in saying, 'our daughters, sisters, and wives do not go for *hajira* (wage work).' This gendered moral distinction had particular meaning imbued by past labour recruitment practices in the tea industry of Assam and North Bengal. As Jayeeta Sharma and Piya Chatterjee have both noted, sexualized and racial tropes accompanied plantation labour recruitment, which occurred mostly among tribal groups in east–central India.[16] In the postcolonial period, however, there has been a divergence in the identity politics of specific tea producing communities in terms of how they situate themselves vis-à-vis these racialized and sexualized histories of plantation work. In Darjeeling, women plantation workers are also stigmatized as sexually immoral and alcoholic.

These specific stereotypes have shaped a gendered moral terrain of critical distinctions where women who do not work on plantations but live nearby—like the smallholder women tea farmers discussed here—distinguish themselves from women plantation workers and their families, even though they likewise cultivate tea. Because among Nepali Hindu families the withdrawal of women from formal labour force participation marks upward mobility, these smallholder women tea farmers identified themselves as housewives and engaged in practices of social mobility. Women tea farmers also realized the limitations of this role identification. Despite their entrepreneurial ventures they were seen as housewives not capable of organized business ventures and hence, as discussed, were denied Fair Trade resources. The spatial manifestation

[16] Chatterjee (2001) and Sharma (2011).

of these gender ideologies also put severe limitations on their ability to procure resources for their families, since middlemen used these ideological tropes to discipline women.

In their daily chores, smallholder women tea farmers performed as obedient housewives or good sisters who always asked for permission to go to town. They also knew the social and economic limitations these performances placed on them. This tension shaped their subjectivities; they lived this contradiction and found ways to question it when they engaged in conflict with the cooperative. The women reminded cooperative members of the importance of their petty trade for nourishing families in the community.

This form of spatial and ideological control hurt the poorest smallholder women tea farmers the most. Whereas comparatively wealthy households in the cooperative could afford to have the wives and sisters stay at home, poorer women were desperate to venture out of their homes to sell produce. For these women, absolute confinement to home-based work was not economically feasible. Their families tolerated some amount of non-farm-related economic activities, like loan-taking and selling produce in the village. However, the non-farm activities of these women were confined to the space of the village which prevented them from forming sustainable links with the market. The persistence of gender ideologies not only confined women's economic activities to certain spaces; it gave some middlemen the moral resources to strategically question the actions of women who attempted to challenge the monopoly of middlemen in the village, by going directly to the market.[17] Thus, the smallholder women tea farmers were determined to defend their Women's Wing, as I show in the next section.

From Debating to Contesting Fair Trade

Despite its aim of creating a better alternative to neoliberal trade and development, Fair Trade relies on technical interventions resembling the liberal methods of conventional development practice. For example, certification involves checklist-style, top-down bureaucratic procedures for monitoring and inspecting farms and farming techniques, for examining on-farm labour relations, for tracking the use of Fair Trade premiums by farming communities, and for implementing empowerment directives from Fair Trade inspectors. I have argued elsewhere that

[17] See also Lynch (2007).

these governance schemes make for interesting biopolitics where people and processes are measured against liberal notions of empowerment and development.

Smallholder women tea farmers encountered the technical rationality undergirding Fair Trade in the form of yearly inspection visits by a male Fair Trade inspector from New Delhi. Each community vying for certification had to pass the annual Fair Trade inspection. International Fair Trade monitoring organizations like FLO also sent inspectors to check whether producer organizations like cooperatives were run democratically. Depending on how cooperative members fared in the inspection interviews, FLO inspectors decided whether a producer organization (such as the tea cooperative) could continue to receive Fair Trade premium funds for economic development. Due to their significant consequences, inspections were tense times in the community.

In December 2006, I had the opportunity to witness one such inspection, as well as dynamics in the cooperative as members prepared for it. In the days preceding the one-day inspection, male cooperative members were busy organizing documentation of tea sales and the cooperative budget. Women's Wing members were given the task of informing cooperative members' families about the meaning and benefits of Fair Trade because cooperative heads wanted to ensure that cooperative members would be able to answer basic questions about Fair Trade and organic production if the inspector decided to interview average members. The women were also charged with cleaning and decorating the cooperative office, and preparing meals for the inspector.

The inspector spent most of his time with the cooperative board. I interviewed him soon after the inspection and witnessed his interactions with male and some female cooperative members. During the interview he made a notable comment about the women:

> *Inspector*: Women in Darjeeling are much more 'forward' than women in other parts of India, where society is more patriarchal.
>
> *DS*: Why do you think women are more forward here?
>
> *Inspector*: At least you see them sit in the meeting when you come for inspection, and they even answer my questions correctly. They are 'more free.'

I was struck by the inspector's comments about women farmers' freedom, considering that he spent a total of two days in Darjeeling and six hours in the cooperative, talking mostly to the male board members.

Moreover, the inspector was from New Delhi and did not speak Nepali, the local language; most of his conversations with cooperative members were in Hindi, which the majority of cooperative members did not understand. Still, during his routine inspection, the Fair Trade inspector was impressed by the awareness and enthusiasm of smallholder women tea farmers within this male-dominated cooperative.

The aforementioned Women's Wing consisted of smallholder women tea farmers who were relatives of the male cooperative members. The Women's Wing operated at a level below the cooperative. The cooperative governing board made the major decisions about its operation and the management of tea within the cooperative community. Women's Wing members were involved in micro-credit and assisted the cooperative by cooking for major events, running trainings, and the like. The inspector sensed this hierarchy. He wanted the smallholder women tea farmers to dissolve the Women's Wing and join the governing board in larger numbers. The inspector argued that women were ready for 'more empowerment' and ought to be members of the main cooperative.

During our conversation, the inspector remarked that Darjeeling was not as patriarchal as the rest of India, which was borne out by the demographic fact that the sex ratio in Darjeeling was higher than elsewhere in India—that is, there were more women in the population. He had observed numerous women-owned businesses in the marketplace. In addition, local women did not observe strict norms of *purdah* (veiling) like women did in other parts of north India. Consequently, he assumed that smallholder women tea farmers would welcome his 'Fair Trade' directives as guaranteeing them more political presence in the community and ensuring a more equitable distribution of Fair Trade resources, such as the annual Fair Trade premium to each certified community. Hence he used the word 'forward' to imply that women were more advanced in Darjeeling.

Members of the Women's Wing, in contrast, did not endorse the Fair Trade directives. During my participant observation, I picked up terms women commonly associated with empowerment, such as *aghi badnu* (to move forward/progress), *bato dekhaunu* (showing the way forward), swaccha vyapar *garnu* (doing clear/transparent/fair business), thulo yojana *banaunu* (making big business/big plan), and *baliyo hunu* (to become strong). All these phrases invoke notions of empowerment based on equality and imply particular kinds of economic action. Joining the governing body of the cooperative was never associated with these concepts or viewed as empowering. I wondered why the suggestion of joining the governing body did not sit well with the Women's Wing. Why did they not want to make this potentially empowering move and give up their women's group? What were women trying to achieve collectively by defying the inspector's directive, when they knew that such defiance could lead to the loss of certification and subsequently Fair Trade funds for their community?

Through their persistence, women wanted to publicly demonstrate their disillusionment with the governing board and the problematic operation of Fair Trade within their community. It was a way to publicly express their doubt about Fair Trade's potential to break the monopoly of middlemen in the cooperative and ensure transparent business in their communities. This was evident in their constant contrasting of Fair Trade and swaccha vyapar. In the end, the cooperative's Fair Trade certification and funds were not revoked because of the Women's Wing's defiance. The coop's certification was given a probationary status with a warning to straighten out matters within the cooperative, especially with the Women's Wing. The fact that the cooperative received 'probationary action' not a full-fledged 'pass' pleased Women's Wing members. It was a symbolic victory for them.

Binu further explained that if the Women's Wing dissolved and joined the main cooperative, the women would never get any money for this separate business. The middlemen in the cooperative would never allow the women a separate share of the money to start a business, arguing that funds spent on the entire community would benefit everyone. Women's Wing members like Binu were proud that they preserved their group and that the male governing board had to deal with 'probationary action' because of their resolve. This was a key moment. The women felt they had received some redress for the cooperative's unwillingness to share any monetary resources with them.

Binu elaborated:

> We go for all sorts of training so that we can move forward. Then why not give us the money now, when we can gain some real training to better ourselves? It is okay if they want us to be on the cooperative governing board, but we really want to have our own organization. We women have *laj* (modesty, shame) and we can support each other, even if it is just five of us. I know the men in the cooperative must have jumped at the inspector's suggestions because this was a way for them to wipe out our existence so that the cooperative would not have to share money with

> us again. By the time the secretary finally gave us the money, things had become bitter, but he told us then that this was the last time we were going to get our demands met.

Other women in the Women's Wing shared Binu's reading of the Fair Trade directive as collusion between male cooperative board members and the inspector. They interpreted the Fair Trade directive as the final step in wiping out the Women's Wing in retaliation for their request for the Fair Trade premium money that the male-dominated cooperative governing board wished to monopolize. They saw the recommendation that they join the board as a way for middlemen to retain their voice in the cooperative, since a few women on the board could be easily silenced. The few women board members would hesitate to stand up for themselves based on local codes of honour and modesty that the women themselves invested in. Women in the cooperative community had a bigger battle in mind. They feared that dissolving the Women's Wing and joining the cooperative leadership might lead to middlemen co-opting their business plan, destroying the collective space where they resisted male domination, and shaming them.

The Women's Wing, which on the surface seemed contrary to Fair Trade's goals of empowering women within the cooperative, in reality, represented women's collective aspirations for economic justice at the community level. Smallholder women tea farmers understood that the success of the cooperative was important for getting a good price for their tea and for the general development of their community. But they also saw the Fair Trade-certified cooperative as standing in the way of their business ventures. Therefore they coded the cooperative as a men's domain that discriminated against them.

I am not arguing that FLO's vision of empowerment is inherently depoliticizing, because the inspector did recognize the hierarchies within the community. However, his directive was based on the liberal modernist ideal of equal gender representation in numbers, without considering the context of empowerment. Hence his suggestion that it was important to have 'more' physical presence of women on the cooperative governing body failed to recognize that the effectiveness of their presence was questionable.

Examining how these women questioned the depoliticizing tendencies of Fair Trade as they charted out their own plan of empowerment and community participation revealed the significance of emerging forms of collective self-governance among women in rural India amidst but against the market.[18] In recent years feminist scholars have used the transnational feminist framework to analyse aspects of the emerging global morality market and its specific manifestations.[19] Feminist anthropologists and other social scientists have been preoccupied with issues around transnational justice regimes and the possibilities for local actors to connect their struggles to its promises.[20] Aihwa Ong draws our attention to the workings of modern justice regimes, the particular places that subjects of justice occupy in their own struggles, and the nuances of how these modern schemes of justice work. Commenting on the burgeoning justice initiatives in the transnational sphere she writes: 'Increasingly, a diversity of multilateral systems—multinational companies, religious organizations, UN agencies, and other NGOs—intervene to deal with specific, situated, and practical problems of abused, naked, and flawed bodies. The non-state administration of excluded humanity is an emergent transnational phenomenon, despite its discontinuous, disjointed, and contingent nature.'[21]

Ong characterizes these new justice regimes run by non-state agencies as new 'techno-ethical regimes' trying to bring justice to morally deserving yet excluded populations around the world.[22] Fair Trade's efforts resemble 'techno-ethical regimes' in that they have devised technical directives for empowering marginalized producers. The Fair Trade label speaks for quality, sustainable agricultural products, and for well-governed people who understand and work within Fair Trade guidelines. Such a label, in turn, reassures socially conscious consumers that marginalized producer communities are enjoying the material benefits of Fair Trade, such as social development premiums, and are operating in a democratic way. The process of certification thereby becomes a technical fix for existing inequalities in producer communities. I take Ong's logic further by noting how women producers both reject elements of and take advantage of these 'techno-ethical regimes' to gain prominence in their local communities, while all parties are working within Fair Trade-certified institutions. Ethnographic attention to the gendered cultural politics around certification[23] also closes a major gap in the

[18] Klenk (2004); Moodie (2008); Subramaniam (2006); Sharma (2008).
[19] Chowdhury (2011).
[20] Merry (2006).
[21] Ong (2006: 24).
[22] Ong (2006: 24–5).
[23] Mutersbaugh and Lyon (2010); Mutersbaugh et al. (2005: 381–8).

interdisciplinary literature on Fair Trade certification, by providing a more nuanced understanding of how the broader goals of techno-ethical regimes do and do not translate at the local level, and how such translations are gendered.

Through public disputes (like the one with the cooperative board discussed earlier) and also through household level conversations (detailed in my book, *Everyday Sustainability*, 2017), women consciously reminded community members and interlocutors like me that their labour is critical to sustaining their families and community. These reminders are responses to both shaming practices that entrepreneurial women were subject to, and are key strategies for gaining resource access and recognition for their everyday entrepreneurial work.

In the winter of 2015, I returned to this area to see women's entrepreneurialism take on a new avatar. After many tribulations and struggle with the cooperative, the most active members of the Women's Wing had formed 'Makhmali SHG', which sold crafts, household produce, and even dry illegal tea to visitors and towns people. The business was running well for these 12 women and they were planning to access local bank or panchayat loans based on their savings. I asked Binu, why the name Makhmali? She quickly grabbed my hand and took me outside her house pointing at the bushes of purple flowers called Makhmali. Makhmali flowers looked fragile but endured the harshness of winter bringing colour and charm to the garden before spring arrived. The emphasis, in Binu's explanation, was on beauty, endurance, and survival. 'We could not find a more befitting name,' she said, 'it's like our ambitions and work, which survive the dictates of the cooperative's men.'

The ethnographic details of existing gendered resource struggles in producer communities and events surrounding Fair Trade provide us with an opportunity not only to understand the place-based gendered interpretations of Fair Trade in producer communities, but also to glimpse emerging modalities of women's collective self-governance in Darjeeling, which are in critical dialogue with market-based 'progressive' trade initiatives aimed at giving women more voice. As this chapter illustrates, women are using available opportunities to insert themselves into the global history of Fair Trade and expand its static frames of empowerment. Their efforts to juxtapose Fair Trade and swaccha vyapar were thus a catachrestic effort to demonstrate the limitations of the value frame of Fair Trade. This process reveals how subjects of justice have to re-politicize the technical directives of the Fair Trade movement to defend their own dreams of development.

The gendered resource battles around Fair Trade directives opened up a space for women to enact their collective entrepreneurial desires by refusing to give up their women's group. The Women's Wing was a public reminder to their community of women's refusal to fit themselves within the narrow frame of empowerment, and of their long-standing efforts to sustain family and community—at times at the detriment of their own safety. In the process, they also drew attention to the inadequacy of Fair Trade to address deeper gender-based structural inequalities in their community that maintained the hold of middlemen over people's lives. While removing intermediaries is one of the central aims of Fair Trade, in Darjeeling the inspector did not recognize their domination because he was approaching the situation from a technical, results-oriented perspective.

What is perhaps more critical is that women used their knowledge from previous engagements with market-based development ventures, such as micro-credit, to interpret the significance of Fair Trade as a market-based justice movement. Through micro-credit, women learned the hardships of repaying loans. For them, Fair Trade offered an opportunity to avoid the burden of loans, while planning a more sustainable collective business that would assist them to avoid being singled out through shaming practices of local patriarchs. Creative engagement with Fair Trade directives was a way for them to limit men's economic control of their lives and to reduce their dependence on micro-credit loans.

An understanding of rural women's mobilization within the market has to acknowledge their complex desires around development,[24] which they collectively attempt to further by questioning the directives of the transnational Fair Trade campaign. While Western consumer-activists desire progressive social change in global trade, these reflexive desires are translated through technical inspections that leave larger procedural inequalities in Fair Trade-certified communities intact. In Darjeeling's rural areas, women did not believe that Fair Trade would enable

[24] For similar assertions see Klenk (2004); Sen 2017; Grewal and Kaplan (1994); Ramamurthy (2003, 2011).

swaccha vyapar through a meaningless 'empowerment fix.' And therefore, they engaged in re-politicizing Fair Trade rules. In analysing the background and circumstances of this struggle and the negotiations around certification, this chapter thus illuminates the ways in which women's collective agency[25] in rural Darjeeling is emerging within market-based production systems and how they navigate inequities.

[25] See Naples and Desai (2002); Purkayastha and Subramaniam (2004).

Afterword

Tanka Subba

Having known many of the contributors to this volume, writing the Afterword to *Darjeeling Reconsidered* proved irresistible. This book is unique for several reasons: first, it focuses on a place rather than people or society, which most anthropologists and sociologists are wont to do. Second, the contributors are young and promising scholars. Indeed, all of them hail from a generation after mine. Third, the volume carries a sense of narrative cohesion across the chapters. Hence, it is a matter of pleasure as well as pride to be associated with this book. But being what I am, I will also not be able to stop myself from taking some of the claims in the book with a pinch of salt.

The book comes at a timely moment for Darjeeling and the study thereof. Having lived in Sikkim the past four and a half years I have become acutely aware of the shift of national and international focus from Darjeeling to Sikkim. Today the leaders of Darjeeling come to Sikkim to meet the visiting dignitaries from New Delhi. Sikkim's achievements in almost every field have been spectacular during the past four decades, be it in the field of education, culture, environment, arts, music, or social welfare measures making the people of Darjeeling working in Sikkim feel inferior—much the same way as the people of Sikkim felt vis-à-vis the people of Darjeeling until about four decades ago. This book might be the last tribute to Darjeeling if the number of Indian and foreign scholars interested to study Sikkim is anything to go by. Had there been not so many restrictions on foreigners and even Indians to visit some parts of Sikkim, the academic focus would have already shifted completely from Darjeeling to Sikkim.

This collection of essays provokes, for me, a number of questions. Reading the colonial critiques within this volume, one must ask: Was everything about colonialism bad for Darjeeling? After all, aren't most of the roads and bridges on which we travel even today built by them? Aren't the best schools and hospitals of Darjeeling all established by the colonial rulers? Are the tea gardens, which are an important focus of this book, not established by them as well? At times I wonder what we added to Darjeeling after we became independent in 1947 except congestion of roads, scarcity of water, filth, unplanned urban growth and the like? Have we done one thing good for Darjeeling after Independence? So when *Darjeeling Reconsidered* takes the position it has taken about colonial rule I wonder if the authors have been fair to the colonial rulers. It is always easy to take on those who are not around to defend themselves. Had the contributors been historians of a 'nationalist'—read Hindutva—brand, I would not be surprised. Yet I am indeed a little surprised that even this new generation of scholars, who did not see and experience the birth pangs of an independent India, is in a way more critical of the colonial than perhaps those who lived in colonial times.

Relatedly, the book raises important questions about the continuity between the colonial and the postcolonial, which is acknowledged in various chapters, albeit not as strongly as one would have desired. This continuity is more visible in tea gardens than in the agricultural areas of, say, Kalimpong, which remain somewhat peripheral to the essays' primary focus on Darjeeling itself. Indeed, if part of this volume's aim is to introduce the broadly conceived 'Darjeeling hills' to postcolonial studies, then Kalimpong's unique history offers an important means to internally differentiate that conversation.

In venturing such a conversation, it's worth questioning the degree to which the so-called postcolonial constructs of Darjeeling are really postcolonial. The analytic allure of postcolonial theory is exciting—particularly for the younger generations—but there is the risk of over-indulgence. But is all that these authors are doing even postcolonial? One such example comes with the consideration of the colonial infrastructure of Darjeeling's water and roads, which we all know have failed, much like Darjeeling's allure for tourists. Having done a small study on Darjeeling's tourism about three decades ago, I may say with some confidence that the allure depends on the class and nationality of international tourists, and the tourists' gaze is often beyond the fog-clothed pine trees. For some such tourists, Darjeeling is not really the destination but a place for business meetings for which they take the travel all the way to Darjeeling, braving the ill-managed narrow roads, bearing the traffic jam, and other such challenges that are increasing with each succeeding year. For many domestic tourists, it is the view of Mount Kanchendzonga that is located in Sikkim but very much visible from Darjeeling, which attracts them.

The book offers a unique look into the interplays of identity and politics in the hills—Gorkha, tribal, and otherwise. While it is true that about a dozen communities are engaged in rediscovering their tribalness in their bid to be recognized as Scheduled Tribes, one must simultaneously remember that the Gorkha issue has neither been buried nor put on the backburner. The most common demands made by the leaders of GJM before visiting dignitaries from New Delhi are recognition of the aforementioned communities' demands for ST recognition, a separate state of Gorkhaland, and a central university—but not necessarily in that order of priority. While the demand for ST status may be fulfilled in the near future, the political class in Darjeeling must make many more concerted efforts for the latter two demands than they have managed to date. This is difficult to expect from the GJM leaders who themselves have been charge-sheeted (that is indicted) in former opposition leader Madan Tamang's murder case, and a whimsical political leadership in the state of West Bengal.

The editors of the book contend: 'So long as the legend of Darjeeling continues to cast its long shadows across the hills, the postcolonial romance with this 'queen of the hills' will continue to obscure and occlude understandings of this region—and more importantly, the prospects of those who call it home.' As one who calls it home, I do feel hopeless when I look at the present situation—which has once again escalated since June 2017. But I think the situation is what it is, not only because of the reasons alluded to in the book, but also because of the lack of vision and concern of a West Bengal government that has always treated

Darjeeling as its colony. Locally, even satraps like Ghisingh and Gurung have done precious little, although they may have a dozen justifications for not being able to do anything. In the last four decades or so, the region's forests have vanished, ironically under the West Bengal Forest Development Corporation. Tea gardens have been reduced to less than half their number at the turn of the nineteenth century—having suffered badly during the chaotic situation of 1985–8. But if Darjeeling is to be resurrected, in my humble opinion, its people need to use the brand name of Darjeeling to achieve what they wish to achieve. But the crucial fact remains that without local stakeholders' ownership of tea, tourism, and timber—the three Ts for which Darjeeling is famous—nothing is possible.

The book brings together the three most important issues plaguing the Nepalis/Gorkhas of Darjeeling today—history, politics, and the environment. Historically, something that hurts the Nepalis of Darjeeling the most is to be called an immigrant from Nepal, and worse still, a foreigner. But I think the Nepalis of Darjeeling have been defensive for far too long, trying their best to convince other Indians that they came to India with the land, that they were there since the days of the Mahabharata and Ramayana, that they were Kiratas—the earliest known people to have inhabited this region since prehistoric times—and so on. They have also tried evoking the great number of Nepalis who died in India's freedom movement or while defending the country's borders. Others wish to remind their fellow Indians that the tune of the national anthem of India was composed by a Nepali and the signature tune of the first national television was composed by a Nepali, and so on. There are also today a small group of people who are, perhaps tired of arguing along the above lines, saying: 'Yes, our forefathers came from Nepal. So what? If we are citizens of India, we must be treated as such.' This exudes self–confidence, which characterizes the new generation, well–educated, and well–travelled Nepalis from Darjeeling. History is no doubt important, as it is linked with their citizenship and rights, but creating a counter-discourse, no matter how feeble, is equally important, especially when they are repeatedly told that they came from Nepal only the other day.

It is this perception of most Indians that makes one wonder if the issues of their national identity would be resolved if they achieved statehood with Gorkhaland. The votaries of the movement of course vouch as much, but others in Darjeeling remain doubtful. Some worry about the harassment that the members of their community may have to face in other parts of India, as Nepali-speakers are found in almost every state of India. The Nepalis of Darjeeling and Sikkim need not worry on this count so long as they are within this region, as no one with their wits about them asks if they are from Nepal. But they often have to face this question, often discreetly, in other parts of India. For the people of Darjeeling, it is often painfully easy to know what their fellow Indians assume about their national identity, but this is exactly what hurts and irritates them and motivates them to seek a clear answer to the question of their national identity.

The attainment of a clear national identity is an issue that is not likely to be resolved anytime soon. The formation of an Empowered Persons' Groups (EPG) to review the Indo-Nepalese Peace and Friendship Treaty of 1950 is perhaps more a concession extended to the leaders of Nepal when Prime Minister Narendra Modi first visited Nepal in 2014 rather than a realization of the changed situation between the two friendly countries. More often than not, it was the people of Nepal, especially under the Maoist leader Pushpa Kamal Dahal (alias Prachanda) who have called it an unequal treaty. Ghisingh, the leader of the GNLF that ruled Darjeeling for two decades from 1988, also condemned Articles VI and VII of the treaty, and so did some Gorkha organizations of Assam some decades ago. However, there has been no concerted and vociferous demand for its abrogation or amendment from any quarters in India.

Most Nepalis of Darjeeling do not even know what the Indo-Nepalese Peace and Friendship Treaty contains, let alone what they might want to change in the treaty. Importantly, any change in it may significantly change the issues of their citizenship and nationality in the future. This is of course a wild guess for it is not likely that the EPG will even consult the stakeholders of which the Nepalis in Darjeeling and Nepalese of Indian origin in Nepal are equal claimants. There are three possibilities: one, the treaty will be left as it is, in which case there will be no change in the status of the Nepalis in Darjeeling; two, the treaty may be abrogated, in which case the Nepalis of Darjeeling stand to gain so far as their wish to be delinked from Nepal is concerned. But what will happen to the Darjeeling Nepalis working in Nepal's boarding schools and hotels or to the labourers from Nepal working in various mining and construction sites in India is not clear; and three, the treaty is amended to regulate the flow of people between India and Nepal, which may be done at the border with the help of some citizenship documents. The last option is perhaps most desirable but also most challenging in view of the long and porous border.

The idea of fencing the border with Bangladesh, Pakistan, and Myanmar is not the same as fencing the border with Nepal. India will never endorse that idea because it is not in its national strategic interest to push Nepal towards China. India is aware of the pro-China elements in Nepal and the inroads that China is making to connect itself better with Nepal. But it is high time India stops thinking that the high glacial mountains create an impenetrable natural barrier between China and Nepal. India should also stop relying on the ancient and deep historical, cultural, religious, and linguistic connections between Nepal and India, as such connections fly in the air when real politics comes into play, as it did after the Nepal blockade in late 2015. Prime Minister Modi, who was the tallest hero of Nepal, became its biggest villain after the blockade.

I therefore feel that the issues of Nepali national identity are going to bother the people of Darjeeling for a much longer time than they can imagine. I also do not believe that a separate state of Gorkhaland is going to help them much. They will be told to go to Gorkhaland instead of being told to go to Nepal (as is often the case now), wherever and whenever there is an ethnic conflict with the local majority population and they are forced to leave the way they did from various parts of North-East India in the 1980s and from Bhutan in the 1990s. Some of them, perhaps the unscrupulous among them, will take the reins of power in the state of Gorkhaland, will amass wealth for themselves, and perpetuate backwardness of the majority much the same way it is done under West Bengal.

So what should the Nepalis of Darjeeling do for their future? The Gorkhaland path is certainly one the GJM and its supporters will take. The Sixth Schedule path is touted by the GNLF, but the GNLF does not have any credible leader at present. The Union Territory path is also suggested by some, but the political leaders of Darjeeling do not see how they are going to be relevant under this system. Merger with Sikkim is certainly one great idea, but it is not an option because Sikkim will never agree to it. More districts and more development boards may be created by the state, but such a piecemeal approach will not be able to address the complex issues of Darjeeling. Similarly, the future of Darjeeling is bleak without Siliguri. If Bengali becomes a compulsory language in the hills of Darjeeling, as proclaimed by the state government recently, Darjeeling may not even be able to protect its lingua franca, Nepali. It was such linguistic chauvinism of Bengal that pushed Assam away from Bengal Province at the end of nineteenth century and a similar linguistic chauvinism of Assam led to the division of Assam into several states after India's Independence. So if the linguistic chauvinism of West Bengal results in the separation of Darjeeling, the credit should go to West Bengal's current Chief Minister Mamata Bannerjee. So, in this sense and actually more, she holds the future for the Nepalis/Gorkhas of Darjeeling.

Glossary

B = Bengali; H = Hindi; L = Lepcha; N = Nepali; T = Tibetan

adivasi (N; H)	indigenous; indigenous person
aat (N)	courage
adhiar (N)	sharecropper
aphno manche (N)	own people (used to describe political networks)
aghi badnu (N)	to move forward/progress
antim ladhai (N)	final fight
artha (N)	worldly interests, economics
Arya Samaj	Hindu reform movement
asha (N)	hope
ayo (N)	has come
babu (B) [see also *bhadralok*]	Bengali gentleman
baliyo hunu (N)	to become strong
bandh (N)	general strike
bathi (N)	clever, cunning

bato dekhaunu (N)	showing the way forward
begari (N, H)	forced labour
bhadralok (B) [see also *babu*]	Bengali colonial elite
bhajan mandali	prayer meetings
bhariya (N)	porter
bidi (N)	cigarettes
burra sahib (H)	big (head) manager
chanda (N)	tax, donation
chota sahib (H)	little (assistant) manager
chaubandi choli (N)	Traditional Nepali women's shirt
coolie kam (N)	menial or plantation labour
coolie (N)	plantation labourer
dada (N)	Literally slang for 'big brother'; 'big boss' or authority figure
dajyu (N)	elder brother
dalal (N)	broker
daura suruwal (N)	traditional Nepali men's dress
dhamki (N)	threat
dharma (N)	moral code; religion
dhuri (N)	household
ekrupta (N)	uniformity
gau samaj (N)	village societies (residential organizations)
gherao (B; H)	siege; encirclement
goonda (H)	thug; gangster
gothala (N)	shepherd
gram panchayat (H)	unit of local governance
hazira (H)	wage labour
jamindar (H; N)	landed gentry
janajati (N)	ethnic groups
jati (N)	community
jati unnati (N)	community upliftment
Josmani	alternative religious movement
kalyan (N)	welfare
kaman (N)	tea garden
kamila prakriya (N)	way of the ants (insects)
kamila (N)	ants (insects)
kanya/kaiyas (N)	traders; moneylenders from the plains

khata (T)	Tibetan silk scarves
khetala (N)	farmhand
kutniti (N)	dirty politics
lathi (N, H)	police baton
laj (N)	modesty, shame
mandal (N)	village headman
matwali (N)	alcohol drinkers
mauri prakriya (N)	swarming of bees
mauri (N)	bees
mazdoor (H)	wage earner
mik thuk (L)	'those who poke with their eyes'
mlechha (N)	barbarian
mouza (H)	an administrative unit; one *mouza* comprises several *gram panchayats*
mutanchi rong kup rum kup (L)	'children of the snowy peaks' (Lepcha name for themselves)
pad yatra (N)	foot marches; i.e. political pilgrimage
pakhure (N)	field hand
panchayat (H; N)	system of local governance in India
panche baja (N)	traditional Nepali music band consisting of five players equipped with drums, cybals, folk trumpets, and folk oboes
pattadar (H)	landlord
peti (N)	petty
pravasi (H)	non-resident
punjibadi vargiya swartha (N)	capitalist class interest
rajniti (N)	politics
raksi (N)	homemade rice wine
Ramrajya (N)	reign of lord Rama from the epic Ramayana; paternalistic control of the people or subject by a benevolent ruler
rowdy, rowdies (N)	gangster
ryot	colonial term for native cultivators
samaj (N)	community-based organizations
samanti byavastha ko soshan (N)	feudal exploitation
sardar (H; N)	labour agent; overseer

sarvahara varga (N)	proletariat
sipahi (H; N)	corps
sramajibi (N)	working class
swaccha vyapar (N)	clear/transparent/fair business
thulo jat (N)	upper caste
thulo yojana (N)	big plan, big business
tika (N)	coloured powder placed on the forehead as a religious offering
topi (N)	traditional Nepali men's hat
vargiya swartha (N)	class interest

Bibliography

Abrams, Philip. 1988. 'Notes on the Difficulty of Studying the State.' *Journal of Historical Sociology*, 1: 58–89.

'Mount Everest Expedition'. 1921. *The Geographical Journal*, 58 (1): 56–8.

Adler, Judith. 1989. 'Origins of Sightseeing.' *Annals of Tourism Research*, 16 (1): 7–29.

Aguiar, Marian. 2011. *Tracking Modernity: India's Railway and the Culture of Mobility*. Minneapolis: University of Minnesota Press.

Alexander, Jeffrey C. 2011. *Performance and Power*. Cambridge: Polity Press.

Alm, Björn. 2006. 'The Un/selfish Leader: Changing Notions in a Tamil Nadu Village.' Ph.D. dissertation. Stockholm University.

Anand, Nikhil. 2011. 'Pressure: The PoliTechnics of Water Supply in Mumbai.' *Cultural Anthropology*, 26 (4): 542–64.

———. 2012. 'Municipal Disconnect: On Abject Water and Its Urban Infrastructures.' *Ethnography*, 13: 487–509.

Appadurai, Arjun. 1993. 'Number in the Colonial Imagination.' In Carol A. Breckenridge and Peter Van der Veer (eds), *Orientalism and the Post-Colonial Predicament: Perspectives on South Asia*, pp. 314–39. New Delhi: Oxford University Press.

Asad, Talal (ed.). 1973. *Anthropology and the Colonial Encounter*. London: Ithaca Press.

Augé, Marc. 2008. *Non-Places: Introduction to an Anthropology of Supermodernity*. New York: Verso.

Avery, Mary. 1878. *Up in the Clouds, or Darjeeling and its Surroundings: Historical and Descriptive*. Calcutta: W. Newman & Company.

Bagchi, Romit. 2012. *Gorkhaland: Crisis of Statehood*. New Delhi: SAGE.

Baildon, Samuel. 1882. *The Tea Industry in India: A Review of Finance and Labour and a Guide for Capitalists*. London: W.H. Allen and Company.

Bald, Claud. 1903. *Indian Tea: Its Culture and Manufacture, Being a Textbook on the Cultivation and Manufacture of Tea*. Calcutta: Thacker, Spink, and Company.

Banerjee, Abhijit, Pranab Bardhan, Kaushik Basu, and Mrinal Datta Chaudhuri. 2002. 'Strategy for Economic Reform in West Bengal.' *Economic and Political Weekly*, 37 (41): 4203–18.

Banerjee, Amitav. 2012. 'Barfi! Emerges as Darjeeling's Brand Ambassador.' *Hindustan Times*, September 24.

Banerjee, Barundeb. 1993. *Tea Production and Processing*. New Delhi: IBH Publishing Company.

Banerjee, Mukulika. 2011. 'Elections as Communitas.' *Social Research*, 78 (1): 75–99.

Banerjee, Sandeep. 2014. "Not Altogether Unpicturesque': Samuel Bourne and the Landscaping of the Victorian Himalaya.' *Victorian Literature and Culture*, 42 (3): 351–68.

Banerjee, Sandeep and Subho Basu. 2015. 'Secularizing the Sacred, Imagining the Nation-Space: The Himalaya in Bengali Travelogues, 1856–1901.' *Modern Asian Studies*, 49 (3): 609–49.

Banerji, Sumanta. 1986. 'Gorkhaland Agitation–Cynical Politicking.' *Economic and Political Weekly*, 21 (40): 1770–21.

Basu, Amrita. 2001. 'The Dialectics of Hindu Nationalism.' In Atul Kohli (ed.), *The Success of India's Democracy*, pp. 163–89. Cambridge: Princeton University Press.

Baviskar, Amita. 2006. 'The Politics of Being "Indigenous".' In B.G. Karlsson and Tanka Bahadur Subba (eds), *Indigeneity in India*, pp. 33–50. London: Kegan Paul.

———. 2011. 'What the Eye Does Not See: The Yamuna in the Imagination of Delhi.' *Economic and Political Weekly*, 46 (50): 45–53.

Bayley, S. 1895–6. 'Tea Planting in Darjeeling.' *Society of Arts Journal*, 44: 645.

Behal, Rana P. 2006. 'Power Structure, Discipline, and Labour in Assam Tea Plantations under Colonial Rule.' *International Review of Social History*, 51 (S14): 143–72.

Bennike, Rune. 2017. 'Frontier Commodification: Governing Land, Labour and Leisure in Darjeeling, India.' *South Asia: Journal of South Asian Studies*, 40 (2): 256–71.

Bentley, J. 2015. 'Rituals and Negotiated Belonging among the Lepcha: Culture, Sacred Landscape, Territory, and Ethno-Political Action in a Transnational Himalayan Community.' Unpublished Doctoral Thesis. University of Zürich, Zürich.

Berenschot, Ward. 2011. 'On the Usefulness of Goondas in Indian Politics: "Moneypower" and "Musclepower" in a Gujarati Locality.' *South Asia: Journal of South Asian Studies*, 34 (2): 255–75.

Besky, Sarah. 2008. 'Can a Plantation Be Fair? Paradoxes and Possibilities in Fair Trade Darjeeling Tea Certification.' *Anthropology of Work Review*, 29 (1): 1–9.

———. 2013. *The Darjeeling Distinction: Labor and Justice on Fair-Trade Tea Plantations in India*. Berkeley: University of California Press.

———. 2015. 'Inheriting the Hill Station.' *Edge Effects*, May 19.

Bhandari, P.L. 2003. 'Evolution and Growth of the Nepali Community in Northeast India.' In Awadhesh Coomar Sinha and Tanka Bahadur Subba (eds), *The Nepalese in Northeast India: A Community in Search of Indian Identity*, pp. 106–23. New Delhi: Indus.

Bhattacharya, Nandini. 2012. *Contagion and Enclaves: Tropical Medicine in Colonial India*. Liverpool: University of Liverpool Press.

Bhowmik, Sharit Kumar. 1981. 'Recruitment and Migration Policy in Tea Plantations in West Bengal.' *Bulletin of the Cultural Research Institute*, 15 (1–2): 22–33.

———. 1996. 'Tea Plantation Workers in West Bengal.' in Sharit Kumar Bhowmik, Virginius Xaxa, and M.A Kalam (eds), *Tea Plantation Labour in India*, pp. 43–80. New Delhi: Friedrich Ebert Stiftung.

———. 2016. 'Tribal Labour in the Tea Plantations of West Bengal: Problems of Migration and Settlement.' In Meena Radhakrishna (ed.), *First Citizens: Studies on Adivasis, Tribals, and Indigenous Peoples in India*. New Delhi: Oxford University Press.

Bisen, J.S. and A.K. Singh. 2012. 'Impact of Inorganic to Organic Cultivation Practices on Yield of Tea in Darjeeling Hills: A Case Study.' *Indian Journal of Horticulture*, 69 (2): 288–91.

Biswas, Kumud Ranjan. 2001. 'A Summer Place.' In Government of West Bengal (ed.), *Bengal District Gazetteer: Darjeeling by L.S.S. O'Malley*, pp. v–xvii. Calcutta: Government of West Bengal.

Biswas, Sanjay and Barun Roy. 2003. *Fallen Cicadas: Unwritten History of Darjeeling*. Darjeeling: Barun Roy.

Boer, Liekel. 2011. *Perennial Springs of Darjeeling: A Survey to Community Based Conservation*. Darjeeling: Ashoka Trust for Research in Ecology and the Environment.

Bomjan, D.S. 2008. *Darjeeling–Dooars People and Place under Bengal's Neo-Colonial Rule*. Darjeeling: Bikash Jana Sahitya Kendra.

Bomjan, Pemba. 2008. 'Gorkha Dukha Niwarak Sammelan ko Sthapana: Etihasik Paksha.' *Khoji*, 3 (6): 46–50.

Booth, Chelsea L. 2011. '"These People Deprived of this Country": Language and the Politics of Belonging among Indians of Nepali Descent.' Ph.D. dissertation, Rutgers, The State University of New Jersey.

Bourdieu, Pierre. 1977. *Outline of a Theory of Practice*. Translated by Richard Nice. Cambridge: Cambridge University Press.

———. 1984. *Distinction: A Social Critique of the Judgment of Taste*. Translated by Richard Nice. London: Routledge.

———. 1986. 'The Forms of Capital.' In J. Richardson (ed.), *Handbook of Theory and Research for the Sociology of Education*, pp. 241–58. Westport, CT: Greenwood.

———. 1991. *Language and Symbolic Power*. Translated by Gino Raymond and Matthew Adamson. UK: Polity Press.

Brass, Paul R. 1990. *The Politics of India Since Independence*. Cambridge: Cambridge University Press.

Breckenridge, Carol Appadurai, and Peter van der Veer. 1993. *Orientalism and the Postcolonial Predicament: Perspectives on South Asia*. Philadelphia: University of Pennsylvania Press.

Briggs, Charles. 1996. 'The Politics of Discursive Authority in Research on the Invention of Tradition.' *Cultural Anthropology*, 11 (4): 435–69.

Brown, Trent. 2015. 'Youth Mobilities and Rural–Urban Tensions in Darjeeling, India.' *South Asia: Journal of South Asian Studies*, 32 (2): 263–75.

Brown, Trent, Ruchira Ganguly–Scrase, and Timothy J. Scrase. 2016. 'Urbanization, Rural Mobility, and New Class Relations in Darjeeling, India.' *Critical Asian Studies*, 48 (2): 235–56.

Bruce, C.G. 1934. *Himalayan Wanderer*. London: Alexander Maclehose & Co.

Butler, Judith. 1997. *The Psychic Life of Power: Theories of Subjection*. Stanford, CA: Stanford University Press.

Byrne, Sarah and Bart Klem. 2015. 'Constructing Legitimacy in Post-War Transition: The Return of "Normal" Politics in Nepal and Sri Lanka?' *Geoforum*, 66: 224–33.

Caine, William Sproston. 1891. *Picturesque India: A Handbook for European Travellers*. London: G. Routledge & Sons.

Cameron, Ian. 1984. *Mountains of the Gods*. London: Century.

Candea, Matei. 2011. '"Our Division of the Universe": Making a Space for the Non-Political in the Anthropology of Politics.' *Current Anthropology*, 52 (3): 309–34.

Caplan, Lionel. 1995a. *Warrior Gentleman: 'Gurkhas' in Western Imagination*. New York: Berghahn Books.

———. 1995b. 'Martial Gurkhas: The Persistence of a Military Discourse on Race.' In Peter Robb (ed.), *The Concept of Race in South Asia*, pp. 260–81. New Delhi: Oxford University Press.

Chakrabarti, Dyutis. 1988. 'Gorkhaland: Evolution of Politics of Segregation.' Special Lecture–10. University of North Bengal: Centre for Himalayan Studies.

Chakrabarty, Subhas Ranjan. 2005. 'Silence under Freedom: The Strange Story of Democracy in the Darjeeling Hills.' In Ranabir Samaddar (ed.), *The Politics of Autonomy*, pp. 173–95. New Delhi: SAGE.

Chalmers, Rhoderick. 2003a. 'The Quest for *Ekrupta*: Unity, Uniformity and the Delineation of the Nepali Community in Darjeeling.' In A.C. Sinha and T.B. Subba (eds), *The Nepalis in North-East India: A Community in Search of Indian Identity*, pp. 339–59. New Delhi: Indus.

———. 2003b. '"We Nepalis": Language, Literature, and the Formation of a Nepali Public Sphere in India 1914–1940.' Ph.D. dissertation. SOAS, University of London.

———. 2009. 'Education, Institutions, and Elite Building and Bounding Nepali Public Life in Early Twentieth Century India.' In T.B. Subba, A.C. Sinha, G.S. Nepal, and D.R. Nepal (eds), *Indian Nepalis: Issues and Perspectives*, pp. 109–47. New Delhi: Concept Publishing Company.

Chandra, Bipan. 2002 [1993]. *Essays on Indian Nationalism*. New Delhi: Har–Anand Publications Pvt. Ltd.

Chandra, Kanchan. 2004. *Why Ethnic Parties Succeed: Patronage and Ethnic Headcounts in India*. Cambridge: Cambridge University Press.

Chapman, Graham, and Michael Thompson (eds). 1995. *Water and the Quest for Sustainable Development in the Ganga Valley*. New York: Mansell.

Chatterjee, Partha. 2004. *The Politics of the Governed: Reflections on Popular Politics in Most of the World*. New York: Columbia University Press.

———. 2008. 'Democracy and Economic Transformation in India.' *Economic and Political Weekly*, 43 (16): 53–62.

Chatterjee, Piya. 2001. *A Time for Tea: Women, Labour, and Post/Colonial Politics on an Indian Plantation*. London: Duke University Press.

———. 2007. 'Tea's Fortunes and Famines: Global Capital, Women Workers, and Survival in Indian Plantation Country.' In A. Cabezas (ed.), *The Wages of Empire: Neoliberal Policies, Repression and Women's Poverty*, pp. 57–72. Boulder: Paradigm Publishers.

Chatterji, Joya. 1999. 'The Fashioning of a Frontier: The Radcliffe Line and Bengal's Border Landscape, 1947–52.' *Modern Asian Studies*, 33 (1): 185–242.

———. 2007. *The Spoils of Partition: Bengal and India, 1947–1967*. Cambridge: Cambridge University Press.

Chettri, Mona. 2013. 'Choosing the Gorkha: At the Crossroads of Class and Ethnicity in the Darjeeling Hills.' *Asian Ethnicity*, 14 (3): 1–16.

———. 2014. 'Interpreting Democracy: Ethnic Politics and Democracy in the Eastern Himalaya.' *Studies in Nepali History and Society*, 19 (2): 205–29.

———. 2015. 'Engaging the State: Ethnic Patronage and Cultural Politics in the Eastern Himalayan Borderland.' *South Asia: Journal of South Asian Studies*, 38 (4): 1–16.

———. 2017. *Ethnicity and Democracy in the Eastern Himalayan Borderland*. Amsterdam: Amsterdam University Press.

Chhetri, Nilamber. 2016. 'Restructuring the Past, Reimagining the Future: Ethnic Renewal Process and Claims for Recognition as Scheduled Tribes in Darjeeling.' *Asian Ethnicity*, published online June 27.

Chowdhury, Ellora H. 2011. *Transnationalism Reversed: Women Organizing Against Gendered Violence in Bangladesh*. Albany: SUNY Press.

Christison, G.W. 1895–6. 'Tea Planting in Darjeeling.' *Society of Arts Journal*, 44: 623–44.

Clifford, James. 1997. *Routes: Travel and Translation in the Late Twentieth Century*. Cambridge: Harvard University Press.

Cohen, Anthony P. 1985. *The Symbolic Construction of Community*. London: Ellis Horwood Ltd.

Cohn, Bernard S. 1987. *An Anthropologist Among the Historians and Other Essays*. New Delhi: Oxford University Press.

———. 1996. *Colonialism and its Forms of Knowledge: The British in India*. Princeton, NJ: Princeton University Press.

Coombe, Rosemary J. 2007. 'The Work of Rights at the Limits of Governmentality.' *Anthropologica*, 49 (2): 284–9.

Cosgrove, Denis E. 1984. *Social Formation and Symbolic Landscape*. London: Croom Helm.

Cowan, Jane K, Marie–Bénédicte Dembour, and Richard Wilson (eds). 2001. *Culture and Rights: Anthropological Perspectives*. Cambridge: Cambridge University Press.

———. 2006. 'Culture and Rights after Culture and Rights.' *American Anthropologist*, 108 (1): 9–24.

Cresswell, Tim. 2004. *Place: A Short Introduction*. Malden, MA: Blackwell.

Crick, Bernard. 2007. *In Defence of Politics*. First South Asian Edition, London: Continuum.

Dahal, Narbahadur. 2011. *Ganga Prasad Pradhan*. New Delhi: Sahitya Aakademi.

Darjeeling Ladenla Road Prerana. 2003a. *Area and Issue Profile of Darjeeling and Sikkim*. Report prepared by Mashqura Fareedi and Pasang Dorjee Lepcha. Darjeeling: Regional Community Development Center Hayden Hall.

Darjeeling Ladenla Road Prerana. 2003b. *Small Farmers Organic Tea and Sanjukta Vikas Cooperative: A Case Study from Darjeeling Hills*. Conference paper for Regional Community Development Center by Navin Tamang. Darjeeling: Regional Community Development Center Hayden Hall.

Darjeeling Waterworks Department. n.d. *A Report on Water Supply System of Darjeeling Municipal Area*. Darjeeling: Darjeeling Municipality.

Dasgupta, Atis. 1999. 'Ethnic Problems and Movements for Autonomy in Darjeeling.' *Social Scientist*, 27 (11–12): 47–68.

Dasgupta, Manas. 1988. 'The Gorkhaland Agitation in Darjeeling: Some Political and Economic Dimensions.' Special Lecture, No. IX, Centre for Himalayan Studies, University of North Bengal (India).

Datta, Prabhat. 1991. 'The Gorkhaland Agitation in West Bengal.' *The Indian Journal of Political Science*, 52 (2): 225–41.

Datta, Tarun Kumar. 2010. *Advantages, Constraints and Key Success Factors in Establishing Origin and Tradition-linked Quality Signs: The Case of Darjeeling Tea, India*. Indian Institute of Management, Kolkata: Food and Agriculture Organisation of the United Nations.

de Certeau, Michel. 1984. *The Practice of Everyday Life*. Berkeley: University of California Press.

Deleuze, Gilles and Félix Guattari. 1988. *A Thousand Plateaus: Capitalism and Schizophrenia*. Translated by Brian Massumi. Minneapolis: University of Minnesota Press.

Denjongpa, Anna Balikci. 2002. 'Kangchendzonga: Secular and Buddhist Perceptions of the Mountain Deity of Sikkim among the Lhopo.' *Bulletin of Tibetology*, 2 (1): 5–37.

Des Chene, Mary. 1991. 'Relics of Empire: A Cultural History of the Gurkhas, 1815–1987.' Ph.D. dissertation. Stanford University.

———. 1999. 'Military Ethnology in British India.' *South Asia Research*, 19 (2): 121–35.

Desai, A.R. 1991 [1948]. *Social Background of Indian Nationalism*. Bombay: Popular Prakashan.

Development and Planning Department, Government of West Bengal. 2004. *West Bengal Human Development Report*. Kolkata: Government of West Bengal. http://hdr.undp.org/sites/default/files/india_west_bengal_2004_en.pdf.

Dhakal, Rajendra. 2009. 'The Urge to Belong: An Identity in Waiting.' In D.R. Nepal, G.S. Nepal, A.C Sinha, and T.B. Subba (eds), *Indian Nepalis: New Perspectives*, pp. 148–67. New Delhi: Concept Publishing House.

Directorate of Census Operations, West Bengal. 2011. *District Census Handbook Darjiling*. Delhi: Census of India. Available at http://www.censusindia.gov.in/2011census/dchb/1901_PART_B_DCHB_DARJILING.pdfbh.

Dirks, Nicholas B. 2001. *Castes of Mind: Colonialism and the Making of Modern India*. Princeton, NJ: Princeton University Press.

———. 2004. 'The Ethnographic State.' In Saurabh Dube (ed.), *Postcolonial Passages: Contemporary History Writing in India*, pp. 70–88. New Delhi: Oxford University Press.

Dixit, Kanak Mani. 2003. 'The Myth–Making of Greater Nepal.' In Awadhesh Coomar Sinha and Tanka Bahadur Subba (eds), *The Nepalese in Northeast India: A Community in Search of Indian Identity*, pp. 321–38. New Delhi: Indus.

Dolan, C.S. 2010. 'Virtual Moralities: The Mainstreaming of Fairtrade in Kenyan Tea Fields.' *Geoforum*, 41: 33–43.

Dolan, Catherine S. 2008. 'In the Mists of Development: Fairtrade in Kenyan Tea Fields.' *Globalizations*, 5 (2): 305–18.

Donahue, John, and Barbara Rose Johnston. 1998. *Water, Culture, and Power: Local Struggles in a Global Context*. Washington, D.C.: Island Press.

Dowler, Lorraine, Josephine Carubia, and Bonj Szczygiel. 2005. *Gender and Landscape: Renegotiating Morality and Space*. London: Routledge.

Dozey, E.C. 1922. *A Concise History of the Darjeeling District since 1835, with a Complete Itinerary of Tours in Sikkim and the District, Etc. (Second Edition)*. Calcutta: N. Mukherjee.

Driver, Felix. 2015. 'Intermediaries and the Archive of Exploration.' In Shino Konishi, Maria Nugent, and Tiffany Shellam (eds), *Indigenous Intermediaries*, pp. 1–10. Canberra: Australian National University Press. Available at http://press.anu.edu.au/publications/aboriginal–history–monographs/indigenous–intermediaries/download (accessed 1 January 2016).

Duara, Prasenjit. 1995. *Rescuing History from the Nations: Questioning Narratives of Modern China*. Chicago: Chicago University Press.

Dudley-Jenkins, Laura. 2003. *Identity and Identification in India*. New York: Routledge.

Dumont, L. 1980. *Homo Hierarchicus: The Caste System and Its Implications*. Chicago: University of Chicago Press.

Duncan, James S. and Nancy Duncan. 2001. 'The Aestheticization of the Politics of Landscape Preservation.' *Annals of the Association of American Geographers*, 91 (2): 387–409.

———. 2004. *Landscapes of Privilege: Aesthetics and Affluence in an American Suburb*. New York: Routledge.

Dunn, Elizabeth Cullen. 2012. 'The Chaos of Humanitarianism: Adhocracy in the Republic of Georgia.' *Humanity* 3 (1): 1–23.

Dutt, Kant. 1981. 'Migration and Development: The Nepalese in Northeast.' *Economic and Political Weekly*, 13 June 1981, pp. 1053–63.

Elyachar, Julia. 2012. 'Before (and After) Neoliberalism: Tacit Knowledge, Secrets of the Trade, and the Public Sector in Egypt.' *Cultural Anthropology*, 27 (1): 76–96.

Endersby, Jim. 2008a. 'Joseph Hooker: A Philosophical Botanist.' *Journal of Biosciences*, 33 (2): 163–9.

———. 2008b. *Imperial Nature: Joseph Hooker and the Practices of Victorian Science*. Chicago: University of Chicago Press.

Ferguson, James. 1990. *The Anti-Politics Machine: 'Development', Depoliticization, and Bureaucratic Power in Lesotho*. Cambridge: Cambridge University Press.

Fielder, C.H. 1868–9. 'On Tea Cultivation in India.' *Society of Arts Journal*, 17: 291–2.

Foning, A.R. 1987. *Lepcha, My Vanishing Tribe*. Kalimpong: Chy–Pandi Farm.

Foucault, M. 1978. *The History of Sexuality: An Introduction. Vol. I.* New York: Vintage.

Fraser, W.M. 1935. *The Recollections of a Tea Planter.* London: The Tea and Rubber Mail.

Fuller, C. and V. Bénéï (eds.). 2000. *The Everyday State and Society in Modern India.* London: Hurst.

Fuller, C.J. and John Harriss. 2000. 'For an Anthropology of the Modern Indian State.' In C.J. Fuller and Véronique Bénéï (eds), *The Everyday State and Society in Modern India*, pp. 1–30. New Delhi: Social Science Press.

Ganguly-Scrase, Ruchira, and Timothy J. Scrase. 2015. 'Darjeeling Re-made: The Cultural Politics of Charm and Heritage.' *South Asia: A Journal of South Asian Studies*, 38 (2): 246–62.

Gellner, David. 2007. 'Caste, Ethnicity and Inequality in Nepal.' *Economic and Political Weekly*, 42 (20): 1823–8.

———. 2013. 'Warriors, Workers, Traders and Peasants: The Nepali/Gorkhali Diaspora since the Nineteenth Century.' In Joya Chatterjee and David Washbrook (eds), *Routledge Handbook of the South Asian Diaspora*, pp. 136–50. New York: Routledge.

Gerke, Barbara. 2012. *Long Lives and Untimely Deaths: Life-span Concepts and Longevity Practices among Tibetans in the Darjeeling Hills, India.* Leiden: Brill Academic Publishers.

Ghosh, Kaushik. 1999. 'A Market for Aboriginality: Primitivism and Race Classification in the Indentured Labour Market of Colonial India.' In Gautam Bhadra, Gyan Prakash, and Susie Tharu (eds), *Subaltern Studies X.*, pp. 8–48. New Delhi: Oxford University Press.

———. 2006. 'Global Flows and Local Dams: Indigenousness, Locality, and the Transnational Sphere in Jharkhand, India.' *Cultural Anthropology*, 21 (4): 501–34.

Gibbs, H.R.K. 1943. *The Gurkha Soldier.* Calcutta: Thacker, Spink & Co Ltd.

Gilmartin, David. 1994. 'Scientific Empire and Imperial Science: Colonialism and Irrigation Technology in the Indus Basin.' *The Journal of Asian Studies*, 53 (4): 1127–49.

GJM. 2008. 'The case for Gorkhaland: Creating a New State out of Darjeeling District and the Dooars.' Presented at the tripartite talks between Government of India, Government of West Bengal and Gorkha Janamukti Morcha, New Delhi, 8 September. Darjeeling: Gorkha Janamukti Morcha.

———. 2009. *Why Gorkhaland?* Darjeeling: Gorkha Janamukti Morcha, Central Committee.

Golay, Bidhan. 2006. 'Rethinking Gorkha Identity: Outside the Imperium of Discourse, Hegemony, and History.' *Peace and Democracy in South Asia*, 2 (1–2): 23–49.

———. 2009. 'Rethinking Gorkha Identity: Outside the Imperium of Discourse, Hegemony, and History.' In Tanka B. Subba, A.C. Sinha,

G.S. Nepal, and D.R. Nepal (eds), *Indian Nepalis: Issues and Perspectives*, pp. 73–94. New Delhi: Concept Publishing.

Goldthorpe, J.H. (in collaboration with Llewellyn, C. and Payne, C.) 1987. *Social Mobility and Class Structure in Modern Britain*. 2nd edition. Oxford: Clarendon Press.

Goldthorpe, John M., and Gordon Marshall. 1992. 'The Promising Future of Class Analysis: A Response to Recent Critiques.' *Sociology*, 26 (3): 381–400.

Gooptu, Nandini. 2007. 'Economic Liberalisation, Work and Democracy: Industrial Decline and Urban Politics in Kolkata.' *Economic and Political Weekly*, 42 (21): 1922–33.

Gordon, Milton. 1949. 'Social Class in American Sociology.' *American Journal of Sociology*, 55 (3): 262–8.

Goswami, Manu. 2004. *Producing India: From Colonial Economy to National Space*. Chicago: University of Chicago Press.

Government of West Bengal Director of Information (ed.). 1986. *Gorkhaland Agitation: The Issues: An Information Document*. Calcutta: Government of West Bengal.

Grewal, Inderpal and Caren Kaplan (eds). 1994. *Scattered Hegemonies: Postmodernity and Transnational Feminist Practices*. Minneapolis: University of Minnesota Press.

Gross, Llewellyn. 1949. 'The Use of Class Concepts in Sociological Research.' *American Journal of Sociology*, 54 (5): 409–421.

Gudavarthy, Ajay. 2013. *Politics of Post-Civil Society: Contemporary History of Political Movements in India*. New Delhi: SAGE.

Gupta, Akhil. 1999. *Postcolonial Developments: Agriculture in the Making of Modern India*. Delhi: Oxford University Press.

Gupta, Akhil and James Ferguson (eds). 2001. *Culture, Power, Place: Explorations in Critical Anthropology*. Durham: Duke University Press.

Gupta, Akhil and James Ferguson. 1992. 'Beyond Culture: Space, Identity and the Politics of Difference', *Cultural Anthropology*, 7: 6–23.

———. 2002. 'Spatializing States: Toward an Ethnography of Neoliberal Governmentality.' *American Ethnologist*, 29 (4): 981–1002.

Gupta, Akhil and Aradhana Sharma (eds). 2006. *The Anthropology of State: A Reader*. Oxford: Blackwell.

Gupta, Akhil and Kalyanakrishnan Sivaramakrishnan (eds). 2011. *The State in India after Liberalization: Interdisciplinary Perspectives*. London: Routledge.

Gurung, Bimal. 2007. Speech. Motor stand at Darjeeling's main bazaar, October 7.

Gurung, Bimal. 2008. Speech. Mass meeting, Siliguri, May 7.

Guyer, Jane. 2007. 'Prophecy and the Near Future: Thoughts on Macroeconomic, Evangelical, and Punctuated Time.' *American Ethnologist*, 34 (3): 409–21.

Gyr, Ueli. 2010. 'The History of Tourism Structures on the Path to Modernity.' *European History Online (EGO)*. Available at http://www.ieg–ego.eu/gyru–2010–en.

Hajra, N. Ghosh. 2001. *Tea Cultivation: A Comprehensive Treaty*. Lucknow: International Book Distributing Company.

Hangen, Susan. 2010. *The Rise of Ethnic Politics in Nepal*. London: Routledge.

Hansen, Peter. 1999. 'Partners, Guides, and Sherpas.' In Jas Elsner and Joan–Pau Rubies (eds), *Voyages and Visions: Towards a Cultural History of Travel*, pp. 210–31. London: Reaktion.

Hansen, Peter. 2013. *The Summits of Modern Man: Mountaineering after the Enlightenment*. Cambridge, MA: Harvard University Press.

Hansen, Thomas Blom, and Finn Stepputat. 2006. 'Sovereignty Revisited.' *Annual Review of Anthropology*, 35: 295–315.

Hansen, Thomas Blom. 2001. *Wages of Violence: Naming and Identity in Postcolonial Bombay*. Princeton: Princeton University Press.

Hansen, Thomas Bloom and Finn Stepputat (eds). 2001. *States of Imagination: Ethnographic Explorations of the Postcolonial State*. Durham: Duke University Press.

Harris, Tina. 2013. *Geographical Diversions: Tibetan Trade, Global Transactions*. Athens: University of Georgia Press.

Harris, Tina, Amy Holmes–Tagchungdarpa, Jayeeta Sharma, and Markus Viehbeck. 2016. 'Global Encounters, Local Places. Connected Histories of Darjeeling, Kalimpong, and the Himalayas—An Introduction.' *Transcultural Studies*, 12 (1): 43–53.

Hathorn, J.G. 1863. *A Handbook of Darjeeling: With Brief Notes on the Culture and Manufacture of Tea, and Rules for the Sale of Unassessed Waste Lands etc.* Calcutta: Lepage.

Hechter, Michael. 1978. 'Group Formation and the Cultural Division of Labour.' *American Journal of Sociology*, 84 (2): 293–318.

Herbert, J.D. 1830. *Report on Darjeeling, A Place in the Sikkim Mountains, Proposed as A Sanatorium, or Station of Health*. Calcutta: Baptist Mission Press.

———. 2000 [1830]. 'Particulars of a Visit to the Siccim Hills with Some Account of Darjiling.' in Fred Pinn (ed.), *Travelling to Darjeeling*. Bath: Pagoda Tree Press.

Hermanns, Fr. Matthias. 1954. *The Indo–Tibetans: The Indo–Tibetan and Mongoloid Problem in the Southern Himalaya and North–North-East India*. Bombay: Examiner Press.

Hetherington, F.A. 1994. *The Diary of a Tea Planter*. Sussex: The Book Guild, Ltd.

Hodgson, Brian. 1847. *On the Kocch, Bódo and Dhimál Tribes*. Calcutta: Baptist Mission Press.

———. 1880. *Miscellaneous Essays Relating to Indian Subjects*. London: Trübner & Company.

Höfer, Andreas. 1979. *The Caste Hierarchy and the State in Nepal: A Study of the Muluki Ain of 1854*. Patan: Himal Books.

Holland, Dorothy, and Jean Lave. 2001. 'History in Person: An Introduction.' In Dorothy Holland and Jean Lave (eds), *History in Person: Enduring Struggles, Contentious Practice, Intimate Identities*, pp. 3–36. Santa Fe: School of American Research Press.

Holmberg, David, Kathryn March, and Suryaman Tamang. 1999. 'Local Production/Local Knowledge: Forced Labour from Below.' *Studies in Nepali History and Society*, 4 (1): 5–64.

Hooker, J.D. 1849. *Rhododendrons of the Sikkim Himalaya: Being an Account, Botanical and Geographical, of the Rhododendrons recently Discovered in the Mountains of Eastern Himalaya, from Drawings and Descriptions made on the Spot, during a Government Botanical Mission to that Country*. London: Reeve, Benham, and Reeve.

———. 2002 [1854]. *Himalayan Journals*. London: Blackmask Online. Available at http://www.hudsoncress.net/hudsoncress.org/html/library/history–travel/Hooker,%20JD%20–%20Himalayan%20Journals.pdf.

Hunter, William Wilson. 1876. *A Statistical Account of Bengal Vol. X: Districts of Darjeeling and Jalpaiguri, and State of Kuch Behar*. London: Trübner & Company.

———. 1896 [1991]. *The Life of Brian Houghton Hodgson*. New Delhi: Asian Educational Services.

Hussain, Imdad. 2003. 'Soldiers and Settlers: The Recruitment of Gorkhas.' In Tanka B. Subba and A.C. Sinha (eds), *The Nepalis in North-East India*, pp. 67–105. New Delhi: Indus.

Hutt, Michael. 1997. 'Being Nepali without Nepal: Reflections on a South Asian Diaspora.' In David Gellner, Joanna Pfaff–Czarnecka and John Whelpton (eds), *Nationalism and Ethnicity in a Hindu Kingdom: The Politics of Culture in Contemporary Nepal*, pp. 101–44. Amsterdam: Harwood Academic Publishers.

———. 1998. 'Going to Mugalan: Nepali Literary Representations of Migration to India and Bhutan.' *South Asia Research*, 18 (2): 195–214.

———. 2003. *Unbecoming Citizens: Culture, Nationhood, and the Flight of Refugees from Bhutan*. Oxford: Oxford University Press.

Jaffrelot, Christophe. 2002. 'Indian Democracy: The Rule of Law on Trial.' *India Review*, 1 (1): 77–121.

Jayal, N.G. 1999. *Democracy and the State: Welfare, Secularism and Development in Contemporary India*. New Delhi: Oxford University Press.

Jeffrey, Craig. 2010. *Timepass: Youth, Class and the Politics of Waiting in India*. Stanford: Stanford University Press.

Jeffrey, Craig, Patricia Jeffery, and Roger Jeffery. 2008. *Degrees without Freedom? Education, Masculinities, and Unemployment in North India*. Stanford: Stanford University Press.

Johnson, Reginald. 1953. *Johnson's Note Book for Tea Planters: A Complete Up-to-Date Guide on Tea Planting, Tea Manufacture, Tea Tasting, Estate Book Keeping & Accountancy*. Santa Cruz: Santa Cruz Press.

Johnston, Barbara Rose. 2005. 'The Commodification of Water and the Human Dimensions of Manufactured Scarcity.' In Linda Whiteford, and Scott Whiteford (eds), *Globalization, Water, and Health: Resource Management in Times of Scarcity*, pp. 133–52. Santa Fe: School of American Research Advanced Seminar Series.

Joshi, Deepa. 2014. 'Feminist Solidary? Women, Water, and Politics in Darjeeling Himalaya.' *Mountain Research and Development*, 34 (3): 243–55.

Kabeer, Naila. 1999. 'Resources, Agency, Achievements: Reflections on the Measure of Women's Empowerment.' *Development and Change*, 30: 435–64.

Kaplan, Caren. 1996. *Questions of Travel: Postmodern Discourses of Displacement*. Durham: Duke University Press.

Kar, D.P. 2009. *Gorkhaland Movement: A Clandestine Invasion*. Siliguri: Janachetana.

Karim, Lamia. 2011. *Microfinance and Its Discontents: Women and Debt in Bangladesh*. Minneapolis: University of Minnesota Press.

Karlsson, B.G. 2013. 'The Social Life of Categories: Affirmative Action and Trajectories of the Indigenous.' *Focaal—Journal of Global and Historical Anthropology*, 65: 33–41.

Kaviraj, Sudipta. 1992. 'The Imaginary Institutions of India.' In Partha Chatterjee and Gyanendra Pandey (eds), *Subaltern Studies VII*, pp. 1–39. New Delhi: Oxford University Press.

Kellas, A.M. 1917. 'A Consideration of the Possibility of Ascending the Loftier Himalaya.' *The Geographical Journal*, 49 (1): 26–46.

Kennedy, Dane Keith. 1996. *The Magic Mountains: Hill Stations and the British Raj*. Berkeley: University of California Press.

Kenny, Judith T. 1995. 'Climate, Race, and Imperial Authority: The Symbolic Landscape of the British Hill Station in India.' *Annals of the Association of American Geographers*, 85 (4): 694–714.

Khilnani, Sunil. 1997. *The Idea of India*. Harmondsworth: Penguin Books.

Klenk, Rebecca M. 2004. "Who Is a Developed Woman?' Women as Category of Development Discourse in Kumaon, India.' *Development and Change*, 35: 57–78.

Kothari, Rajni. 1985. 'The Non-Party Political Process.' *Praxis International*, 3: 333–49.

Kulick, Don. 1993. 'Heroes from Hell: Representations of 'Rascalism' in a Papua New Guinean Village.' *Anthropology Today*, 9 (3): 9–14.

Kumar, Anup. 2011. *The Making of a Small State. Populist Social Mobilisation and the Hindi Press in the Uttarakhand Movement*. New Delhi: Orient Blackswan.

Lacina, Bethany. 2009. 'The Problem of Political Stability in North-East India: Local Ethnic Autocracy and the Rule of Law.' *Asian Survey*, 49 (6): 998–1020.

———. 2014. 'India's Stabilizing Segment States.' *Ethnopolitics*, 13 (1): 13–27.

———. 2017. *Rival Claims: Ethnic Violence and Territorial Autonomy under Indian Federalism*. Ann Arbor, MI: University of Michigan Press.

Lahiri-Dutt, Kuntala (ed.). 2006. *Fluid Bonds: Views on Gender and Water*. Kolkata: Stree Publishers.

Lal, S. 1987. *India: Current Party Politics (Also Refers to Gorkhaland and Mizo Accord)*. New Delhi: Election Archives.

Lama, Mahendra P. (ed.). 1996. *Gorkhaland Movement: Quest for an Identity*. Darjeeling: Department of Information and Cultural Affairs, Darjeeling Gorkha Hill Council.

Lama, Niraj. 2006. 'Mountain Autocrat, Still.' *Himal Southasian*, July, 67–9.

Lefebvre, Henri. 1991. *The Production of Space*. Translated by Donald Nicholson-Smith. Oxford: Blackwell.

Li, Tania Murray. 2000. 'Articulating Indigenous Identity in Indonesia: Resource Politics and the Tribal Slot.' *Comparative Studies in Society and History*, 42 (1): 149–79.

Liechty, Mark. 2002. *Suitably Modern: Making Middle-Class Culture in a New Consumer Society*. Princeton: Princeton University Press.

Longley, P.R.H. 1969. *Tea Planter Sahib: The Life and Adventures of a Tea Planter in North East India*. Auckland: Tonson Publishing House.

Ludden, David. 1993. 'Orientalist Empiricism: Transformations of Colonial Knowledge.' In Carol A. Breckenridge and Peter van der Veer (eds), *Orientalism and the Postcolonial Predicament*, pp. 250–78. Philadelphia: Univeristy of Pennsylvania Press.

Lynch, Caitrin. 2007. *Juki Girls, Good Girls: Gender and Cultural Politics in Sri Lanka's Global Garment Industry*. Ithaca: Cornell University Press.

Lyon, Sarah. 2008. 'Fair Trade Coffee and Human Rights in Guatemala.' *Journal of Consumer Policy*, 30: 241–61.

Mahajan, Gurpreet. 1998. *Identities and Rights, Aspects of Liberal Democracy in India*. New Delhi: Oxford.

Manor, James. 2002. 'Changing State, Changing Society in India.' *South Asia: Journal of South Asian Studies*, 25 (2): 231–56.

Marshall, T.H. 1934. 'Social Class: A Preliminary Analysis.' *The Sociological Review*, 26 (1): 55–76.

Marx, Karl. 1978. 'Capital.' In Robert C Tucker (eds), *The Marx–Engels Reader*, pp. 294–442. New York: W.W. Norton and Company.

McDuie-Ra Duncan. 2016. *Borderland City in New India: Frontier to Gateway*. Amsterdam: Amsterdam University Press.

McGowan, Alexander. 1860. *Tea Planting in the Outer Himalaya*. London: Smith, Elder, and Company.

McGranahan, Carole. 2010. *Arrested Histories: Tibet, the CIA, and Memories of a Forgotten War*. Durham: Duke University Press.

Mehta, Uday Singh. 1999. *Liberalism and Empire*. Chicago: University of Chicago Press.

Mell, Ian C. and John Sturzaker. 2014. 'Sustainable Urban Development in Tightly Constrained Areas: A Case Study of Darjeeling, India.' *International Journal of Urban Sustainable Development*, 6 (1): 65–88.

Merry, Sally. 2006. *Human Rights and Gender Violence*. Chicago: University of Chicago Press.

Metcalf, Thomas R. 1995. *Ideologies of the Raj*. Cambridge: Cambridge University Press.

Michelutti, Lucia. 2014. 'Kingship without Kings in Northern India.' In Anastasia Piliavsky (ed.), *Patronage as Politics in South Asia*, pp. 288–302. Cambridge: Cambridge University Press.

Michelutti, Lucia. 2007. 'The Vernacularization of Democracy: Political Participation and Popular Politics in North India.' *Journal of the Royal Anthropological Institute*, 13: 639–56.

———. 2010. 'Wrestling with (Body) Politics: Understanding 'Goonda' Political Styles in North India.' In Pamela Price and Arild Engelsen Ruud (eds), *Power and Influence in India: Bosses, Lords and Captains*, pp. 44–69. Delhi: Routledge.

Middleton, Townsend. 2010. 'Beyond Recognition: Ethnology, Belonging, and the Refashioning of the Ethnic Subject in Darjeeling, India.' Ph.D. dissertation. Cornell University.

———. 2011. 'Across the Interface of State Ethnography: Rethinking Ethnology and its Subjects in Multicultural India.' *American Ethnologist*, 38 (2): 249–66.

———. 2013a. 'Anxious Belongings: Anxiety and the Politics of Belonging in Subnationalist Darjeeling.' *American Anthropologist*, 115 (4): 608–21.

———. 2013b. 'Scheduling Tribes: A View from Inside India's Ethnographic State.' *Focaal—Journal of Global and Historical Anthropology*, 65: 13–22.

———. 2013c. 'States of Difference: Refiguring Ethnicity and Its "Crisis" at India's Borders.' *Political Geography*, 35 (Special Issue: Geographies at the Margins: Interrogating Borders in South Asia): 14–24.

———. 2015. *The Demands of Recognition: State Anthropology and Ethnopolitics in Darjeeling*. Stanford: Stanford University Press.

———. 2018. 'The Afterlives of a Killing: Assassination, Thanatos, and the Body Politic in South Asia.' *Public Culture*, 30 (1): 85–112.

Middleton, Townsend and Sara Shneiderman. 2008. 'Reservations, Federalism and the Politics of Recognition in Nepal.' *Economic and Political Weekly*, 43 (19): 39–45.

Misra, B.P. 1986. 'Behind Gorkhaland Agitation.' *Mainstream*, 25 (7): 15–20.

Mitchell, Don. 1996. *The Lie of the Land: Migrant Workers and the California Landscape*. Minneapolis: University of Minnesota Press.

Moberg, M. and S. Lyon. 2010. 'What's Fair? The Paradox of Seeking Justice Through Markets.' In S. Lyon and M. Moberg (eds), *Fair Trade and Social Justice: Global Ethnographies*, pp. 1–27. New York: New York University Press.

Moktan, R. 2004. *Sikkim: Darjeeling Compendium of Documents*. Varanasi: Gopal Press.

Moodie, Megan. 2008. 'Enter Microcredit: A New Culture of Women's Empowerment in Rajasthan?' *American Ethnologist*, 35 (3): 454–65.

Morris, C.G. 1933. *Gurkhas*. Delhi: Manager of Publications for Government of India.

Mullard, Saul. 2011. *Opening the Hidden Land: State Formation and the Construction of Sikkimese History*. Leiden: Brill.

Mutersbaugh, Tad and Sarah Lyon. 2010. 'Transparency and Democracy in Certified Ethical Commodity Networks.' *Geoforum*, 41: 27–32.

Mutersbaugh, Tad, Daniel Klooster, Mary Renard, and Philip Taylor. 2005. 'Certifying Rural Spaces: Quality-Certified Products and Rural Governance.' *Journal of Rural Studies*, 21 (4): 381–8.

Nag, Dipak Kumar. 2000. *Political Culture of the Tea Garden Workers*. Calcutta: Minerva Associates.

Nag, Soumen. 2007. 'The Role of Tea Planters in Creating the Demand of Separate Gorkhaland.' In Sailen Debnath (ed.), *Social and Political Tensions in North Bengal (Since 1947)*, pp. 207–18. Siliguri: N.L. Publishers.

Nagel, Joane. 1994. 'Constructing Ethnicity: Creating and Recreating Ethnic Identity and Culture.' *Social Problems*, 41: 152–76.

———. 1995. 'American Indian Ethnic Renewal: Politics and the Resurgence of Identity.' *American Sociological Review*, 60 (6): 947–65.

Nanda, Sugata. 2010. 'Constructing the Criminal: Politics of Social Imagery of the "Goonda,"' *Social Scientist*, 38 (3–4): 37–54.

Naples, Nancy and Manisha Desai (eds). 2002. *Women's Activism and Globalization: Linking Local Struggles and Transnational Politics*. New York: Routledge.

Newman & Company. 1900. *Newman's Guide to Darjeeling and Its Surroundings, Historical & Descriptive, with Some Account of the Manners and Customs of the Neighbouring Hill Tribes*. London: W.H. Allen and Company.

Norgay, Tenzing and James Ramsay Ullman. 1955. *Tiger of the Snows*. New York: Putnam.

Notes on Tea in Darjeeling by a Planter. 1888. Calcutta: Military Orphan Press.

O'Leary, Heather. 2016. 'Between Stagnancy and Affluence: Reinterpreting Water Poverty and Domestic Flows in Delhi, India.' *Society & Natural Resources*, 29 (6): 639–53.

O'Malley, L.L.S. 1907. *Bengal District Gazetteers: Darjeeling*. Calcutta: Bengal Secretariat Book Depot, Indian Civil Service.

———. 2001 [1907]. *Bengal District Gazetteers: Darjeeling*. Calcutta: Government of West Bengal.

Ong, Aihwa. 2006. *Neoliberalism as Exception: Mutations in Citizenship and Sovereignty*. Durham: Duke University Press.

Onta, Pratyoush. 1996a. 'Creating a Brave Nepali Nation in British India: The Rhetoric of Jati Improvement, Rediscovery of Bhanubhakta and the Writing of Bir History.' *Studies in Nepali History and Society*, 1 (1): 37–76.

———. 1996b. 'The Politics of Bravery: A History of Nepali Nationalism.' Ph.D. dissertation. University of Pennsylvania.

———. 2006. 'The Growth of the Adivasi Janajati Movement in Nepal after 1990.' *Studies in Nepali History and Society*, 11 (2): 303–54.

Oppitz, Michael. 1974. 'Myths and Facts: Reconsidering some Data Concerning the Clan History of the Sherpas.' *Kailash*, 1: 1–2.

Ortner, Sherry. 1989. *High Religion: A Cultural and Political History of Sherpa Buddhism*. Princeton: Princeton University.

———. 1999. *Life and Death on Mt. Everest*. Princeton: Princeton University Press.

Panikkar, K.N. 2001 [1995]. *Culture, Ideology, Hegemony: Intellectuals and Social Consciousness in Colonial India*. New Delhi: Tulika.

Papers on the Tea Factories and Plantations in Kumaon and Gurhwal. 1854. Agra: Secundra Orphan Press.

Pardo, Italo. 2000. 'Introduction: Morals of Legitimacy: Interplay between Responsibility, Authority and Trust.' In Italo Pardo (ed.), *Morals of Legitimacy: Between Agency and System*, pp. 1–26. New York: Berghahn Books.

Parkin, Frank. 1972. *Class Inequality and Political Order*. London: Paladin.

———. 1974. 'Strategies of Social Closure in Class Formation.' In Frank Parkin (ed.), *The Social Analysis of Class Structure*, pp. 1–18. London: Tavistock.

———. 1979. *Marxism and Class Theory*. London: Tavistock.

Parry, Jonathan P. 2000. 'The "Crisis of Corruption' and 'the Idea of India."' In Italo Pardo (ed.), *Morals of Legitimacy: Between Agency and System*, pp. 27–56. New York: Berghahn Books.

Pels, Peter and Oscar Salemink (eds). 2000. *Colonial Subjects: Essays on the Practical History of Anthropology*. Ann Arbor: University of Michigan Press.

Perry, Cindy. 1997. *Nepali Around the World*. Kathmandu: Ekta Books.

Piliavsky, Anastasia and Tommaso Sbriccoli. 2016. 'The Ethics of Efficacy in North India's Goonda Raj (rule of Toughs).' *Journal of the Royal Anthropological Institute*, 22: 1–19.

Piliavsky, Anastasia. 2014.'Introduction.' In Anastasia Piliawsky (ed.), *Patronage as Politics in South Asia*, pp. 1–38. Cambridge: Cambridge University Press.

Pokharel, Madhav. 2009. 'Origin and Development of the Nepali Language.' In A.C. Sinha and T.B. Subba (eds), *Indian Nepalis: Issues and Perspectives*, pp. 325–38. New Delhi: Concept Publishing Company.

Porter, E.A. 1933. *Extracts Copy from the Book of Census of India, 1931, Vol. V. Bengal and Sikkim Part–I. Report*. Calcutta: Central Publication Branch.

Povinelli, Elizabeth A. 2002. *The Cunning of Recognition: Indigenous Alterities and the Making of Australian Multiculturalism*. Durham: Duke University Press.

———. 2011. *Economies of Abandonment. Social Belonging and Endurance in Late Liberalism*. Durham: Duke University Press.

Pradhan, Alina. 2012. 'Language Movement in the Darjeeling Himalayas: Special Reference to the Lepcha Language.' *Language Today*, 12: 3.

Pradhan, Kumar. 1982. *Pahilo Prahar*. Darjeeling: Sajha Prakashan.

———. 1984. *A History of Nepali Literature*. New Delhi: Sahitya Academy.

———. 1991. *The Gorkha Conquests: The Process and Consequence of the Unification of Nepal, with Particular Reference to Eastern Nepal*. Calcutta: Oxford University Press.

———. 2004. 'Darjeelingma Nepali Jati ra Janajatiya Chinarika naya Udan haru.' The Mahesh Chandra Regmi Lecture, Social Science Baha, Lalitpur (Nepal).

———. 2005 [1982]. 'Agam Singh Giriko Kavitama Jatiya Bhavan.' In Kumar Pradhan (ed.), *Adhiti Kehi*, pp. 109–33. Siliguri: Purnima Prakashan.

Pradhan, Sandeep. 2012. *Gorkha Dukh Niwarak Sammelan (Darjeeling)*. Darjeeling: Gama Prakashan.

Prakash, Karat. 1973. *Language and Nationality Politics in India*. Bombay: Orient Longman.

Price, Pamela. 2007. 'Honor and Morality in Contemporary Rural India.' In Lauren Joseph, Matthew Mahler, and Javier Auyero (eds), *New Perspectives in Political Ethnography*, pp. 88–109. New York: Springer.

Price, Pamela and Arild Engelsen Ruud. 2010. 'Introduction.' In Pamela Price and Arild Engelsen Ruud (eds), *Power and Influence in India: Bosses, Lords and Captains*, pp. xix–xxxiv. New Delhi: Routledge.

Purkayastha, Bandana and Mangala Subramaniam (eds). 2004. *The Power of Women's Informal Networks: Lessons in Social Change from South Asia and West Africa*. Lanham, MD: Lexington Books.

Rademacher, Anne. 2011. *Reigning the River: Urban Ecologies and Political Transformation in Kathmandu*. Durham: Duke University Press.

Rai, Indrabahadur. 1984. *Darjeelingma Nepali Natak ko Aadha Satabdi*. Darjeeling: Sajha Prakashan.

Ramamurthy, Priti. 2003.'Material Consumers, Fabricating Subjects: Perplexity, Global Connectivity Discourses, and Transnational Feminist Research.' *Cultural Anthropology*, 18 (4): 524–50.

Ramamurthy, Priti. 2011. 'Rearticulating Caste: The Global Cottonseed Commodity Chain and the Paradox of Smallholder Capitalism in South India.' *Environment and Planning*, 43 (5): 1035–56.

Ramsden, A.R. 1945. *Assam Planter: Tea Planting and Hunting in the Assam Jungle*. London: John Gifford Limited.

Ranadive, B.T. 1986. *Gorkhaland Agitation: A Part of Imperialist Plot in the East.* Calcutta: West Bengal State Committee, Communist Party of India (Marxist).

Rankin, Katharine N. 2004. *The Cultural Politics of Markets: Economic Liberalization and Social Change in Nepal.* Toronto: University of Toronto Press.

Rayner, Hugh (ed.). 2009. *Photographic Journeys in the Himalayas by Samuel Bourne*. Bath: Pagoda Tree Press.

Rhodes, Nicholas and Deki Rhodes. 2006. *A Man of the Frontier: S.W. Laden La (1876–1936)*. Kolkata: Progressive Art House.

Ricalton, James. 1900. *India through the Stereoscope: A Journey through Hindusthan*. Underwood & Underwood: New York. Available at https://archive.org/details/indiathroughste00ricagoog/ (accessed June 1, 2016).

Rojek, Chris. 1997.'Indexing, Dragging, and the Social Construction of Tourist Sights.' In Chris Rojek and John Urry (eds), *Touring Cultures: Transformations of Travel and Theory*, pp. 52–74. London: Routledge.

Rose, Leo E. 1994. 'The Nepali Ethnic Community in the North-East of the Sub–Continent.' *Ethnic Studies Report*, 12 (1): 103–20.

Rose, Nikolas and Peter Miller. 1992. 'Political Power Beyond State: Problematics of Government.' *British Journal of Sociology*, 43 (2): 173–205.

Ruud, Arild Engelsen. 2000. 'Talking Dirty about Politics: A View from a Bengali Village.' In C.J. Fuller and Véronique Bénéï (eds), *The Everyday State and Society in Modern India*, pp. 115–36. New Delhi: Social Science Press.

———. 2014. 'The Political Bully in Bangladesh.' In Anastasia Piliavsky (ed.), *Patronage as Politics in South Asia*, pp. 305–25. Cambridge: Cambridge University Press.

Rycroft, Daniel J. and Sangeeta Dasgupta. 2011. *The Politics of Belonging in India: Becoming Adivasi*. New York: Routledge.

Samanta, Amiya K. 2000. *Gorkhaland Movement: A Study in Ethnic Separatism*. New Delhi: A.P.H. Publishing Corporation.

Sanchez, Andrew. 2012.'Questioning Success: Dispossession and the Criminal Entrepreneur in Urban India.' *Critique of Anthropology*, 32 (4): 435–57.

Sarkar, Dilip Kumar, and Dhruba Jyoti Bhaumik. 2000. *Empowering Darjeeling Hills: An Experience with Darjeeling Gorkha Hill Council*. Delhi: Indian Publishers Distributors.

Sarkar, Sumit. 1973. *The Swadeshi Movement in Bengal*. New Delhi: People's Publishing House.

Sarkar, Swatahsiddha. 'Dress, Difference and Dissent in the Darjeeling Hills.' *South Asian Citizen's Web*, 2008. Available at http://www.sacw.net/article442.html.

———. 2010. 'The Land Question and Ethnicity in the Darjeeling Hills.' *Journal of Rural Social Sciences*, 25 (2): 81–121.

———. 2013. *Gorkhaland Movement: A Study on Ethnic Conflict and State Response*. New Delhi: Concept Publishing House.

———. 2014. 'Obituary: Kumar Pradhan (1937–2013).' *Himalaya: the Journal of the Association for Nepal and Himalayan Studies*, 34 (1): 137–41.

———. 2016. 'How (Not) to Write Hill History: Gorkhaland and Telangana Are Not Similar.' *Economic and Political Weekly*, 51 (5): 94–5.

Schmitt, Carl. 1985. *Political Theology: Four Chapters on the Concept of Sovereignty*. Translated by G. Schwab. Chicago: University of Chicago Press.

Schumpeter, Joseph. 1951. *Imperialism and Social Classes*. New York: Augustus M. Kelley.

Scott, James C. 1998. *Seeing Like a State: How Certain Schemes to Improve the Human Condition Have Failed*. New Haven: Yale University Press.

Scrase, Timothy, Mario Rutten, Ruchira Ganguly-Scrase, and Trent Brown. 2015. 'Beyond the Metropolis—Regional Globalisation and Town Development in India: An Introduction.' *South Asia: Journal of South Asian Studies*, 38 (2): 216–29.

Scrase, Timothy, Ruchira Ganguly-Scrase, and Andrew Deuchar. 2016. 'Young Men, Education and Ethnicity in Contemporary Darjeeling.' *South Asia Research*, 36 (10): 98–114.

Sen, Debarati. 2014. 'Fair trade vs. Swaccha Vyāpār: Women's Activism and Transnational Justice Regimes in Darjeeling, India.' *Feminist Studies*, 40 (2): 444–72.

———. 2016. 'Affective Solidarities? Participating in and Witnessing Fair Trade and Women's Empowerment in Transnational Communities of Practice.' *Anthropology in Action*, 23 (2): 13–18.

———. 2017. *Everyday Sustainability: Gender Justice and Fair Trade Tea in Darjeeling*. Albany: State University of New York Press.

Sen, Debarati and Sarasij Majumder. 2011. 'Fair Trade and Fair Trade Certification of Agricultural Commodities: Promises, Pitfalls and Possibilities.' *Environment and Society: Advances in Research*, 2: 29–47.

Sen, Samita. 2010. 'Commercial Recruiting and Informal Intermediation: Debate over the Sardari System in Assam Tea Plantations, 1860–1900.' *Modern Asian Studies*, 44 (1): 3–28.

Sharma, Aradhana. 2008. *Logics of Empowerment: Development, Gender and Governance in Neoliberal India*. Minneapolis: University of Minnesota Press.

Sharma, Janaklal. 2020 v.s. *Josmani Santa Parampara ra Sahitya*. Lalitpur: Sajha Prakashan.

Sharma, Jayeeta. 2009. '"Lazy" Natives, Coolie Labour, and the Assam Tea Industry.' *Modern Asian Studies*, 43 (6): 1287–1324.

———. 2011. *Empire's Garden: Assam and the Making of Modern India*. Durham: Duke University Press.

———. 2016a. 'A Space That Has Been Laboured On: Mobile Lives and Transcultural Circulation around Darjeeling and the Eastern Himalayas.' *Transcultural Studies*, 12 (1): 54–85.

———. 2016b. 'Producing Himalayan Darjeeling: Mobile People and Mountain Encounters.' *Himalaya: the Journal of the Association for Nepal and Himalayan Studies*, 35 (2): 87–101.

Shneiderman, Sara. 2009. 'Ethnic (P)reservations: Comparing Thangmi Ethnic Activism in Nepal and India.' In David N. Gellner (ed.), *Ethnic Activism and Civil Society in South Asia*, pp. 115–41. New Delhi: SAGE.

———. 2013. 'Developing a Culture of Marginality: Nepal's Current Classificatory Moment.' *Focaal—Journal of Global and Historical Anthropology*, 65: 42–55.

———. 2015. *Rituals of Ethnicity: Thangmi Identities Between Nepal and India*. Philadelphia: University of Pennsylvania Press.

Shneiderman, Sara and Mark Turin. 2006. 'Seeking the Tribe: Ethno-Politics in Darjeeling and Sikkim.' *Himal*, 18 (5): 54–8.

Sibley, David. 1995. *Geographies of Exclusion: Society and Difference in the West*. New York: Routledge.

Shrestha, Ananda. 2003. 'Political Murders Rock Darjeeling.' *Nepali Times*, June 15–29.

Singh, I.D. 2005. *The Tea Planter's Guide to Tea Culture and Manufacture*. New Delhi: NB Modern Agencies.

Singh, Prerna. 2015. 'Subnationalism and Social Development: A Comparative Analysis of Indian States.' *World Politics*, 67 (3): 506–62.

Sinha, Awadhesh Coomar. 2003. 'The Indians of Nepali Origin and Security of North-East India.' In Awadhesh Coomar Sinha and Tanka Bahadur Subba (eds), *The Nepalese in North-East India: A Community in Search of Indian Identity*, pp. 360–77. New Delhi: Indus.

Sinha, Suvadip. 2013. 'Vernacular Masculinity and Politics of Space in Contemporary Bollywood Cinema.' *Studies in South Asian Film and Media*, 5 (2): 131–45.

Snellinger, Amanda T. 2006. 'Commitment as an Analytic: Reflections on Nepali Student Activists Protracted Struggle.' *PoLAR (Political and Legal Anthropology Review)*, 29 (2): 351–64.

Sökefeld, Martin. 2005. 'From Colonialism to Postcolonial Colonialism: Changing Modes of Domination in the Northern Areas of Pakistan.' *Journal of Asian Studies*, 64: 939–74.

Sonntag, Selma K. 1999. 'Autonomous Councils in India: Contesting the Liberal Nation-State.' *Alternatives*, 24 (3): 415–34.

Spencer, Jonathan. 2007. *Anthropology, Politics and the State. Democracy and Violence in South Asia*. Cambridge: Cambridge University Press.

Spivak, Gayatri Chakrabarti. 1993. *Outside in the Teaching Machine*. New York: Routledge.

Sprigg, R.K. 1982. 'The Lepcha Language and Three Hundred Years of Tibetan Influence in Sikkim.' *Journal of the Asiatic Society of India*, 24 (1–4): 16–31.

———. 1998. 'Dr. Hooker's Lepcha Treasurer (1848–49).' *Aachuley: A Quarterly Lepcha Bilingual News Magazine*, 2 (3): 5.

States Reorganisation Commission. 1955. *Report*. India: SRC.

Stone, Ian. 1984. *Canal Irrigation in British India*. New York: Cambridge University Press.

Subba, T.B. 1985. *The Quiet Hills: A Study of Agrarian Relations in Hill Darjeeling*. Delhi: ISPCK.

———. 1986. 'Agrarian Relations and Development in Sikkim.' Paper presented in National Seminar on Rural Development in Eastern and North Eastern India, Kolkata: IIM Joka Campus, 8–10 May.

———. 1989a. *Dynamics of a Hill Society*. Delhi: Mittal.

———. 1989b. 'Sociological Consequences of Tourism in Darjeeling.' In S.C Singh (ed.), *Impact of Tourism on Mountain Environment*, pp. 305–14. Meerut: Research India Publications.

———. 1992. *Ethnicity, State, and Development: A Case Study of the Gorkhaland Movement in Darjeeling*. New Delhi: Vikas Publishing House.

———. 2003. 'The Nepalese in North-East India: Political Aspirations and Ethnicity.' In Awadhesh Coomar Sinha and Tanka Bahadur Subba (eds), *The Nepalese in North-East India: A Community in Search of Indian Identity*, pp. 54–66. New Delhi: Indus.

———. 2008. 'Living Nepali Diaspora in India: An Anthropological Essay.' *Zeitschrift fur Ethnologie*, 133: 213–32.

Subba, T.B., A.C. Sinha, G.S. Nepal, and D.R. Nepal (eds). 2009. *Indian Nepalis: Issues and Perspectives*. New Delhi: Concept Publishing Company.

Subba, T.B., and A.C. Sinha (eds). 2003. *The Nepalis in North-East India*. New Delhi: Indus.

———. 2016. *Nepali Diaspora in a Globalized World*. New Delhi: Routledge.

Subramaniam, M. 2006. *The Power of Women's Informal Organizing: Gender, Caste and Class in India*. Lanham: Lexington Books.

Sultana, Farhana. 2009. 'Fluid Lives: Subjectivities, Water, and Gender in Bangladesh.' *Gender, Place, and Culture*, 16 (4): 427–44.

———. 2010. 'Living in Hazardous Waterscapes: Gendered Vulnerabilities and Experiences of Floods and Disasters.' *Environmental Hazards*, 9 (1): 43–53.

———. 2011. 'Suffering for Water, Suffering from Water: Emotional Geographies of Resource Access, Control, and Conflict.' *Geoforum*, 42 (2): 163–72.

Sundar, Nandini. 1997. *Subalterns and Sovereigns: An Anthropological History of Bastar (1854–1996)*. New Delhi: Oxford University Press.

———. 2000. 'Caste as Census Category: Implications for Sociology.' *Current Sociology*, 48 (3): 111–26.

Swyngedouw, Eric. 2004. *Social Power and the Urbanization of Water: Flows of Power*. New York: Oxford University Press.

Talukdar, Shashwati. 2010. 'Picturing Mountains as Hills: Hill Station Postcards and the Tales They Tell.' Tasveer Ghar: A Digital Archive of South Asian Popular Visual Culture http://tasveerghar.net/cmsdesk/essay/102/.

Tea Cultivation. 1865. Calcutta: Military Orphan Press.

Thapa, Namrata. 2012. *Employment Status and Human Development of Tea Plantation Workers in West Bengal: NRPPD Discussion Paper 11*, pp. 41–2. http://www.cds.edu/wpcontent/uploads/2012/11/NRPPD11.pdf. Accessed March 11, 2013.

Thapa, Rudraman. 1997. 'Movement for Nepali Identity in Assam.' In Girin Phukon and Nikunjalata Dutta (eds), *Politics of Identity and Nation Building in North-East India*, pp. 165–78. Denver: International Academic.

The Scotsman. 1924. 'Expedition. General Bruce Reports All Well.' Edinburgh: Johnston Publishing, April 16. From ProQuest Historical Newspapers, *The Scotsman (1817–1950)* (accessed 1 July 2016).

The Tea Cyclopaedia: Articles on Tea, Tea Science, Blights, Soils and Manures, Cultivation, Buildings, Manufacture, & c. with Tea Statistics. 1882. London: W.B. Whittingham & Co.

Thompson, E. P. 1991 [1963]. *The Making of the English Working Class*. Toronto: Penguin Books.

Tillin, Louise. 2013. *Remapping India: New States and Their Political Origins*. London: Hurst & Company.

Tillyris, D. 2016. 'After the Standard Dirty Hands Thesis: Towards a Dynamic Account of Dirty Hands in Politics.' *Ethical Theory and Moral Practice*, 19 (1): 161–75. https://doi.org/10.1007/s10677-015-9604-6.

Timsina, S.R. 1992. *Nepali Community in India*. Delhi: Manak Publicaions Pvt. Ltd.

Tirkey, Prem Lal. 2005. 'Tea Plantations in Darjeeling District, India: Geo–Ecological and Socio-Economic Impacts in Post-Independence Period.' Ph.D. dissertation. University of Manitoba.

Truelove, Yaffa. 2011. '(Re)Conceptualizing Water Inequality in Delhi, India through a Feminist Political Ecology Framework.' *Geoforum*, 42 (2): 143–52.

Turin, Mark. 2014. 'Mother Tongues and Language Competence: The Shifting Politics of Linguistic Belonging in the Himalayas.' In Gérard Toffin Joanna

Pfaff-Czarnecka (ed.), *Facing Globalization in the Himalayas: Belonging and the Politics of the Self*, pp. 372–96. New Delhi: SAGE.

Uberoi, Patricia, Nandini Sundar, and Satish Deshpande (eds). 2008. *Anthropology in the East: Founders of Indian Sociology and Anthropology*. Oxford: Seagull Books.

Ukers, William. 1935. *All about Tea: Volumes 1 and 2*. New York: Tea and Coffee Trade Journal Company.

Urry, John. 2001. *The Tourist Gaze: Second Edition*. London: SAGE.

Vaishnav, Milan. 2012.'The Merits of Money and'Muscle': Essays on Criminality, Elections and Democracy in India.' Ph.D. dissertation. Columbia University.

van Beek, Martijn. 2000. 'Beyond Identity Fetishism: 'Communal' Conflict in Ladakh and the Limits of Autonomy.' *Cultural Anthropology*, 15 (4): 529–69.

van Schendel, Willem. 2005. *The Bengal Borderland: Beyond State and Nation in South Asia*. London: Anthem.

van Spengen, Wim. 1992. *Tibetan Border Worlds: A Geo-historical Analysis of Trade and Traders*. London: Kegan Paul International.

Vandenhelsken, Mélanie, and Bengt G. Karlsson. 2015. 'Fluid attachments in Northeast India: Introduction.' *Asian Ethnicity*, 17 (3): 330–9.

Vansittart, Lieutenant–Colonel Eden. 1890. *Notes on Goorkhas: Being a Short Account of their Country, History, Characteristics, Class, etc.* Calcutta: Superintendent of Government Printing.

Viehbeck, Markus, ed. 2017. *Transcultural Encounters in the Himalayan Borderlands: Kalimpong as 'Contact Zone'*. Heidelberg: Heidelberg University Publishing.

W. Newman & Co. 1900. *Newman's Guide to Darjeeling and Its Surroundings.* Calcutta: W. Newman and Company.

Walzer, M. 1973. 'Political Action: The Problem of Dirty Hands.' *Philosophy & Public Affairs*, 2 (2): 160–80. Available at https://doi.org/10.2307/2265139.

Warner, Catherine. 2014. 'Flighty Subjects: Sovereignty, Shifting Cultivators, and the State in Darjeeling, 1830–1856.' *Himalaya: The Journal of the Association for Nepal and Himalayan Studies*, 34 (1): 23–35.

Wedeen, Lisa. 1999. *Ambiguities of Domination: Politics, Rhetoric, and Symbols in Contemporary Syria*. Chicago: University of Chicago Press.

Wenner, Miriam. 2013. 'Challenging the State by Reproducing its Principles: The Demand for "Gorkhaland" between Regional Autonomy and the National Belonging.' *Asian Ethnology*, 72 (2): 199–220.

———. 2015. 'Legitimization through Patronage? Strategies for Political Control beyond Ethno-Regional Claims in Darjeeling, India.' *Geoforum*, 66: 234–43.

Wenner, M. (2018): '"Breaking Bad" or Being Good? Moral Conflict and Political Conduct in Darjeeling.' *Contemporary South Asia*, 26 (1): 2–17.

West, John B. 1989. 'A.M. Kellas: Pioneer Himalayan Physiologist and Mountaineer.' *The Alpine Journal*, 94: 207–13.

West, Paige. 2012. *From Modern Production to Imagined Primitive: The Social World of Coffee From Papua New Guinea*. Durham: Duke University Press.

Whelpton, John. 2005. *A History of Nepal*. Cambridge: Cambridge University Press.

Whitcombe, Elizabeth. 1972. *Agrarian Conditions in Northern India*. Berkeley: University of California Press.

Wimmer, Andreas and Nina Glick Schiller. 2002. 'Methodological Nationalism and Beyond: Nation-State Building, Migration and the Social Sciences.' *Global Networks*, 2 (4): 301–34.

Young, Martin. 1999. 'The Social Construction of Tourist Places.' *Australian Geographer*, 30 (3): 373–89.

Zivkovic, Tanya. 2013. *Death and Reincarnation in Tibetan Buddhism: In-Between Bodies*. London: Routledge.

Index

Editors and Contributors

Rune Bennike, post-doctoral fellow, Cross–Cultural and Regional Studies, University of Copenhagen, Copenhagen, Denmark

Sarah Besky, assistant professor, Anthropology & Watson Institute, Brown University, Providence, Rhode Island, USA

Mona Chettri, post-doctoral research fellow, Aarhus University, Aarhus, Denmark

Nilamber Chhetri, assistant professor, Sociology, Maharashtra National Law University, Mumbai, Maharashtra, India

Georgina Drew, senior lecturer, Department of Anthropology and Development Studies, University of Adelaide, Adelaide, Australia

Babika Khawas, PhD candidate, Department of Sociology, University of North Bengal, Siliguri, West Bengal, India

Bethany Lacina, assistant professor, Department of Political Science, University of Rochester, Rochester, New York, USA

Townsend Middleton, assistant professor, Department of Anthropology, University of North Carolina at Chapel Hill, Chapel Hill, North Carolina, USA

Roshan P. Rai, development practitioner, DLR Prerna, Darjeeling, West Bengal, India

Swatahsiddha Sarkar, assistant professor, Department of Sociology, University of North Bengal, Siliguri, West Bengal, India

Debarati Sen, associate professor, Anthropology and International Conflict Management, Kennesaw State University, Kennesaw, Georgia, USA

Jayeeta Sharma, associate professor, Department of History, University of Toronto, Toronto, Ontario, Canada

Sara Shneiderman, associate professor, Department of Anthropology and School of Public Policy & Global Affairs/Institute of Asian Research, University of British Columbia, Vancouver, Canada

Tanka Subba, vice chancellor, Sikkim University, Gangtok, Sikkim, India

Miriam Wenner, post-doctoral teaching & research assistant, Department of Geography, University of Göttingen, Göttingen, Germany